ANNOTATED

General
MAR
Prof
The Queen's University of Belfast

Editorial Board

PROFESSOR B. W. DOWNS
Christ's College, Cambridge

V. DE SOLA PINTO
Professor Emeritus, University of Nottingham

F. W. BATESON
*Fellow and University Lecturer in English
Corpus Christi College, Oxford*

M. L. BURCHNALL
Senior English Master, Winchester College

M & E ANNOTATED STUDENT TEXTS

Available

TENNYSON: POEMS OF 1842: ed. C. Ricks
WORDSWORTH AND COLERIDGE: LYRICAL BALLADS: ed. D. S. Roper
BROWNING: DRAMATIS PERSONAE: ed. F. B. Pinion
HAZLITT: THE SPIRIT OF THE AGE: ed. E. D. Mackerness
KEATS: POEMS OF 1820: ed. D. G. Gillham
BYRON: DON JUAN (1819): ed. Brian Lee
RUSKIN: 'UNTO THIS LAST': ed. P. M. Yarker
BLAKE: SONGS OF INNOCENCE AND OF EXPERIENCE AND OTHER WORKS: ed. R. B. Kennedy
SHELLEY: ALASTOR AND OTHER POEMS: ed. P. H. Butter
POPE: ESSAY ON CRITICISM; THE RAPE OF THE LOCK; MORAL ESSAY: ed. Raymond Southall
DRYDEN: ABSALOM AND ACHITOPHEL; THE MEDAL; MACFLECKNOE; RELIGIO LAICI: ed. Philip Roberts
EDWARD THOMAS: POEMS AND LAST POEMS: ed. Edna Longley

M & E ANNOTATED STUDENT TEXTS

ALFRED TENNYSON

Poems of 1842

Edited by

CHRISTOPHER RICKS, B.Litt., M.A.
*Professor of English,
University of Bristol*

MACDONALD & EVANS LTD
8 John Street, London WC1N 2HY

First published 1968
Reprinted September 1975

ISBN: 0 7121 01519

Editorial material

© Christopher Ricks, 1968

This book is copyright and may not be reproduced in whole *or in part* (except for purposes of review) without the express permission of the publishers in writing.

This book is sold subject to the condition that it shall not, by way of *trade or otherwise*, be lent, resold, hired out or otherwise *circulated* without the publisher's prior consent in any form of binding or cover other than that in which it is published *and without a similar condition including this condition being imposed on the subsequent purchaser.*

Printed in Great Britain
at the
University Printing House, Cambridge
(Euan Phillips, University Printer)

General Preface

This series has two principal aims:
1. To meet the needs of both sixth-formers and undergraduates;
2. To encourage the student to *read the text* of the author he is studying rather than have recourse to substitutes which will tell him (as he hopes) 'what he ought to think'.

The annotation, accordingly, is designed as a tool with which to read the text. The conventional introduction has been eliminated and is replaced by a brief preface indicating the principal topics that scholars and critics discuss in connection with an author's work.

Authors are not represented in this series by volumes of selections of the kind that is now so familiar. Selections are in any case of limited use to the serious student. But there is the further point that in a volume of selections the pieces selected and the context they create for other pieces exercise a great influence upon the reader's impression of the author. When the present series was planned, it was felt that it would be much better to choose from an author's work, not individual pieces, but what are by common consent key *volumes*, so that each piece might appear in its original context. In this way, the overall impression of each volume is put firmly back in the hands of its author.

Editors have been asked to produce 'standard' texts on conventional lines, and the text of a poem in one of these volumes, therefore, will normally be that which the reader

GENERAL PREFACE

is most likely to meet in other contexts. Each editor, however, has been given a wide measure of freedom to make what seems to him the most sensible decision in the case of his own particular text, and the textual status of each volume is fully described in the Note on the Text with which it begins. In addition, important variants are recorded in the Notes.

MARK ROBERTS

Contents

Note on the Text of this Edition	9
Preface	11
Principal Dates of Tennyson's Life	13
Poems of 1842	15
Notes	275
Critical Extracts	365
Bibliography	376
Index of Titles	381
Index of First Lines	383

Acknowledgments

The editors and publishers would like to thank the following authors, publishers and owners of copyright who have given permission for material to be quoted in this book.

Chatto and Windus Ltd. for an extract from *The Poetry of Experience* by Robert Langbaum; Faber and Faber Ltd. for an extract from 'In Memoriam' in *Essays, Ancient and Modern* by T. S. Eliot; Macmillan and Co.Ltd. for the use of *The Eversley Edition of the Works of Tennyson*, edited by Hallam, Lord Tennyson; Sir Harold Nicolson for an extract from his book, *Tennyson*; The Trustees of the Hopkins Estate for an extract from *Further Letters of Gerard Manley Hopkins* published by Oxford University Press.

Note on the Text of this Edition

THE POEMS are here printed in the order of *1842*, but the text is that of the Eversley edition (1907-8), which has been collated with the 1894 edition (see Bibliography, p. 376). Tennyson's mature practice as to *-t* and the sounded and unsounded *ed* has been retained; he differentiated *'d/ed*. But he sensibly made local exceptions to this where the root-word itself ended with or required an *e*. Thus he left 'died', 'tongued', 'cried', as monosyllables, and 'storied' as two syllables. Common sense points out such exceptions. His original practice in *1830* and *1832* had been to differentiate *ed/éd, èd*; where the footnotes below quote variants that are in *1830* and *1832*, they therefore follow Tennyson's earlier practice (which serves to remind one that these are early readings).

Only a selection from the published variants could be given in this compass, except where specifically noted otherwise. In a few cases where variants are extensively but not fully quoted, a further warning has been added. Quotations from Tennyson, Hallam Tennyson, and Edward FitzGerald are from the Eversley edition, except where otherwise stated. On other occasions (e.g., the statement that a particular book was in the library of the Tennysons), the authority is that provided by the materials in the Tennyson Research Centre at Lincoln. The Tennysonian scholars quoted (i) are given full references; or (ii) will be found in the Bibliography; or (iii) have not been given a full reference because their point has been sufficiently made in the footnote itself (e.g. a comparison of a line of Tennyson with a line of Shelley). Acknowledgments to such scholars are given when a point was made by them (and for the first

NOTE ON THE TEXT

time) during the last 30 years or so; it has not seemed necessary to acknowledge by name the earlier discoverers.

My edition of *The Poems of Tennyson* (in the series 'Longmans' Annotated English Poets', General Editor: F. W. Bateson, published 1968) includes all the published variants, a generous selection from manuscript variants, and full notes on sources, composition, publication, parallel passages, etc.

Preface

TENNYSON'S TWO VOLUMES of *Poems* (*1842*) established him as the foremost poet of his generation, the Victorian generation which succeeded Keats, Shelley and Byron. The first volume of *1842* brought together the best poems of Tennyson's previous two volumes (*1830* and *1832*), among them *The Lady of Shalott*, *Mariana*, and *Mariana in the South*. The second volume published much of Tennyson's finest work, including *Morte d'Arthur*, *St. Simeon Stylites*, *Ulysses*, and *The Two Voices*. Not that it included everything which Tennyson had written by 1842. He had already written much of *In Memoriam*; he had created the 'germ' of *Maud* ('O that 'twere possible'); and he had drafts of many poems which he did not perfect till much later—for example, *Tithonus* was drafted in 1833-4, but published in 1860. Yet no better evidence of the variety of Tennyson's skills and concerns could exist than the collection of *1842*.

Those skills and concerns have been discussed by the critics who are listed in the Bibliography (p. 376), from some of whom this edition prints extracts (p. 365). What are the questions which have provoked discussion? The central problem has always been seen as simply whether or not Tennyson had very much to say. 'His gift of utterance is truly golden', agreed Gerard Manley Hopkins, 'but go further home and you come to thoughts commonplace and wanting in nobility.' (But does 'truly golden' have a rather poetical sound? Perhaps a major poet ought to resemble the whole range of metals.) Is it true that Tennyson is more notable for skill with words than for any profound insight into the important experiences in life? And what precisely is it that we would point to in order to show Tennyson's skill at work? It is easy to sense that he is a skilful poet—but not easy to demonstrate in what the skill consists.

Walt Whitman insisted that 'Tennyson shows more than

any poet I know (perhaps has been a warning to me) how much there is in finest verbalism.' But how are we to take that word 'warning'? And could it be that Tennyson shows not only 'how much' but also ultimately how little there is in 'finest verbalism'? Was Matthew Arnold right to accuse Tennyson of 'dawdling with the painted shell of the universe'? Does his work go beyond verbal and metrical expertise into greatness? No one would argue that a poet should be indifferent to beauty, but was Tennyson inordinately preoccupied with Beauty? Was he in his poetry (though not, certainly not, in person) too much of an aesthete?

Or perhaps too much of an aesthete except when being too much of a sententious moralist? 'Go further home and you come to thoughts commonplace', said Hopkins. But then what is the dividing line between an empty commonplace and a profoundly simple truth? After all, Gray's 'Elegy in a Country Churchyard' is made up of commonplace thoughts, but it is not a commonplace poem.

Then there is Tennyson's Victorianism. Some think that the Victorians were complacent (but didn't their writers make exactly the attacks which we now make on some things in Victorian society?). Whitman believed that Tennyson's 'moral line is local and conventional'—yet he went on, unexpectedly, 'but it is vital and genuine'. Do we now believe that there can be such a thing? (If not, why not?) In any case, is it true that the author of *Maud* and *Aylmer's Field* was smugly at one with the society he lived in?

Other critics, most notably Sir Harold Nicolson, have argued that there were two Tennysons—the rather hollow one who produced public poetry, patriotic and insensitive, concerned above all to do what was expected of him; and the true poet, a man of deep and private fears, 'a morbid and unhappy mystic'. But is it true that all of Tennyson's poems on public themes are hollow? Or that his only great poems are poems of fear and deprivation? Can we so neatly slice this poet in two?

Principal Dates of Tennyson's Life

1809 August 6, Alfred Tennyson born, fourth son of Rev. George Clayton Tennyson, Rector of Somersby, Lincolnshire.

1815 Educated at Louth Grammar School until 1820, when (with his brothers and sisters) he was privately taught at home by their father.

1827 *Poems by Two Brothers*, a volume by Alfred and his brother Charles, with a few poems by the brother Frederick. (Reissued by Macmillan, 1893.) In November, he joined Frederick at Trinity College, Cambridge (from which he went down without a degree early in 1831).

1829 Joined the debating society, 'The Apostles', after meeting the man who was to be his closest friend, Arthur Henry Hallam. In June, he won the Chancellor's Medal for his poem *Timbuctoo*.

1830 *Poems, Chiefly Lyrical*. (This included 23 poems which Tennyson did not subsequently reprint, as well as 7 poems which he did not reprint in *1842* but reprinted later.) In the summer, he toured the Pyrenees with Hallam.

1831 March. His father died. By this date Hallam was deeply in love with Tennyson's sister Emily, somewhat to the distress of his father, Henry Hallam.

1832 In the summer he toured the Rhine country with Hallam. In December, he published *Poems*, dated 1833 on the title-page. (This included 7 poems which Tennyson did not subsequently reprint, as well as 7 poems which he did not reprint in *1842* but reprinted later.)

1833 Hallam's engagement to Emily Tennyson recognized by his family. Tennyson set to work revising the poems of *1830* and *1832*. Apart from a few poems in annuals, he was to publish nothing until *1842*, partly because of hostile reviews. In September, Hallam died in Vienna.

1833-4 Tennyson began writing *In Memoriam* and created many of the most notable poems of *1842*.

PRINCIPAL DATES OF TENNYSON'S LIFE

1836 Tennyson fell in love with Emily Sellwood; the engagement was recognized in 1838, but broken off in 1840 (partly because of Tennyson's financial insecurity).

1837 The Tennysons had to leave Somersby, and lived at High Beech, Epping.

1840-1 Invested his fortune (about £3,000) in a wood-carving scheme which collapsed.

1842 *Poems*. The first volume consists of some of the poems of *1830* and *1832*, together with a few written about 1833. The second volume is entirely new poems.

1840s Tennyson suffered from very bad health and nervous depression.

1847 *The Princess*.

1850 June, *In Memoriam A. H. H.* (published anonymously). Married the same month to Emily Sellwood. In November, appointed Poet Laureate (Wordsworth had died in April).

1853 Made his home at Farringford, Isle of Wight.

1855 *Maud, and Other Poems*.

1859 *Idylls of the King*. Four idylls: *Enid, Vivien, Elaine,* and *Guinevere*. The sequence was gradually built up; the last of the idylls was not published till 1885.

1864 *Enoch Arden, etc.*

1869 December, *The Holy Grail and Other Poems*, dated 1870 on the title-page. In 1869 he established another home at Aldworth.

1872 *Gareth and Lynette*.

1875 *Queen Mary*. The first of his plays, followed by *Harold* (1877), *Becket* (1884), *The Cup and The Falcon* (1884), *The Promise of May* (1886), and *The Foresters* (1892).

1880 *Ballads and Other Poems*.

1883 Accepted a barony.

1885 *Tiresias and Other Poems*.

1886 *Locksley Hall Sixty Years After, Etc.*

1889 *Demeter and Other Poems*.

1892 October 6, died at Aldworth. Posthumous publication of *The Death of Œnone, Akbar's Dream, and Other Poems*.

Poems of 1842

VOLUME ONE

CLARIBEL	19
LILIAN	20
ISABEL	21
MARIANA ✓	23
TO ——	26
MADELINE	27
SONG—THE OWL	28
SECOND SONG—TO THE SAME	29
RECOLLECTIONS OF THE ARABIAN NIGHTS	30
ODE TO MEMORY	35
SONG [A SPIRIT]	39
ADELINE	40
A CHARACTER	42
THE POET	43
THE POET'S MIND	45
THE DYING SWAN	46
A DIRGE	47
LOVE AND DEATH	49
THE BALLAD OF ORIANA	50
CIRCUMSTANCE	53
THE MERMAN	53
THE MERMAID	55
TO J.M.K.	57
THE LADY OF SHALOTT ✓	57
MARIANA IN THE SOUTH	63
ELEÄNORE	66
THE MILLER'S DAUGHTER	71
FATIMA	79

ŒNONE	80
THE SISTERS	88
TO— WITH THE FOLLOWING POEM	90
THE PALACE OF ART	91
LADY CLARA VERE DE VERE	101
THE MAY QUEEN	104
NEW-YEAR'S EVE	106
CONCLUSION	109
THE LOTOS-EATERS	112
A DREAM OF FAIR WOMEN	118
MARGARET	128
THE BLACKBIRD	130
THE DEATH OF THE OLD YEAR	131
TO J.S.	133
'YOU ASK ME, WHY, THO' ILL AT EASE'	136
'OF OLD SAT FREEDOM ON THE HEIGHTS'	137
'LOVE THOU THY LAND, WITH LOVE FAR-BROUGHT'	138
THE GOOSE	141

VOLUME TWO

THE EPIC	143
MORTE D'ARTHUR	145
THE GARDENER'S DAUGHTER	154
DORA	163
AUDLEY COURT	168
WALKING TO THE MAIL	171
ST. SIMEON STYLITES	174
THE TALKING OAK	181
LOVE AND DUTY	191
ULYSSES	194
LOCKSLEY HALL	196

POEMS OF 1842

GODIVA	209
THE TWO VOICES	211
THE DAY-DREAM	228
PROLOGUE	228
THE SLEEPING PALACE	229
THE SLEEPING BEAUTY	231
THE ARRIVAL	232
THE REVIVAL	233
THE DEPARTURE	234
MORAL	235
L'ENVOI	236
EPILOGUE	238
AMPHION	238
ST. AGNES' EVE	242
SIR GALAHAD	243
EDWARD GRAY	246
WILL WATERPROOF'S LYRICAL MONOLOGUE	247
LADY CLARE	256
THE LORD OF BURLEIGH	259
SIR LAUNCELOT AND QUEEN GUINEVERE	262
A FAREWELL	263
THE BEGGAR MAID	264
THE VISION OF SIN	265
THE SKIPPING-ROPE	272
'MOVE EASTWARD, HAPPY EARTH, AND LEAVE'	273
'BREAK, BREAK, BREAK'	273
THE POET'S SONG	274

CLARIBEL

A MELODY

I

Where Claribel low-lieth
  The breezes pause and die,
    Letting the rose-leaves fall:
But the solemn oak-tree sigheth,
    Thick-leaved, ambrosial, 5
  With an ancient melody
  Of an inward agony,
Where Claribel low-lieth.

II

At eve the beetle boometh
  Athwart the thicket lone: 10
At noon the wild bee hummeth
  About the moss'd headstone:
At midnight the moon cometh,
  And looketh down alone.
Her song the lintwhite swelleth, 15
The clear-voiced mavis dwelleth,
  The callow throstle lispeth,
The slumbrous wave outwelleth,
  The babbling runnel crispeth,
The hollow grot replieth 20
  Where Claribel low-lieth.

---

15. *lintwhite:* linnet   16-7. *mavis, throstle:* song-thrush
           19. *crispeth:* curleth

LILIAN

I

Airy, fairy Lilian,
  Flitting, fairy Lilian,
When I ask her if she love me,
Claps her tiny hands above me,
  Laughing all she can;
She'll not tell me if she love me,
  Cruel little Lilian.

II

  When my passion seeks
  Pleasance in love-sighs,
She, looking thro' and thro' me
Thoroughly to undo me,
  Smiling, never speaks:
So innocent-arch, so cunning-simple,
From beneath her gathered wimple
  Glancing with black-beaded eyes,
Till the lightning laughters dimple
  The baby-roses in her cheeks;
  Then away she flies.

III

Prythee weep, May Lilian!
  Gaiety without eclipse
Wearieth me, May Lilian:
Thro' my very heart it thrilleth
  When from crimson-threaded lips
Silver-treble laughter trilleth:
  Prythee weep, May Lilian.

---

14. *wimple:* head-cloth

IV

Praying all I can,
If prayers will not hush thee,
   Airy Lilian,
Like a rose-leaf I will crush thee,
   Fairy Lilian.   30

ISABEL

I

EYES not down-dropt nor over-bright, but fed
  With the clear-pointed flame of chastity,
Clear, without heat, undying, tended by
  Pure vestal thoughts in the translucent fane
Of her still spirit; locks not wide-dispread,   5
  Madonna-wise on either side her head;
  Sweet lips whereon perpetually did reign
The summer calm of golden charity,
Were fixed shadows of thy fixed mood,
  Revered Isabel, the crown and head,   10
The stately flower of female fortitude,
  Of perfect wifehood and pure lowlihead.

II

The intuitive decision of a bright
  And thorough-edged intellect to part
    Error from crime; a prudence to withhold;   15
  The laws of marriage character'd in gold
Upon the blanched tablets of her heart;
A love still burning upward, giving light
To read those laws; an accent very low
In blandishment, but a most silver flow   20

---

4. *fane*: temple

Of subtle-paced counsel in distress,
Right to the heart and brain, tho' undescried,
　　Winning its way with extreme gentleness
Thro' all the outworks of suspicious pride;
A courage to endure and to obey; 25
A hate of gossip parlance, and of sway,
Crown'd Isabel, thro' all her placid life,
The queen of marriage, a most perfect wife.

III

The mellow'd reflex of a winter moon;
A clear stream flowing with a muddy one, 30
　Till in its onward current it absorbs
　　With swifter movement and in purer light
　　　The vexed eddies of its wayward brother:
　A leaning and upbearing parasite,
　　Clothing the stem, which else had fallen quite 35
With cluster'd flower-bells and ambrosial orbs
　Of rich fruit-bunches leaning on each other—
　　Shadow forth thee:—the world hath not another
(Tho' all her fairest forms are types of thee,
And thou of God in thy great charity) 40
Of such a finish'd chasten'd purity.

---

26. *gossip:* silly woman's

MARIANA

> 'Mariana in the moated grange.'
> *Measure for Measure*

WITH blackest moss the flower-plots
    Were thickly crusted, one and all:
The rusted nails fell from the knots
    That held the pear to the gable-wall.
The broken sheds look'd sad and strange: 5
    Unlifted was the clinking latch;
    Weeded and worn the ancient thatch
Upon the lonely moated grange.
        She only said, 'My life is dreary,
           He cometh not,' she said;   10
        She said, 'I am aweary, aweary,
           I would that I were dead!'

Her tears fell with the dews at even;
    Her tears fell ere the dews were dried;
She could not look on the sweet heaven,   15
    Either at morn or eventide.
After the flitting of the bats,
    When thickest dark did trance the sky,
    She drew her casement-curtain by,
And glanced athwart the glooming flats.   20
        She only said, 'The night is dreary,
           He cometh not,' she said;
        She said, 'I am aweary, aweary,
           I would that I were dead!'

Upon the middle of the night,   25
    Waking she heard the night-fowl crow:
The cock sung out an hour ere light:
    From the dark fen the oxen's low

Came to her: without hope of change,
  In sleep she seem'd to walk forlorn,
  Till cold winds woke the gray-eyed morn
About the lonely moated grange.
    She only said, 'The day is dreary,
      He cometh not,' she said;
    She said, 'I am aweary, aweary,
      I would that I were dead!'

About a stone-cast from the wall
  A sluice with blacken'd waters slept,
And o'er it many, round and small,
  The cluster'd marish-mosses crept.
Hard by a poplar shook alway,
  All silver-green with gnarled bark:
  For leagues no other tree did mark
The level waste, the rounding gray.
    She only said, 'My life is dreary,
      He cometh not,' she said;
    She said, 'I am aweary, aweary,
      I would that I were dead!'

And ever when the moon was low,
  And the shrill winds were up and away,
In the white curtain, to and fro,
  She saw the gusty shadow sway.
But when the moon was very low,
  And wild winds bound within their cell,
  The shadow of the poplar fell
Upon her bed, across her brow.
    She only said, 'The night is dreary,
      He cometh not,' she said;
    She said, 'I am aweary, aweary,
      I would that I were dead!'

All day within the dreamy house,
  The doors upon their hinges creak'd;
The blue fly sung in the pane; the mouse
  Behind the mouldering wainscot shriek'd,
Or from the crevice peer'd about.
  Old faces glimmer'd thro' the doors,
  Old footsteps trod the upper floors,
Old voices called her from without.
    She only said, 'My life is dreary,
      He cometh not,' she said;
    She said, 'I am aweary, aweary,
      I would that I were dead!'

The sparrow's chirrup on the roof,
  The slow clock ticking, and the sound
Which to the wooing wind aloof
  The poplar made, did all confound
Her sense; but most she loathed the hour
  When the thick-moted sunbeam lay
  Athwart the chambers, and the day
Was sloping toward his western bower.
    Then, said she, 'I am very dreary,
      He will not come,' she said;
    She wept, 'I am aweary, aweary,
      Oh God, that I were dead!'

TO

I

CLEAR-HEADED friend, whose joyful scorn,
   Edged with sharp laughter, cuts atwain
     The knots that tangle human creeds,
   The wounding cords that bind and strain
     The heart until it bleeds,   5
Ray-fringed eyelids of the morn
     Roof not a glance so keen as thine:
     If aught of prophecy be mine,
Thou wilt not live in vain.

II

Low-cowering shall the Sophist sit;   10
   Falsehood shall bare her plaited brow:
   Fair-fronted Truth shall droop not now
With shrilling shafts of subtle wit.
Nor martyr-flames, nor trenchant swords
   Can do away that ancient lie;   15
   A gentler death shall Falsehood die,
Shot thro' and thro' with cunning words.

III

Weak Truth a-leaning on her crutch,
   Wan, wasted Truth in her utmost need,
   Thy kingly intellect shall feed,   20
     Until she be an athlete bold,
And weary with a finger's touch
   Those writhed limbs of lightning speed;
Like that strange angel which of old,
   Until the breaking of the light,   25
Wrestled with wandering Israel,
   Past Yabbok brook the livelong night,
And heaven's mazed signs stood still
In the dim tract of Penuel.

MADELINE

I

Thou art not steep'd in golden languors,
　　No tranced summer calm is thine,
　　　　Ever varying Madeline.
　　Thro' light and shadow thou dost range,
　　Sudden glances, sweet and strange,　　　　5
Delicious spites and darling angers,
　　And airy forms of flitting change.

II

Smiling, frowning, evermore,
Thou art perfect in love-lore.
Revealings deep and clear are thine　　　　10
Of wealthy smiles: but who may know
Whether smile or frown be fleeter?
Whether smile or frown be sweeter,
　　　　Who may know?
Frowns perfect-sweet along the brow　　　　15
Light-glooming over eyes divine,
Like little clouds sun-fringed, are thine,
　　　　Ever varying Madeline.
　　Thy smile and frown are not aloof
　　　　From one another,　　　　20
　　　Each to each is dearest brother;
　　Hues of the silken sheeny woof
　　　　Momently shot into each other.
　　　　All the mystery is thine;
Smiling, frowning, evermore,　　　　25
Thou art perfect in love-lore,
　　　　Ever varying Madeline.

III

A subtle, sudden flame,
  By veering passion fann'd,
    About thee breaks and dances: 30
  When I would kiss thy hand,
The flush of anger'd shame
  O'erflows thy calmer glances,
And o'er black brows drops down
A sudden-curved frown: 35
But when I turn away,
Thou, willing me to stay,
  Wooest not, nor vainly wranglest;
    But, looking fixedly the while,
  All my bounding heart entanglest 40
    In a golden-netted smile;
Then in madness and in bliss,
If my lips should dare to kiss
Thy taper fingers amorously,
Again thou blushest angerly; 45
And o'er black brows drops down
A sudden-curved frown.

SONG—THE OWL

I

When cats run home and light is come,
  And dew is cold upon the ground,
And the far-off stream is dumb,
  And the whirring sail goes round,
  And the whirring sail goes round; 5
    Alone and warming his five wits,
    The white owl in the belfry sits.

II

When merry milkmaids click the latch,
  And rarely smells the new-mown hay,
And the cock hath sung beneath the thatch
  Twice or thrice his roundelay,
  Twice or thrice his roundelay;
    Alone and warming his five wits,
    The white owl in the belfry sits.

SECOND SONG

TO THE SAME

I

Thy tuwhits are lull'd, I wot,
  Thy tuwhoos of yesternight,
Which upon the dark afloat,
  So took echo with delight,
  So took echo with delight,
    That her voice untuneful grown,
    Wears all day a fainter tone.

II

I would mock thy chaunt anew;
  But I cannot mimick it;
Not a whit of thy tuwhoo,
  Thee to woo to thy tuwhit,
  Thee to woo to thy tuwhit,
    With a lengthen'd loud halloo,
    Tuwhoo, tuwhit, tuwhit, tuwhoo-o-o.

RECOLLECTIONS OF THE ARABIAN NIGHTS

WHEN the breeze of a joyful dawn blew free
In the silken sail of infancy,
The tide of time flow'd back with me,
  The forward-flowing tide of time;
And many a sheeny summer-morn, 5
Adown the Tigris I was borne,
By Bagdat's shrines of fretted gold,
High-walled gardens green and old;
True Mussulman was I and sworn,
  For it was in the golden prime 10
  Of good Haroun Alraschid.

Anight my shallop, rustling thro'
The low and bloomed foliage, drove
The fragrant, glistening deeps, and clove
The citron-shadows in the blue: 15
By garden porches on the brim,
The costly doors flung open wide,
Gold glittering thro' lamplight dim,
And broider'd sofas on each side:
  In sooth it was a goodly time, 20
  For it was in the golden prime
  Of good Haroun Alraschid.

12. *shallop:* open boat

Often where clear-stemm'd platans guard
The outlet, did I turn away
The boat-head down a broad canal 25
From the main river sluiced, where all
The sloping of the moon-lit sward
Was damask-work, and deep inlay
Of braided blooms unmown, which crept
Adown to where the water slept. 30
  A goodly place, a goodly time,
    For it was in the golden prime
      Of good Haroun Alraschid.

A motion from the river won
Ridged the smooth level, bearing on 35
My shallop thro' the star-strown calm,
Until another night in night
I enter'd, from the clearer light,
Imbower'd vaults of pillar'd palm,
Imprisoning sweets, which, as they clomb 40
Heavenward, were stay'd beneath the dome
  Of hollow boughs.—A goodly time,
    For it was in the golden prime
      Of good Haroun Alraschid.

Still onward; and the clear canal 45
Is rounded to as clear a lake.
From the green rivage many a fall
Of diamond rillets musical,
Thro' little crystal arches low
Down from the central fountain's flow 50
Fall'n silver-chiming, seemed to shake
The sparkling flints beneath the prow.
  A goodly place, a goodly time,
    For it was in the golden prime
      Of good Haroun Alraschid. 55

23. *platans:* plane-trees   47. *rivage:* bank

Above thro' many a bowery turn
A walk with vary-colour'd shells
Wander'd engrain'd. On either side
All round about the fragrant marge
From fluted vase, and brazen urn   60
In order, eastern flowers large,
Some dropping low their crimson bells
Half-closed, and others studded wide
　With disks and tiars, fed the time
　With odour in the golden prime   65
　　Of good Haroun Alraschid.

Far off, and where the lemon grove
In closest coverture upsprung,
The living airs of middle night
Died round the bulbul as he sung;   70
Not he: but something which possess'd
The darkness of the world, delight,
Life, anguish, death, immortal love,
Ceasing not, mingled, unrepress'd,
　Apart from place, withholding time,   75
　But flattering the golden prime
　　Of good Haroun Alraschid.

Black the garden-bowers and grots
Slumber'd: the solemn palms were ranged
Above, unwoo'd of summer wind: 80
A sudden splendour from behind
Flush'd all the leaves with rich gold-green,
And, flowing rapidly between
Their interspaces, counterchanged
The level lake with diamond-plots   85
　Of dark and bright. A lovely time,
　For it was in the golden prime
　　Of good Haroun Alraschid.

Dark-blue the deep sphere overhead,
Distinct with vivid stars inlaid, 90
Grew darker from that under-flame:
So, leaping lightly from the boat,
With silver anchor left afloat,
In marvel whence that glory came
Upon me, as in sleep I sank 95
In cool soft turf upon the bank,
   Entranced with that place and time,
   So worthy of the golden prime
     Of good Haroun Alraschid.

Thence thro' the garden I was drawn— 100
A realm of pleasance, many a mound,
And many a shadow-chequer'd lawn
Full of the city's stilly sound,
And deep myrrh-thickets blowing round
The stately cedar, tamarisks, 105
Thick rosaries of scented thorn,
Tall orient shrubs, and obelisks
   Graven with emblems of the time,
   In honour of the golden prime
     Of good Haroun Alraschid. 110

With dazed vision unawares
From the long alley's latticed shade
Emerged, I came upon the great
Pavilion of the Caliphat.
Right to the carven cedarn doors, 115
Flung inward over spangled floors,
Broad-based flights of marble stairs
Ran up with golden balustrade,
   After the fashion of the time,
   And humour of the golden prime 120
     Of good Haroun Alraschid.

       105. *tamarisks:* shrubs

The fourscore windows all alight
As with the quintessence of flame,
A million tapers flaring bright
From twisted silvers look'd to shame 125
The hollow-vaulted dark, and stream'd
Upon the mooned domes aloof
In inmost Bagdat, till there seem'd
Hundreds of crescents on the roof
  Of night new-risen, that marvellous time 130
    To celebrate the golden prime
      Of good Haroun Alraschid.

Then stole I up, and trancedly
Gazed on the Persian girl alone,
Serene with argent-lidded eyes 135
Amorous, and lashes like to rays
Of darkness, and a brow of pearl
Tressed with redolent ebony,
In many a dark delicious curl,
Flowing beneath her rose-hued zone; 140
  The sweetest lady of the time,
    Well worthy of the golden prime
      Of good Haroun Alraschid.

Six columns, three on either side,
Pure silver, underpropt a rich 145
Throne of the massive ore, from which
Down-droop'd, in many a floating fold,
Engarlanded and diaper'd
With inwrought flowers, a cloth of gold.
Thereon, his deep eye laughter-stirr'd 150
With merriment of kingly pride,
  Sole star of all that place and time,
  I saw him—in his golden prime,
    THE GOOD HAROUN ALRASCHID.

125. *silvers:* candelabra   140. *zone:* girdle

ODE TO MEMORY

ADDRESSED TO ——

I

Thou who stealest fire,
From the fountains of the past,
To glorify the present; oh, haste,
    Visit my low desire!
Strengthen me, enlighten me!   5
I faint in this obscurity,
Thou dewy dawn of memory.

II

Come not as thou camest of late,
  Flinging the gloom of yesternight
On the white day; but robed in soften'd light   10
    Of orient state.
Whilome thou camest with the morning mist,
  Even as a maid, whose stately brow
The dew-impearled winds of dawn have kiss'd,
    When, she, as thou,   15
Stays on her floating locks the lovely freight
Of overflowing blooms, and earliest shoots
Of orient green, giving safe pledge of fruits,
  Which in wintertide shall star
The black earth with brilliance rare.   20

III

Whilome thou camest with the morning mist,
  And with the evening cloud,
Showering thy gleaned wealth into my open breast
(Those peerless flowers which in the rudest wind
    Never grow sere,   25
When rooted in the garden of the mind,
  Because they are the earliest of the year).

Nor was the night thy shroud.
In sweet dreams softer than unbroken rest
Thou leddest by the hand thine infant Hope.   30
The eddying of her garments caught from thee
The light of thy great presence; and the cope
   Of the half-attain'd futurity,
      Tho' deep not fathomless,
Was cloven with the million stars which tremble   35
O'er the deep mind of dauntless infancy.
Small thought was there of life's distress;
For sure she deem'd no mist of earth could dull
Those spirit-thrilling eyes so keen and beautiful:
Sure she was nigher to heaven's spheres,   40
Listening the lordly music flowing from
         The illimitable years.
   O strengthen me, enlighten me!
   I faint in this obscurity,
   Thou dewy dawn of memory.   45

IV

Come forth, I charge thee, arise,
Thou of the many tongues, the myriad eyes!
Thou comest not with shows of flaunting vines
         Unto mine inner eye,
         Divinest Memory!   50
   Thou wert not nursed by the waterfall
Which ever sounds and shines
   A pillar of white light upon the wall
Of purple cliffs, aloof descried:
Come from the woods that belt the gray hill-side,   55
The seven elms, the poplars four
That stand beside my father's door,
And chiefly from the brook that loves
To purl o'er matted cress and ribbed sand,
Or dimple in the dark of rushy coves,   60

29. dreams: day-dreams

Drawing into his narrow earthen urn,
  In every elbow and turn,
The filter'd tribute of the rough woodland,
  O! hither lead thy feet!
Pour round mine ears the livelong bleat 65
Of the thick-fleeced sheep from wattled folds,
  Upon the ridged wolds,
When the first matin-song hath waken'd loud
Over the dark dewy earth forlorn,
What time the amber morn 70
Forth gushes from beneath a low-hung cloud.

V

Large dowries doth the raptured eye
  To the young spirit present
    When first she is wed;
      And like a bride of old 75
    In triumph led,
      With music and sweet showers
        Of festal flowers,
Unto the dwelling she must sway.
Well hast thou done, great artist Memory, 80
  In setting round thy first experiment
    With royal frame-work of wrought gold;
Needs must thou dearly love thy first essay,
And foremost in thy various gallery
  Place it, where sweetest sunlight falls 85
    Upon the storied walls;
      For the discovery
And newness of thine art so pleased thee,
That all which thou hast drawn of fairest
  Or boldest since, but lightly weighs 90
With thee unto the love thou bearest
The first-born of thy genius. Artist-like,
Ever retiring thou dost gaze
On the prime labour of thine early days:

No matter what the sketch might be; 95
Whether the high field on the bushless Pike,
Or even a sand-built ridge
Of heaped hills that mound the sea,
Overblown with murmurs harsh,
Or even a lowly cottage whence we see 100
Stretch'd wide and wild the waste enormous marsh,
Where from the frequent bridge,
Like emblems of infinity,
The trenched waters run from sky to sky;
Or a garden bower'd close 105
With plaited alleys of the trailing rose,
Long alleys falling down to twilight grots,
Or opening upon level plots
Of crowned lilies, standing near
Purple-spiked lavender: 110
Whither in after life retired
From brawling storms,
From weary wind,
With youthful fancy re-inspired,
    We may hold converse with all forms 115
Of the many-sided mind,
And those whom passion hath not blinded,
Subtle-thoughted, myriad-minded.

My friend, with you to live alone,
Were how much better than to own 120
A crown, a sceptre, and a throne!

O strengthen me, enlighten me!
I faint in this obscurity,
Thou dewy dawn of memory.

SONG

I

A SPIRIT haunts the year's last hours
Dwelling amid these yellowing bowers:
    To himself he talks;
For at eventide, listening earnestly,
At his work you may hear him sob and sigh   5
    In the walks;
    Earthward he boweth the heavy stalks
Of the mouldering flowers:
    Heavily hangs the broad sunflower
        Over its grave i' the earth so chilly;   10
    Heavily hangs the hollyhock,
        Heavily hangs the tiger-lily.

II

The air is damp, and hush'd, and close,
As a sick man's room when he taketh repose
    An hour before death;   15
My very heart faints and my whole soul grieves
At the moist rich smell of the rotting leaves,
    And the breath
    Of the fading edges of box beneath,
And the year's last rose.   20
    Heavily hangs the broad sunflower
        Over its grave i' the earth so chilly;
    Heavily hangs the hollyhock,
        Heavily hangs the tiger-lily.

ADELINE

I

Mystery of mysteries,
    Faintly smiling Adeline,
    Scarce of earth nor all divine,
Nor unhappy, nor at rest,
    But beyond expression fair   5
    With thy floating flaxen hair;
Thy rose-lips and full blue eyes
    Take the heart from out my breast.
Wherefore those dim looks of thine,
Shadowy, dreaming Adeline?   10

II

Whence that aery bloom of thine,
    Like a lily which the sun
Looks thro' in his sad decline,
    And a rose-bush leans upon,
Thou that faintly smilest still,   15
    As a Naiad in a well,
    Looking at the set of day,
Or a phantom two hours old
    Of a maiden past away,
Ere the placid lips be cold?   20
Wherefore those faint smiles of thine,
    Spiritual Adeline?

III

What hope or fear or joy is thine?
Who talketh with thee, Adeline?
    For sure thou art not all alone.   25
    Do beating hearts of salient springs
    Keep measure with thine own?
        Hast thou heard the butterflies
    What they say betwixt their wings?
    Or in stillest evenings   30
With what voice the violet woos

To his heart the silver dews?
  Or when little airs arise,
How the merry bluebell rings
    To the mosses underneath? 35
    Hast thou look'd upon the breath
  Of the lilies at sunrise?
Wherefore that faint smile of thine,
Shadowy, dreaming Adeline?

IV

Some honey-converse feeds thy mind, 40
  Some spirit of a crimson rose
  In love with thee forgets to close
  His curtains, wasting odorous sighs
All night long on darkness blind.
What aileth thee? whom waitest thou 45
With thy soften'd, shadow'd brow,
    And those dew-lit eyes of thine,
    Thou faint smiler, Adeline?

V

Lovest thou the doleful wind
  When thou gazest at the skies? 50
  Doth the low-tongued Orient
    Wander from the side of the morn,
    Dripping with Sabæan spice
  On thy pillow, lowly bent
    With melodious airs lovelorn, 55
Breathing Light against thy face,
While his locks a-drooping twined
  Round thy neck in subtle ring
Make a carcanet of rays,
    And ye talk together still, 60
  In the language wherewith Spring
  Letters cowslips on the hill?
Hence that look and smile of thine,
    Spiritual Adeline.

59. *carcanet:* necklace

A CHARACTER

With a half-glance upon the sky
At night he said, 'The wanderings
Of this most intricate Universe
Teach me the nothingness of things.'
Yet could not all creation pierce
Beyond the bottom of his eye.

He spake of beauty: that the dull
Saw no divinity in grass,
Life in dead stones, or spirit in air;
Then looking as 'twere in a glass,
He smooth'd his chin and sleek'd his hair,
And said the earth was beautiful.

He spake of virtue: not the gods
More purely, when they wish to charm
Pallas and Juno sitting by:
And with a sweeping of the arm,
And a lack-lustre dead-blue eye,
Devolved his rounded periods.

Most delicately hour by hour
He canvass'd human mysteries,
And trod on silk, as if the winds
Blew his own praises in his eyes,
And stood aloof from other minds
In impotence of fancied power.

With lips depress'd as he were meek,
Himself unto himself he sold:
Upon himself himself did feed:
Quiet, dispassionate, and cold,
And other than his form of creed,
With chisell'd features clear and sleek.

THE POET

The poet in a golden clime was born,
    With golden stars above;
Dower'd with the hate of hate, the scorn of scorn,
    The love of love.

He saw thro' life and death, thro' good and ill,   5
    He saw thro' his own soul.
The marvel of the everlasting will,
    An open scroll,

Before him lay: with echoing feet he threaded
    The secretest walks of fame: 10
The viewless arrows of his thoughts were headed
    And wing'd with flame,

Like Indian reeds blown from his silver tongue,
    And of so fierce a flight,
From Calpe unto Caucasus they sung,   15
    Filling with light

And vagrant melodies the winds which bore
    Them earthward till they lit;
Then, like the arrow-seeds of the field flower,
    The fruitful wit   20

Cleaving, took root, and springing forth anew
    Where'er they fell, behold,
Like to the mother plant in semblance, grew
    A flower all gold,

And bravely furnish'd all abroad to fling   25
    The winged shafts of truth,

18. *lit:* alighted

To throng with stately blooms the breathing spring
    Of Hope and Youth.

So many minds did gird their orbs with beams,
    Tho' one did fling the fire.
Heaven flow'd upon the soul in many dreams
    Of high desire.

Thus truth was multiplied on truth, the world
    Like one great garden show'd,
And thro' the wreaths of floating dark upcurl'd,
    Rare sunrise flow'd.

And Freedom rear'd in that august sunrise
    Her beautiful bold brow,
When rites and forms before his burning eyes
    Melted like snow.

There was no blood upon her maiden robes
    Sunn'd by those orient skies;
But round about the circles of the globes
    Of her keen eyes

And in her raiment's hem was traced in flame
    WISDOM, a name to shake
All evil dreams of power—a sacred name.
    And when she spake,

Her words did gather thunder as they ran,
    And as the lightning to the thunder
Which follows it, riving the spirit of man,
    Making earth wonder,

So was their meaning to her words. No sword
    Of wrath her right arm whirl'd,
But one poor poet's scroll, and with *his* word
    She shook the world.

THE POET'S MIND

I

VEX not thou the poet's mind
　With thy shallow wit:
Vex not thou the poet's mind;
　For thou canst not fathom it.
Clear and bright it should be ever,
Flowing like a crystal river;
Bright as light, and clear as wind.

II

Dark-brow'd sophist, come not anear;
　All the place is holy ground;
　　Hollow smile and frozen sneer
　　　Come not here.
　Holy water will I pour
　Into every spicy flower
Of the laurel-shrubs that hedge it around.
The flowers would faint at your cruel cheer.
　In your eye there is death,
　There is frost in your breath
　Which would blight the plants.
　　Where you stand you cannot hear
　　　From the groves within
　　　The wild-bird's din.
In the heart of the garden the merry bird chants.
It would fall to the ground if you came in.
　In the middle leaps a fountain
　　　Like sheet lightning,
　　　Ever brightening
　With a low melodious thunder;
All day and all night it is ever drawn
　From the brain of the purple mountain
　Which stands in the distance yonder:
It springs on a level of bowery lawn,

And the mountain draws it from Heaven above,
And it sings a song of undying love;
And yet, tho' its voice be so clear and full,
You never would hear it; your ears are so dull;   35
So keep where you are: you are foul with sin;
It would shrink to the earth if you came in.

THE DYING SWAN

I

The plain was grassy, wild and bare,
Wide, wild, and open to the air,
Which had built up everywhere
   An under-roof of doleful gray.
With an inner voice the river ran,   5
Adown it floated a dying swan,
     And loudly did lament.
   It was the middle of the day.
Ever the weary wind went on,
     And took the reed-tops as it went.   10

II

Some blue peaks in the distance rose,
And white against the cold-white sky,
Shone out their crowning snows.
   One willow over the river wept,
And shook the wave as the wind did sigh;   15
Above in the wind was the swallow,
     Chasing itself at its own wild will,
     And far thro' the marish green and still
     The tangled water-courses slept,
Shot over with purple, and green, and yellow.   20

III

The wild swan's death-hymn took the soul
Of that waste place with joy
Hidden in sorrow: at first to the ear
The warble was low, and full and clear;
And floating about the under-sky, 25
Prevailing in weakness, the coronach stole
Sometimes afar, and sometimes anear;
But anon her awful jubilant voice,
With a music strange and manifold,
Flow'd forth on a carol free and bold; 30
As when a mighty people rejoice
With shawms, and with cymbals, and harps of gold,
And the tumult of their acclaim is roll'd
Thro' the open gates of the city afar,
To the shepherd who watcheth the evening star. 35
And the creeping mosses and clambering weeds,
And the willow-branches hoar and dank,
And the wavy swell of the soughing reeds,
And the wave-worn horns of the echoing bank,
And the silvery marish-flowers that throng 40
The desolate creeks and pools among,
Were flooded over with eddying song.

A DIRGE

I

Now is done thy long day's work;
Fold thy palms across thy breast,
Fold thine arms, turn to thy rest.
    Let them rave.
Shadows of the silver birk 5
Sweep the green that folds thy grave.
    Let them rave.

5. *birk:* birch.

II

Thee nor carketh care nor slander;
Nothing but the small cold worm
Fretteth thine enshrouded form.
    Let them rave.
Light and shadow ever wander
O'er the green that folds thy grave.
    Let them rave.

III

Thou wilt not turn upon thy bed;
Chaunteth not the brooding bee
Sweeter tones than calumny?
    Let them rave.
Thou wilt never raise thine head
From the green that folds thy grave.
    Let them rave.

IV

Crocodiles wept tears for thee;
The woodbine and eglatere
Drip sweeter dews than traitor's tear.
    Let them rave.
Rain makes music in the tree
O'er the green that folds thy grave.
    Let them rave.

V

Round thee blow, self-pleached deep,
Bramble roses, faint and pale,
And long purples of the dale.
    Let them rave.
These in every shower creep
Thro' the green that folds thy grave.
    Let them rave.

8. *carketh:* vexeth

VI

The gold-eyed kingcups fine;
The frail bluebell peereth over
Rare broidry of the purple clover.
    Let them rave.
Kings have no such couch as thine,   40
As the green that folds thy grave.
    Let them rave.

VII

Wild words wander here and there:
God's great gift of speech abused
Makes thy memory confused: 45
    But let them rave.
The balm-cricket carols clear
In the green that folds thy grave.
    Let them rave.

LOVE AND DEATH

WHAT time the mighty moon was gathering light
Love paced the thymy plots of Paradise,
And all about him roll'd his lustrous eyes;
When, turning round a cassia, full in view,
Death, walking all alone beneath a yew,   5
And talking to himself, first met his sight:
'You must begone,' said Death, 'these walks are mine.'
Love wept and spread his sheeny vans for flight;
Yet ere he parted said, 'This hour is thine:
Thou art the shadow of life, and as the tree   10
Stands in the sun and shadows all beneath,
So in the light of great eternity
Life eminent creates the shade of death;
The shadow passeth when the tree shall fall,
But I shall reign for ever over all.'   15

THE BALLAD OF ORIANA

My heart is wasted with my woe,
    Oriana.
There is no rest for me below,
    Oriana.
When the long dun wolds are ribb'd with snow,   5
And loud the Norland whirlwinds blow,
    Oriana,
Alone I wander to and fro,
    Oriana.

Ere the light on dark was growing,   10
    Oriana,
At midnight the cock was crowing,
    Oriana:
Winds were blowing, waters flowing,
We heard the steeds to battle going,   15
    Oriana;
Aloud the hollow bugle blowing,
    Oriana.

In the yew-wood black as night,
    Oriana,   20
Ere I rode into the fight,
    Oriana,
While blissful tears blinded my sight
By star-shine and by moonlight,
    Oriana,   25
I to thee my troth did plight,
    Oriana.

6. *Norland:* northern-region

She stood upon the castle wall,
    Oriana:
She watch'd my crest among them all,
    Oriana:
She saw me fight, she heard me call,
When forth there stept a foeman tall,
    Oriana,
Atween me and the castle wall,
    Oriana.

The bitter arrow went aside,
    Oriana:
The false, false arrow went aside,
    Oriana:
The damned arrow glanced aside,
And pierced thy heart, my love, my bride,
    Oriana!
Thy heart, my life, my love, my bride,
    Oriana!

Oh! narrow, narrow was the space,
    Oriana.
Loud, loud rung out the bugle's brays,
    Oriana.
Oh! deathful stabs were dealt apace,
The battle deepen'd in its place,
    Oriana;
But I was down upon my face,
    Oriana.

They should have stabb'd me where I lay,
    Oriana!
How could I rise and come away,
    Oriana?
How could I look upon the day?

They should have stabb'd me where I lay,
    Oriana—
They should have trod me into clay,
    Oriana.

O breaking heart that will not break,
    Oriana!
O pale, pale face so sweet and meek,
    Oriana!
Thou smilest, but thou dost not speak,
And then the tears run down my cheek,
    Oriana:
What wantest thou? whom dost thou seek,
    Oriana?

I cry aloud: none hear my cries,
    Oriana.
Thou comest atween me and the skies,
    Oriana.
I feel the tears of blood arise
Up from my heart unto my eyes,
    Oriana.
Within thy heart my arrow lies,
    Oriana.

O cursed hand! O cursed blow!
    Oriana!
O happy thou that liest low,
    Oriana!
All night the silence seems to flow
Beside me in my utter woe,
    Oriana.
A weary, weary way I go,
    Oriana.

When Norland winds pipe down the sea,
    Oriana,
I walk, I dare not think of thee,
    Oriana.
Thou liest beneath the greenwood tree,   95
I dare not die and come to thee,
    Oriana.
I hear the roaring of the sea,
    Oriana.

CIRCUMSTANCE

Two children in two neighbour villages
Playing mad pranks along the healthy leas;
Two strangers meeting at a festival;
Two lovers whispering by an orchard wall;
Two lives bound fast in one with golden ease;   5
Two graves grass-green beside a gray church-tower,
Wash'd with still rains and daisy blossomed;
Two children in one hamlet born and bred;
So runs the round of life from hour to hour.

THE MERMAN

I

    Who would be
    A merman bold,
    Sitting alone,
    Singing alone
    Under the sea,
    With a crown of gold,   5
    On a throne?

II

I would be a merman bold,
I would sit and sing the whole of the day;
I would fill the sea-halls with a voice of power;   10
But at night I would roam abroad and play
With the mermaids in and out of the rocks,
Dressing their hair with the white sea-flower;
And holding them back by their flowing locks
I would kiss them often under the sea,   15
And kiss them again till they kiss'd me
    Laughingly, laughingly;
And then we would wander away, away
To the pale-green sea-groves straight and high,
    Chasing each other merrily.   20

III

There would be neither moon nor star;
But the wave would make music above us afar—
Low thunder and light in the magic night—
    Neither moon nor star.
We would call aloud in the dreamy dells,   25
Call to each other and whoop and cry
    All night, merrily, merrily;
They would pelt me with starry spangles and shells,
Laughing and clapping their hands between,
    All night, merrily, merrily: 30
But I would throw to them back in mine
Turkis and agate and almondine:
Then leaping out upon them unseen
I would kiss them often under the sea,
And kiss them again till they kiss'd me   35
    Laughingly, laughingly.
Oh! what a happy life were mine
Under the hollow-hung ocean green!
Soft are the moss-beds under the sea;
We would live merrily, merrily.   40

THE MERMAID

I

Who would be
A mermaid fair,
Singing alone,
Combing her hair
Under the sea,
In a golden curl
With a comb of pearl,
On a throne?

II

I would be a mermaid fair;
I would sing to myself the whole of the day;
With a comb of pearl I would comb my hair;
And still as I comb'd I would sing and say,
'Who is it loves me? who loves not me?'
I would comb my hair till my ringlets would fall
    Low adown, low adown,
From under my starry sea-bud crown
    Low adown and around,
And I should look like a fountain of gold
    Springing alone
    With a shrill inner sound,
    Over the throne
    In the midst of the hall;
Till that great sea-snake under the sea
From his coiled sleeps in the central deeps
Would slowly trail himself sevenfold
Round the hall where I sate, and look in at the gate
With his large calm eyes for the love of me.
And all the mermen under the sea
Would feel their immortality
Die in their hearts for the love of me.

III

But at night I would wander away, away,
   I would fling on each side my low-flowing locks,
And lightly vault from the throne and play
   With the mermen in and out of the rocks;
We would run to and fro, and hide and seek,   35
   On the broad sea-wolds in the crimson shells,
   Whose silvery spikes are nighest the sea.
But if any came near I would call, and shriek,
And adown the steep like a wave I would leap
   From the diamond-ledges that jut from the dells; 40
For I would not be kiss'd by all who would list,
Of the bold merry mermen under the sea;
They would sue me, and woo me, and flatter me,
In the purple twilights under the sea;
But the king of them all would carry me,   45
Woo me, and win me, and marry me,
In the branching jaspers under the sea;
Then all the dry pied things that be
In the hueless mosses under the sea
Would curl round my silver feet silently,   50
All looking up for the love of me.
And if I should carol aloud, from aloft
All things that are forked, and horned, and soft
Would lean out from the hollow sphere of the sea,
All looking down for the love of me.   55

47. *jasper:* precious quartz

TO J. M. K.

My hope and heart is with thee—thou wilt be
A latter Luther, and a soldier-priest
To scare church-harpies from the master's feast;
Our dusted velvets have much need of thee:
Thou art no sabbath-drawler of old saws,   5
Distill'd from some worm-canker'd homily;
But spurr'd at heart with fieriest energy
To embattail and to wall about thy cause
With iron-worded proof, hating to hark
The humming of the drowsy pulpit-drone   10
Half God's good sabbath, while the worn-out clerk
Brow-beats his desk below. Thou from a throne
Mounted in heaven wilt shoot into the dark
Arrows of lightnings. I will stand and mark.

THE LADY OF SHALOTT

PART I

On either side the river lie
Long fields of barley and of rye,
That clothe the wold and meet the sky;
And thro' the field the road runs by
    To many-tower'd Camelot;   5
And up and down the people go,
Gazing where the lilies blow
Round an island there below,
    The island of Shalott.

Willows whiten, aspens quiver,   10
Little breezes dusk and shiver
Thro' the wave that runs for ever
By the island in the river
    Flowing down to Camelot.
Four gray walls, and four gray towers,   15
Overlook a space of flowers,
And the silent isle imbowers
    The Lady of Shalott.

By the margin, willow-veil'd,
Slide the heavy barges trail'd   20
By slow horses; and unhail'd
The shallop flitteth silken-sail'd
    Skimming down to Camelot:
But who hath seen her wave her hand?
Or at the casement seen her stand?   25
Or is she known in all the land,
    The Lady of Shalott?

Only reapers, reaping early
In among the bearded barley,
Hear a song that echoes cheerly   30
From the river winding clearly,
    Down to tower'd Camelot:
And by the moon the reaper weary,
Piling sheaves in uplands airy,
Listening, whispers ''Tis the fairy   35
    Lady of Shalott.'

PART II

THERE she weaves by night and day
A magic web with colours gay.
She has heard a whisper say,
A curse is on her if she stay   40
    To look down to Camelot.

She knows not what the curse may be,
And so she weaveth steadily,
And little other care hath she,
    The Lady of Shalott.

And moving thro' a mirror clear
That hangs before her all the year,
Shadows of the world appear.
There she sees the highway near
    Winding down to Camelot:
There the river eddy whirls,
And there the surly village-churls,
And the red cloaks of market girls,
    Pass onward from Shalott.

Sometimes a troop of damsels glad,
An abbot on an ambling pad,
Sometimes a curly shepherd-lad,
Or long-hair'd page in crimson clad,
    Goes by to tower'd Camelot;
And sometimes thro' the mirror blue
The knights come riding two and two:
She hath no loyal knight and true,
    The Lady of Shalott.

But in her web she still delights
To weave the mirror's magic sights,
For often thro' the silent nights
A funeral, with plumes and lights
    And music, went to Camelot:
Or when the moon was overhead,
Came two young lovers lately wed;
'I am half sick of shadows,' said
    The Lady of Shalott.

PART III

A BOW-SHOT from her bower-eaves,
He rode between the barley-sheaves,
The sun came dazzling thro' the leaves,   75
And flamed upon the brazen greaves
    Of bold Sir Lancelot.
A red-cross knight for ever kneel'd
To a lady in his shield,
That sparkled on the yellow field,   80
    Beside remote Shalott.

The gemmy bridle glitter'd free,
Like to some branch of stars we see
Hung in the golden Galaxy.
The bridle bells rang merrily   85
    As he rode down to Camelot:
And from his blazon'd baldric slung
A mighty silver bugle hung,
And as he rode his armour rung,
    Beside remote Shalott.   90

All in the blue unclouded weather
Thick-jewell'd shone the saddle-leather,
The helmet and the helmet-feather
Burn'd like one burning flame together,
    As he rode down to Camelot.   95
As often thro' the purple night,
Below the starry clusters bright,
Some bearded meteor, trailing light,
    Moves over still Shalott.

76. *greaves:* shin-armour

His broad clear brow in sunlight glow'd; 100
On burnish'd hooves his war-horse trode;
From underneath his helmet flow'd
His coal-black curls as on he rode,
  As he rode down to Camelot.
From the bank and from the river 105
He flash'd into the crystal mirror,
'Tirra lirra,' by the river
  Sang Sir Lancelot.

She left the web, she left the loom,
She made three paces thro' the room, 110
She saw the water-lily bloom,
She saw the helmet and the plume,
  She look'd down to Camelot.
Out flew the web and floated wide;
The mirror crack'd from side to side; 115
'The curse is come upon me,' cried
  The Lady of Shalott.

PART IV

IN the stormy east-wind straining,
The pale yellow woods were waning,
The broad stream in his banks complaining, 120
Heavily the low sky raining
  Over tower'd Camelot;
Down she came and found a boat
Beneath a willow left afloat,
And round about the prow she wrote 125
  The Lady of Shalott.

And down the river's dim expanse
Like some bold seër in a trance,
Seeing all his own mischance—
With a glassy countenance 130
  Did she look to Camelot.

And at the closing of the day
She loosed the chain, and down she lay;
The broad stream bore her far away,
    The Lady of Shalott. 135

Lying, robed in snowy white
That loosely flew to left and right—
The leaves upon her falling light—
Thro' the noises of the night
    She floated down to Camelot: 140
And as the boat-head wound along
The willowy hills and fields among,
They heard her singing her last song,
    The Lady of Shalott.

Heard a carol, mournful, holy, 145
Chanted loudly, chanted lowly,
Till her blood was frozen slowly,
And her eyes were darken'd wholly,
    Turn'd to tower'd Camelot.
For ere she reach'd upon the tide 150
The first house by the water-side,
Singing in her song she died,
    The Lady of Shalott.

Under tower and balcony,
By garden-wall and gallery, 155
A gleaming shape she floated by,
Dead-pale between the houses high,
    Silent into Camelot.
Out upon the wharfs they came,
Knight and burgher, lord and dame, 160
And round the prow they read her name,
    The Lady of Shalott.

Who is this? and what is here?
And in the lighted palace near
Died the sound of royal cheer;   165
And they cross'd themselves for fear,
    All the knights at Camelot:
But Lancelot mused a little space;
He said, 'She has a lovely face;
God in his mercy lend her grace,   170
    The Lady of Shalott.'

MARIANA IN THE SOUTH

WITH one black shadow at its feet,
  The house thro' all the level shines,
Close-latticed to the brooding heat,
  And silent in its dusty vines:
A faint-blue ridge upon the right,   5
  An empty river-bed before,
  And shallows on a distant shore,
In glaring sand and inlets bright.
    But 'Ave Mary,' made she moan,
      And 'Ave Mary,' night and morn,   10
    And 'Ah,' she sang, 'to be all alone,
      To live forgotten, and love forlorn.'

She, as her carol sadder grew,
  From brow and bosom slowly down
Thro' rosy taper fingers drew   15
  Her streaming curls of deepest brown
To left and right, and made appear
  Still-lighted in a secret shrine,
  Her melancholy eyes divine,
The home of woe without a tear.   20

And 'Ave Mary,' was her moan,
  'Madonna, sad is night and morn,'
And 'Ah,' she sang, 'to be all alone,
  To live forgotten, and love forlorn.'

Till all the crimson changed, and past 25
  Into deep orange o'er the sea,
Low on her knees herself she cast,
  Before Our Lady murmur'd she;
Complaining, 'Mother, give me grace
  To help me of my weary load.' 30
  And on the liquid mirror glow'd
The clear perfection of her face.
    'Is this the form,' she made her moan,
      'That won his praises night and morn?'
    And 'Ah,' she said, 'but I wake alone, 35
      I sleep forgotten, I wake forlorn.'

Nor bird would sing, nor lamb would bleat.
  Nor any cloud would cross the vault,
But day increased from heat to heat,
  On stony drought and steaming salt; 40
Till now at noon she slept again,
  And seem'd knee-deep in mountain grass,
  And heard her native breezes pass,
And runlets babbling down the glen.
    She breathed in sleep a lower moan, 45
      And murmuring, as at night and morn,
    She thought, 'My spirit is here alone,
      Walks forgotten, and is forlorn.'

Dreaming, she knew it was a dream:
  She felt he was and was not there. 50
She woke: the babble of the stream
  Fell, and, without, the steady glare
Shrank one sick willow sere and small.
  The river-bed was dusty-white;

POEMS OF 1842

  And all the furnace of the light   55
  Struck up against the blinding wall.
    She whisper'd, with a stifled moan
     More inward than at night or morn,
   'Sweet Mother, let me not here alone
     Live forgotten and die forlorn.'   60

And, rising, from her bosom drew
  Old letters, breathing of her worth,
For 'Love,' they said, 'must needs be true,
  To what is loveliest upon earth.'
An image seem'd to pass the door,   65
  To look at her with slight, and say
  'But now thy beauty flows away,
So be alone for evermore.'
   'O cruel heart,' she changed her tone,
    'And cruel love, whose end is scorn,   70
   Is this the end to be left alone,
    To live forgotten, and die forlorn?'

But sometimes in the falling day
  An image seem'd to pass the door,
To look into her eyes and say,   75
  'But thou shalt be alone no more.'
And flaming downward over all
  From heat to heat the day decreased,
  And slowly rounded to the east
The one black shadow from the wall.   80
   'The day to night,' she made her moan,
    'The day to night, the night to morn,
   And day and night I am left alone
    To live forgotten, and love forlorn.'

At eve a dry cicala sung,   85
  There came a sound as of the sea;
Backward the lattice-blind she flung,

    85. *cicala:* a cricket

And lean'd upon the balcony.
There all in spaces rosy-bright
  Large Hesper glitter'd on her tears, 90
  And deepening thro' the silent spheres
Heaven over Heaven rose the night.
And weeping then she made her moan,
  'The night comes on that knows not morn,
When I shall cease to be all alone, 95
  To live forgotten, and love forlorn.'

ELEÄNORE

I

Thy dark eyes open'd not,
  Nor first reveal'd themselves to English air,
    For there is nothing here,
Which, from the outward to the inward brought,
Moulded thy baby thought. 5
Far off from human neighbourhood,
  Thou wert born, on a summer morn,
A mile beneath the cedar-wood.
Thy bounteous forehead was not fann'd
  With breezes from our oaken glades, 10
But thou wert nursed in some delicious land
  Of lavish lights, and floating shades:
And flattering thy childish thought
  The oriental fairy brought,
    At the moment of thy birth, 15
From old well-heads of haunted rills,
And the hearts of purple hills,
  And shadow'd coves on a sunny shore,
    The choicest wealth of all the earth,
  Jewel or shell, or starry ore, 20
    To deck thy cradle, Eleänore.

II

Or the yellow-banded bees,
Thro' half-open lattices
Coming in the scented breeze,
    Fed thee, a child, lying alone, 25
        With whitest honey in fairy gardens cull'd—
    A glorious child, dreaming alone,
    In silk-soft folds, upon yielding down,
With the hum of swarming bees
    Into dreamful slumber lull'd. 30

III

Who may minister to thee?
Summer herself should minister
    To thee, with fruitage golden-rinded
    On golden salvers, or it may be,
Youngest Autumn, in a bower 35
Grape-thicken'd from the light, and blinded
    With many a deep-hued bell-like flower
Of fragrant trailers, when the air
    Sleepeth over all the heaven,
    And the crag that fronts the Even, 40
    All along the shadowing shore,
Crimsons over an inland mere,
    Eleänore!

IV

How may full-sail'd verse express,
    How may measured words adore 45
    The full-flowing harmony
Of thy swan-like stateliness,
    Eleänore?
    The luxuriant symmetry
Of thy floating gracefulness, 50
    Eleänore?
    Every turn and glance of thine,

42. *mere:* lake

Every lineament divine,
    Eleänore,
And the steady sunset glow, 55
    That stays upon thee? For in thee
Is nothing sudden, nothing single;
Like two streams of incense free
    From one censer in one shrine,
        Thought and motion mingle, 60
Mingle ever. Motions flow
To one another, even as tho'
They were modulated so
    To an unheard melody,
Which lives about thee, and a sweep 65
    Of richest pauses, evermore
Drawn from each other mellow-deep;
    Who may express thee, Eleänore?

V

I stand before thee, Eleänore;
    I see thy beauty gradually unfold, 70
Daily and hourly, more and more.
I muse, as in a trance, the while
    Slowly, as from a cloud of gold,
Comes out thy deep ambrosial smile.
I muse, as in a trance, whene'er 75
    The langours of thy love-deep eyes
Float on to me. I would I were
    So tranced, so rapt in ecstasies,
To stand apart, and to adore,
Gazing on thee for evermore, 80
Serene, imperial Eleänore!

VI

Sometimes, with most intensity
Gazing, I seem to see
Thought folded over thought, smiling asleep,

Slowly awaken'd, grow so full and deep 85
In thy large eyes, that, overpower'd quite,
I cannot veil, or droop my sight,
But am as nothing in its light:
As tho' a star, in inmost heaven set,
Ev'n while we gaze on it, 90
Should slowly round his orb, and slowly grow
To a full face, there like a sun remain
Fix'd—then as slowly fade again,
    And draw itself to what it was before;
    So full, so deep, so slow, 95
    Thought seems to come and go
In thy large eyes, imperial Eleänore.

VII

As thunder-clouds that, hung on high,
    Roof'd the world with doubt and fear,
Floating thro' an evening atmosphere, 100
Grow golden all about the sky;
In thee all passion becomes passionless,
Touch'd by thy spirit's mellowness,
Losing his fire and active might
    In a silent meditation, 105
Falling into a still delight,
    And luxury of contemplation:
As waves that up a quiet cove
    Rolling slide, and lying still
        Shadow forth the banks at will: 110
Or sometimes they swell and move,
  Pressing up against the land,
    With motions of the outer sea:
        And the self-same influence
        Controlleth all the soul and sense 115
Of Passion gazing upon thee.
His bow-string slacken'd, languid Love,

Leaning his cheek upon his hand,
Droops both his wings, regarding thee,
    And so would languish evermore,   120
  Serene, imperial Eleänore.

VIII

But when I see thee roam, with tresses unconfined,
While the amorous, odorous wind
  Breathes low between the sunset and the moon;
    Or, in a shadowy saloon,   125
On silken cushions half reclined;
    I watch thy grace; and in its place
  My heart a charmed slumber keeps,
    While I muse upon thy face;
  And a languid fire creeps   130
    Thro' my veins to all my frame,
Dissolvingly and slowly: soon
    From thy rose-red lips MY name
Floweth; and then, as in a swoon,
  With dinning sound my ears are rife,   135
    My tremulous tongue faltereth,
I lose my colour, I lose my breath,
I drink the cup of a costly death,
Brimm'd with delirious draughts of warmest life.
  I die with my delight, before   140
    I hear what I would hear from thee;
  Yet tell my name again to me,
I *would* be dying evermore,
So dying ever, Eleänore.

THE MILLER'S DAUGHTER

I SEE the wealthy miller yet,
    His double chin, his portly size,
And who that knew him could forget
    The busy wrinkles round his eyes?
The slow wise smile that, round about   5
    His dusty forehead drily curl'd,
Seem'd half-within and half-without,
    And full of dealings with the world?

In yonder chair I see him sit,
    Three fingers round the old silver cup—   10
I see his gray eyes twinkle yet
    At his own jest—gray eyes lit up
With summer lightnings of a soul
    So full of summer warmth, so glad,
So healthy, sound, and clear and whole,   15
    His memory scarce can make me sad.

Yet fill my glass: give me one kiss:
    My own sweet Alice, we must die.
There's somewhat in this world amiss
    Shall be unriddled by and by.   20
There's somewhat flows to us in life,
    But more is taken quite away.
Pray, Alice, pray, my darling wife,
    That we may die the self-same day.

Have I not found a happy earth? 25
 I least should breathe a thought of pain
Would God renew me from my birth
 I'd almost live my life again.
So sweet it seems with thee to walk,
 And once again to woo thee mine— 30
It seems in after-dinner talk
 Across the walnuts and the wine—

To be the long and listless boy
 Late-left an orphan of the squire,
Where this old mansion mounted high 35
 Looks down upon the village spire:
For even here, where I and you
 Have lived and loved alone so long,
Each morn my sleep was broken thro'
 By some wild skylark's matin song. 40

And oft I heard the tender dove
 In firry woodlands making moan;
But ere I saw your eyes, my love,
 I had no motion of my own.
For scarce my life with fancy play'd 45
 Before I dream'd that pleasant dream—
Still hither thither idly sway'd
 Like those long mosses in the stream.

Or from the bridge I lean'd to hear
 The milldam rushing down with noise, 50
And see the minnows everywhere
 In crystal eddies glance and poise,
The tall flag-flowers when they sprung
 Below the range of stepping-stones,
Or those three chestnuts near, that hung 55
 In masses thick with milky cones.

But, Alice, what an hour was that,
   When after roving in the woods
('Twas April then), I came and sat
   Below the chestnuts, when their buds   60
Were glistening to the breezy blue;
   And on the slope, an absent fool,
I cast me down, nor thought of you,
   But angled in the higher pool.

A love-song I had somewhere read,   65
   An echo from a measured strain,
Beat time to nothing in my head
   From some odd corner of the brain.
It haunted me, the morning long,
   With weary sameness in the rhymes,   70
The phantom of a silent song,
   That went and came a thousand times.

Then leapt a trout. In lazy mood
   I watch'd the little circles die;
They past into the level flood,   75
   And there a vision caught my eye;
The reflex of a beauteous form,
   A glowing arm, a gleaming neck,
As when a sunbeam wavers warm
   Within the dark and dimpled beck.   80

For you remember, you had set,
   That morning, on the casement-edge
A long green box of mignonette,
   And you were leaning from the ledge:
And when I raised my eyes, above   85
   They met with two so full and bright—
Such eyes! I swear to you, my love,
   That these have never lost their light.

I loved, and love dispell'd the fear
  That I should die an early death: 90
For love possess'd the atmosphere,
  And fill'd the breast with purer breath.
My mother thought, What ails the boy?
  For I was alter'd, and began
To move about the house with joy, 95
  And with the certain step of man.

I loved the brimming wave that swam
  Thro' quiet meadows round the mill,
The sleepy pool above the dam,
  The pool beneath it never still, 100
The meal-sacks on the whiten'd floor,
  The dark round of the dripping wheel,
The very air about the door
  Made misty with the floating meal.

And oft in ramblings on the wold, 105
  When April nights began to blow,
And April's crescent glimmer'd cold,
  I saw the village lights below;
I knew your taper far away,
  And full at heart of trembling hope, 110
From off the wold I came, and lay
  Upon the freshly-flower'd slope.

The deep brook groan'd beneath the mill;
  And 'by that lamp,' I thought, 'she sits!'
The white chalk-quarry from the hill 115
  Gleam'd to the flying moon by fits.
'O that I were beside her now!
  O will she answer if I call?
O would she give me vow for vow,
  Sweet Alice, if I told her all?' 120

Sometimes I saw you sit and spin;
    And, in the pauses of the wind,
Sometimes I heard you sing within;
    Sometimes your shadow cross'd the blind.
At last you rose and moved the light, 125
    And the long shadow of the chair
Flitted across into the night,
    And all the casement darken'd there.

But when at last I dared to speak,
    The lanes, you know, were white with may, 130
Your ripe lips moved not, but your cheek
    Flush'd like the coming of the day;
And so it was—half-sly, half-shy,
    You would, and would not, little one!
Although I pleaded tenderly, 135
    And you and I were all alone.

And slowly was my mother brought
    To yield consent to my desire:
She wish'd me happy, but she thought
    I might have look'd a little higher; 140
And I was young—too young to wed:
    'Yet must I love her for your sake;
Go fetch your Alice here,' she said:
    Her eyelid quiver'd as she spake.

And down I went to fetch my bride: 145
    But, Alice, you were ill at ease;
This dress and that by turns you tried,
    Too fearful that you should not please.
I loved you better for your fears,
    I knew you could not look but well; 150
And dews, that would have fall'n in tears,
    I kiss'd away before they fell.

I watch'd the little flutterings,
   The doubt my mother would not see;
She spoke at large of many things,   155
   And at the last she spoke of me;
And turning look'd upon your face,
   As near this door you sat apart,
And rose, and, with a silent grace
   Approaching, press'd you heart to heart.   160

Ah, well—but sing the foolish song
   I gave you, Alice, on the day
When, arm in arm, we went along,
   A pensive pair, and you were gay
With bridal flowers—that I may seem,   165
   As in the nights of old, to lie
Beside the mill-wheel in the stream,
   While those full chestnuts whisper by.

> It is the miller's daughter,
>   And she is grown so dear, so dear,   170
> That I would be the jewel
>   That trembles in her ear:
> For hid in ringlets day and night,
> I'd touch her neck so warm and white.
>
> And I would be the girdle   175
>   About her dainty dainty waist,
> And her heart would beat against me,
>   In sorrow and in rest:
> And I should know if it beat right,
> I'd clasp it round so close and tight.   180
>
> And I would be the necklace,
>   And all day long to fall and rise
> Upon her balmy bosom,
>   With her laughter or her sighs,
> And I would lie so light, so light,   185
> I scarce should be unclasp'd at night

A trifle, sweet! which true love spells—
    True love interprets—right alone.
His light upon the letter dwells,
    For all the spirit is his own.   190
So, if I waste words now, in truth
    You must blame Love. His early rage
Had force to make me rhyme in youth,
    And makes me talk too much in age.
And now those vivid hours are gone,   195
    Like mine own life to me thou art,
Where Past and Present, wound in one,
    Do make a garland for the heart:
So sing that other song I made,
    Half-anger'd with my happy lot,   200
The day, when in the chestnut shade
    I found the blue Forget-me-not.

        Love that hath us in the net,
        Can he pass, and we forget?
        Many suns arise and set.   205
        Many a chance the years beget.
        Love the gift is Love the debt.
            Even so.
        Love is hurt with jar and fret.
        Love is made a vague regret.   210
        Eyes with idle tears are wet.
        Idle habit links us yet.
        What is love? for we forget:
            Ah, no! no!

Look thro' mine eyes with thine. True wife,   215
    Round my true heart thine arms entwine
My other dearer life in life,
    Look thro' my very soul with thine!
Untouch'd with any shade of years,
    May those kind eyes for ever dwell!   220
They have not shed a many tears,
    Dear eyes, since first I knew them well.

Yet tears they shed: they had their part
  Of sorrow: for when time was ripe,
The still affection of the heart 225
  Became an outward breathing type,
That into stillness past again,
  And left a want unknown before;
Although the loss had brought us pain,
  That loss but made us love the more, 230

With farther lookings on. The kiss,
  The woven arms, seem but to be
Weak symbols of the settled bliss,
  The comfort, I have found in thee:
But that God bless thee, dear—who wrought 235
  Two spirits to one equal mind—
With blessings beyond hope or thought,
  With blessings which no words can find.

Arise, and let us wander forth,
  To yon old mill across the wolds; 240
For look, the sunset, south and north,
  Winds all the vale in rosy folds,
And fires your narrow casement glass,
  Touching the sullen pool below:
On the chalk-hill the bearded grass 245
  Is dry and dewless. Let us go.

FATIMA

O Love, Love, Love! O withering might!
O sun, that from thy noonday height
Shudderest when I strain my sight,
Throbbing thro' all thy heat and light,
   Lo, falling from my constant mind,   5
   Lo, parch'd and wither'd, deaf and blind.
   I whirl like leaves in roaring wind.

Last night I wasted hateful hours
Below the city's eastern towers:
I thirsted for the brooks, the showers: 10
I roll'd among the tender flowers:
   I crush'd them on my breast, my mouth;
   I look'd athwart the burning drouth
   Of that long desert to the south.

Last night, when some one spoke his name,   15
From my swift blood that went and came
A thousand little shafts of flame
Were shiver'd in my narrow frame.
   O Love, O fire! once he drew
   With one long kiss my whole soul thro'   20
   My lips, as sunlight drinketh dew.

Before he mounts the hill, I know
He cometh quickly: from below
Sweet gales, as from deep gardens, blow
Before him, striking on my brow.   25
   In my dry brain my spirit soon,
   Down-deepening from swoon to swoon,
   Faints like a dazzled morning moon.

        13. *drouth:* drought

The wind sounds like a silver wire,
And from beyond the noon a fire 30
Is pour'd upon the hills, and nigher
The skies stoop down in their desire;
   And, isled in sudden seas of light,
   My heart, pierced thro' with fierce delight,
   Bursts into blossom in his sight. 35

My whole soul waiting silently,
All naked in a sultry sky,
Droops blinded with his shining eye:
I *will* possess him or will die.
   I will grow round him in his place, 40
   Grow, live, die looking on his face,
   Die, dying clasp'd in his embrace.

ŒNONE

[marginalia: Like lotus-eaters — classical myth / separate hand]

THERE lies a vale in Ida, lovelier
Than all the valleys of Ionian hills.
The swimming vapour slopes athwart the glen,
Puts forth an arm, and creeps from pine to pine,
And loiters, slowly drawn. On either hand 5
The lawns and meadow-ledges midway down
Hang rich in flowers, and far below them roars
The long brook falling thro' the clov'n ravine
In cataract after cataract to the sea.
Behind the valley topmost Gargarus 10
Stands up and takes the morning: but in front
The gorges, opening wide apart, reveal
Troas and Ilion's column'd citadel,
The crown of Troas.

                Hither came at noon
Mournful Œnone, wandering forlorn
Of Paris, once her playmate on the hills.
Her cheek had lost the rose, and round her neck
Floated her hair or seem'd to float in rest.
She, leaning on a fragment twined with vine,
Sang to the stillness, till the mountain-shade
Sloped downward to her seat from the upper cliff.

  'O mother Ida, many-fountain'd Ida,
Dear mother Ida, harken ere I die.
For now the noonday quiet holds the hill:
The grasshopper is silent in the grass:
The lizard, with his shadow on the stone,
Rests like a shadow, and the winds are dead.
The purple flower droops: the golden bee
Is lily-cradled: I alone awake.
My eyes are full of tears, my heart of love,
My heart is breaking, and my eyes are dim,
And I am all aweary of my life.

  'O mother Ida, many-fountain'd Ida,
Dear mother Ida, harken ere I die.
Hear me, O Earth, hear me, O Hills, O Caves
That house the cold crown'd snake! O mountain brooks,
I am the daughter of a River-God,
Hear me, for I will speak, and build up all
My sorrow with my song, as yonder walls
Rose slowly to a music slowly breathed,
A cloud that gather'd shape: for it may be
That, while I speak of it, a little while
My heart may wander from its deeper woe.

  'O mother Ida, many-fountain'd Ida,
Dear mother Ida, harken ere I die.
I waited underneath the dawning hills,

Aloft the mountain lawn was dewy-dark,
And dewy-dark aloft the mountain pine:
Beautiful Paris, evil-hearted Paris,
Leading a jet-black goat white-horn'd, white-hooved,
Came up from reedy Simois all alone.   51

  'O mother Ida, harken ere I die.
Far-off the torrent call'd me from the cleft:
Far up the solitary morning smote
The streaks of virgin snow. With down-dropt eyes   55
I sat alone: white-breasted like a star
Fronting the dawn he moved; a leopard skin
Droop'd from his shoulder, but his sunny hair
Cluster'd about his temples like a God's:
And his cheek brighten'd as the foam-bow brightens 60
When the wind blows the foam, and all my heart
Went forth to embrace him coming ere he came.

  'Dear mother Ida, harken ere I die.
He smiled, and opening out his milk-white palm
Disclosed a fruit of pure Hesperian gold,   65
That smelt ambrosially, and while I look'd
And listen'd, the full-flowing river of speech
Came down upon my heart.
                        ' "My own Œnone,
Beautiful-brow'd Œnone, my own soul,
Behold this fruit, whose gleaming rind ingrav'n   70
'For the most fair,' would seem to award it thine,
As lovelier than whatever Oread haunt
The knolls of Ida, loveliest in all grace
Of movement, and the charm of married brows."

  'Dear mother Ida, harken ere I die.   75
He prest the blossom of his lips to mine,
And added "This was cast upon the board,
When all the full-faced presence of the Gods
Ranged in the halls of Peleus; whereupon

Rose feud, with question unto whom 'twere due· 80
But light-foot Iris brought it yester-eve,
Delivering, that to me, by common voice
Elected umpire, Herè comes to-day,
Pallas and Aphroditè, claiming each
This meed of fairest. Thou, within the cave 85
Behind yon whispering tuft of oldest pine,
Mayst well behold them unbeheld, unheard
Hear all, and see thy Paris judge of Gods."

'Dear mother Ida, harken ere I die.
It was the deep midnoon: one silvery cloud 90
Had lost his way between the piney sides
Of this long glen. Then to the bower they came,
Naked they came to that smooth-swarded bower,
And at their feet the crocus brake like fire,
Violet, amaracus, and asphodel, 95
Lotos and lilies: and a wind arose,
And overhead the wandering ivy and vine,
This way and that, in many a wild festoon
Ran riot, garlanding the gnarled boughs
With bunch and berry and flower thro' and thro'. 100

'O mother Ida, harken ere I die.
On the tree-tops a crested peacock lit,
And o'er him flow'd a golden cloud, and lean'd
Upon him, slowly dropping fragrant dew.
Then first I heard the voice of her, to whom 105
Coming thro' Heaven, like a light that grows
Larger and clearer, with one mind the Gods
Rise up for reverence. She to Paris made
Proffer of royal power, ample rule
Unquestion'd, overflowing revenue 110
Wherewith to embellish state, "from many a vale
And river-sunder'd champaign clothed with corn,

112. *champaign:* field

Or labour'd mine undrainable of ore.
Honour," she said, "and homage, tax and toll,
From many an inland town and haven large, 115
Mast-throng'd beneath her shadowing citadel
In glassy bays among her tallest towers."

'O mother Ida, harken ere I die.
Still she spake on and still she spake of power,
"Which in all action is the end of all; 120
Power fitted to the season; wisdom-bred
And throned of wisdom—from all neighbour crowns
Alliance and allegiance, till thy hand
Fail from the sceptre-staff. Such boon from me,
From me, Heaven's Queen, Paris, to thee king-born,
A shepherd all thy life but yet king-born, 126
Should come most welcome, seeing men, in power
Only, are likest gods, who have attain'd
Rest in a happy place and quiet seats
Above the thunder, with undying bliss 130
In knowledge of their own supremacy."

'Dear mother Ida, harken ere I die.
She ceased, and Paris held the costly fruit
Out at arm's-length, so much the thought of power
Flatter'd his spirit; but Pallas where she stood 135
Somewhat apart, her clear and bared limbs
O'erthwarted with the brazen-headed spear
Upon her pearly shoulder leaning cold,
The while, above, her full and earnest eye
Over her snow-cold breast and angry cheek 140
Kept watch, waiting decision, made reply.

' "Self-reverence, self-knowledge, self-control,
These three alone lead life to sovereign power.
Yet not for power (power of herself
Would come uncall'd for) but to live by law, 145

Acting the law we live by without fear;
And, because right is right, to follow right
Were wisdom in the scorn of consequence."

'Dear mother Ida, harken ere I die.
Again she said: "I woo thee not with gifts. 150
Sequel of guerdon could not alter me
To fairer. Judge thou me by what I am,
So shalt thou find me fairest.
      Yet, indeed,
If gazing on divinity disrobed
Thy mortal eyes are frail to judge of fair, 155
Unbias'd by self-profit, oh! rest thee sure
That I shall love thee well and cleave to thee,
So that my vigour, wedded to thy blood,
Shall strike within thy pulses, like a God's,
To push thee forward thro' a life of shocks, 160
Dangers, and deeds, until endurance grow
Sinew'd with action, and the full-grown will,
Circled thro' all experiences, pure law,
Commeasure perfect freedom."
      'Here she ceas'd,
And Paris ponder'd, and I cried, "O Paris, 165
Give it to Pallas!" but he heard me not,
Or hearing would not hear me, woe is me!

'O mother Ida, many-fountain'd Ida,
Dear mother Ida, harken ere I die.
Idalian Aphroditè beautiful, 170
Fresh as the foam, new-bathed in Paphian wells,
With rosy slender fingers backward drew
From her warm brows and bosom her deep hair
Ambrosial, golden round her lucid throat
And shoulder: from the violets her light foot 175
Shone rosy-white, and o'er her rounded form
Between the shadows of the vine-bunches
Floated the glowing sunlights, as she moved.

'Dear mother Ida, harken ere I die.
She with a subtle smile in her mild eyes,
The herald of her triumph, drawing nigh
Half-whisper'd in his ear, "I promise thee
The fairest and most loving wife in Greece,"
She spoke and laugh'd: I shut my sight for fear:
But when I look'd, Paris had raised his arm,
And I beheld great Herè's angry eyes,
As she withdrew into the golden cloud,
And I was left alone within the bower;
And from that time to this I am alone,
And I shall be alone until I die.

'Yet, mother Ida, harken ere I die.
Fairest—why fairest wife? am I not fair?
My love hath told me so a thousand times.
Methinks I must be fair, for yesterday,
When I past by, a wild and wanton pard,
Eyed like the evening star, with playful tail
Crouch'd fawning in the weed. Most loving is she?
Ah me, my mountain shepherd, that my arms
Were wound about thee, and my hot lips prest
Close, close to thine in that quick-falling dew
Of fruitful kisses, thick as Autumn rains
Flash in the pools of whirling Simois.

'O mother, hear me yet before I die.
They came, they cut away my tallest pines,
My tall dark pines, that plumed the craggy ledge
High over the blue gorge, and all between
The snowy peak and snow-white cataract
Foster'd the callow eaglet—from beneath
Whose thick mysterious boughs in the dark morn
The panther's roar came muffled, while I sat
Low in the valley. Never, never more
Shall lone Œnone see the morning mist

Sweep thro' them; never see them overlaid
With narrow moon-lit slips of silver cloud,
Between the loud stream and the trembling stars.   215

'O mother, hear me yet before I die.
I wish that somewhere in the ruin'd folds,
Among the fragments tumbled from the glens,
Or the dry thickets, I could meet with her
The Abominable, that uninvited came   220
Into the fair Peleïan banquet-hall,
And cast the golden fruit upon the board,
And bred this change; that I might speak my mind,
And tell her to her face how much I hate
Her presence, hated both of Gods and men.   225

'O mother, hear me yet before I die.
Hath he not sworn his love a thousand times,
In this green valley, under this green hill,
Ev'n on this hand, and sitting on this stone?
Seal'd it with kisses? water'd it with tears?   230
O happy tears, and how unlike to these!
O happy Heaven, how canst thou see my face?
O happy earth, how canst thou bear my weight?
O death, death, death, thou ever-floating cloud,
There are enough unhappy on this earth,   235
Pass by the happy souls, that love to live:
I pray thee, pass before my light of life,
And shadow all my soul, that I may die.
Thou weighest heavy on the heart within,
Weigh heavy on my eyelids: let me die.   240

'O mother, hear me yet before I die.
I will not die alone, for fiery thoughts
Do shape themselves within me, more and more,
Whereof I catch the issue, as I hear
Dead sounds at night come from the inmost hills,   245
Like footsteps upon wool. I dimly see

My far-off doubtful purpose, as a mother
Conjectures of the features of her child
Ere it is born: her child!—a shudder comes
Across me: never child be born of me, 250
Unblest, to vex me with his father's eyes!

'O mother, hear me yet before I die.
Hear me, O earth. I will not die alone,
Lest their shrill happy laughter come to me
Walking the cold and starless road of Death 255
Uncomforted, leaving my ancient love
With the Greek woman. I will rise and go
Down into Troy, and ere the stars come forth
Talk with the wild Cassandra, for she says
A fire dances before her, and a sound 260
Rings ever in her ears of armed men.
What this may be I know not, but I know
That, wheresoe'er I am by night and day,
All earth and air seem only burning fire.'

THE SISTERS

WE were two daughters of one race:
She was the fairest in the face:
   The wind is blowing in turret and tree.
They were together, and she fell;
Therefore revenge became me well. 5
   O the Earl was fair to see!

She died: she went to burning flame:
She mix'd her ancient blood with shame.
   The wind is howling in turret and tree.

Whole weeks and months, and early and late, 10
To win his love I lay in wait:
   O the Earl was fair to see!

I made a feast; I bad him come;
I won his love, I brought him home.
   The wind is roaring in turret and tree. 15
And after supper, on a bed,
Upon my lap he laid his head:
   O the Earl was fair to see!

I kiss'd his eyelids into rest:
His ruddy cheek upon my breast. 20
   The wind is raging in turret and tree.
I hated him with the hate of hell,
But I loved his beauty passing well.
   O the Earl was fair to see!

I rose up in the silent night: 25
I made my dagger sharp and bright.
   The wind is raving in turret and tree.
As half-asleep his breath he drew,
Three times I stabb'd him thro' and thro'.
   O the Earl was fair to see! 30

I curl'd and comb'd his comely head,
He look'd so grand when he was dead.
   The wind is blowing in turret and tree.
I wrapt his body in the sheet,
And laid him at his mother's feet. 35
   O the Earl was fair to see!

TO ——

WITH THE FOLLOWING POEM

I SEND you here a sort of allegory,
(For you will understand it) of a soul,
A sinful soul possess'd of many gifts,
A spacious garden full of flowering weeds,
A glorious Devil, large in heart and brain, 5
That did love Beauty only, (Beauty seen
In all varieties of mould and mind)
And Knowledge for its beauty; or if Good,
Good only for its beauty, seeing not
That Beauty, Good, and Knowledge, are three sisters 10
That doat upon each other, friends to man,
Living together under the same roof,
And never can be sunder'd without tears.
And he that shuts Love out, in turn shall be
Shut out from Love, and on her threshold lie 15
Howling in outer darkness. Not for this
Was common clay ta'en from the common earth
Moulded by God, and temper'd with the tears
Of angels to the perfect shape of man.

THE PALACE OF ART

I BUILT my soul a lordly pleasure-house,
    Wherein at ease for aye to dwell.
I said, 'O Soul, make merry and carouse,
    Dear soul, for all is well.'

A huge crag-platform, smooth as burnish'd brass   5
    I chose. The ranged ramparts bright
From level meadow-bases of deep grass
    Suddenly scaled the light.

Thereon I built it firm. Of ledge or shelf
    The rock rose clear, or winding stair.   10
My soul would live alone unto herself
    In her high palace there.

And 'while the world runs round and round,' I said,
    'Reign thou apart, a quiet king,
Still as, while Saturn whirls, his stedfast shade   15
    Sleeps on his luminous ring.'

To which my soul made answer readily:
    'Trust me, in bliss I shall abide
In this great mansion, that is built for me,
    So royal-rich and wide.'   20

*   *   *   *

Four courts I made, East, West and South and North,
    In each a squared lawn, wherefrom
The golden gorge of dragons spouted forth
    A flood of fountain-foam.

And round the cool green courts there ran a row 25
    Of cloisters, branch'd like mighty woods,
Echoing all night to that sonorous flow
    Of spouted fountain-floods.

And round the roofs a gilded gallery
    That lent broad verge to distant lands, 30
Far as the wild swan wings, to where the sky
    Dipt down to sea and sands.

From those four jets four currents in one swell
    Across the mountain stream'd below
In misty folds, that floating as they fell 35
    Lit up a torrent-bow.

And high on every peak a statue seem'd
    To hang on tiptoe, tossing up
A cloud of incense of all odour steam'd
    From out a golden cup. 40

So that she thought, 'And who shall gaze upon
    My palace with unblinded eyes,
While this great bow will waver in the sun,
    And that sweet incense rise?'

For that sweet incense rose and never fail'd, 45
    And, while day sank or mounted higher,
The light aërial gallery, golden-rail'd,
    Burnt like a fringe of fire.

Likewise the deep-set windows, stain'd and traced,
    Would seem slow-flaming crimson fires 50
From shadow'd grots of arches interlaced,
    And tipt with frost-like spires.

    ★   ★   ★   ★

Full of long-sounding corridors it was,
    That over-vaulted grateful gloom,
Thro' which the livelong day my soul did pass,
    Well-pleased, from room to room.

Full of great rooms and small the palace stood,
    All various, each a perfect whole
From living Nature, fit for every mood
    And change of my still soul.

For some were hung with arras green and blue,
    Showing a gaudy summer-morn,
Where with puff'd cheek the belted hunter blew
    His wreathed bugle-horn.

One seem'd all dark and red—a tract of sand,
    And some one pacing there alone,
Who paced for ever in a glimmering land,
    Lit with a low large moon.

One show'd an iron coast and angry waves.
    You seem'd to hear them climb and fall
And roar rock-thwarted under bellowing caves,
    Beneath the windy wall.

And one, a full-fed river winding slow
    By herds upon an endless plain,
The ragged rims of thunder brooding low,
    With shadow-streaks of rain.

And one, the reapers at their sultry toil.
    In front they bound the sheaves. Behind
Were realms of upland, prodigal in oil,
    And hoary to the wind.

And one a foreground black with stones and slags,
    Beyond, a line of heights, and higher
All barr'd with long white cloud the scornful crags,
    And highest, snow and fire.

And one, an English home—gray twilight pour'd   85
    On dewy pastures, dewy trees,
Softer than sleep—all things in order stored,
    A haunt of ancient Peace.

Nor these alone, but every landscape fair,
    As fit for every mood of mind,   90
Or gay, or grave, or sweet, or stern, was there
    Not less than truth design'd.

*   *   *   *

Or the maid-mother by a crucifix,
    In tracts of pasture sunny-warm,
Beneath branch-work of costly sardonyx   95
    Sat smiling, babe in arm.

Or in a clear-wall'd city on the sea,
    Near gilded organ-pipes, her hair
Wound with white roses, slept St. Cecily;
    An angel look'd at her.   100

Or thronging all one porch of Paradise
    A group of Houris bow'd to see
The dying Islamite, with hands and eyes
    That said, We wait for thee.

Or mythic Uther's deeply-wounded son   105
    In some fair space of sloping greens
Lay, dozing in the vale of Avalon,
    And watch'd by weeping queens.

Or hollowing one hand against his ear,
 To list a foot-fall, ere he saw 110
The wood-nymph, stay'd the Ausonian king to hear
 Of wisdom and of law.

Or over hills with peaky tops engrail'd,
 And many a tract of palm and rice,
The throne of Indian Cama slowly sail'd 115
 A summer fann'd with spice.

Or sweet Europa's mantle blew unclasp'd,
 From off her shoulder backward borne:
From one hand droop'd a crocus: one hand grasp'd
 The mild bull's golden horn. 120

Or else flush'd Ganymede, his rosy thigh
 Half-buried in the Eagle's down,
Sole as a flying star shot thro' the sky
 Above the pillar'd town.

Nor these alone: but every legend fair 125
 Which the supreme Caucasian mind
Carved out of Nature for itself, was there,
 Not less than life, design'd.

  * * * *

Then in the towers I placed great bells that swung,
 Moved of themselves, with silver sound; 130
And with choice paintings of wise men I hung
 The royal dais round.

For there was Milton like a seraph strong,
 Beside him Shakespeare bland and mild;
And there the world-worn Dante grasp'd his song, 135
 And somewhat grimly smiled.

And there the Ionian father of the rest;
  A million wrinkles carved his skin;
A hundred winters snow'd upon his breast,
  From cheek and throat and chin.   140

Above, the fair hall-ceiling stately-set
  Many an arch high up did lift,
And angels rising and descending met
  With interchange of gift.

Below was all mosaic choicely plann'd   145
  With cycles of the human tale
Of this wide world, the times of every land
  So wrought, they will not fail.

The people here, a beast of burden slow,
  Toil'd onward, prick'd with goads and stings;   150
Here play'd, a tiger, rolling to and fro
  The heads and crowns of kings;

Here rose, an athlete, strong to break or bind
  All force in bonds that might endure,
And here once more like some sick man declined, 155
  And trusted any cure.

But over these she trod: and those great bells
  Began to chime. She took her throne:
She sat betwixt the shining Oriels,
  To sing her songs alone.   160

And thro' the topmost Oriels' coloured flame
  Two godlike faces gazed below;
Plato the wise, and large-brow'd Verulam,
  The first of those who know.

And all those names, that in their motion were 165
    Full-welling fountain-heads of change,
Betwixt the slender shafts were blazon'd fair
    In diverse raiment strange:

Thro' which the lights, rose, amber, emerald, blue,
    Flush'd in her temples and her eyes, 170
And from her lips, as morn from Memnon, drew
    Rivers of melodies.

No nightingale delighteth to prolong
    Her low preamble all alone,
More than my soul to hear her echo'd song 175
    Throb thro' the ribbed stone;

Singing and murmuring in her feastful mirth,
    Joying to feel herself alive,
Lord over Nature, Lord of the visible earth,
    Lord of the senses five; 180

Communing with herself: 'All these are mine,
    And let the world have peace or wars,
'Tis one to me.' She—when young night divine
    Crown'd dying day with stars,

Making sweet close of his delicious toils— 185
    Lit light in wreaths and anadems,
And pure quintessences of precious oils
    In hollow'd moons of gems,

To mimic heaven; and clapt her hands and cried,
    'I marvel if my still delight 190
In this great house so royal-rich, and wide,
    Be flatter'd to the height.

'O all things fair to sate my various eyes!
  O shapes and hues that please me well!
O silent faces of the Great and Wise,
    My Gods, with whom I dwell!

'O God-like isolation which art mine,
  I can but count thee perfect gain,
What time I watch the darkening droves of swine
    That range on yonder plain.

'In filthy sloughs they roll a prurient skin,
  They graze and wallow, breed and sleep;
And oft some brainless devil enters in,
    And drives them to the deep.'

Then of the moral instinct would she prate
  And of the rising from the dead,
As hers by right of full-accomplish'd Fate;
    And at the last she said:

'I take possession of man's mind and deed.
  I care not what the sects may brawl.
I sit as God holding no form of creed,
    But contemplating all.'

    *   *   *   *

Full oft the riddle of the painful earth
  Flash'd thro' her as she sat alone,
Yet not the less held she her solemn mirth,
    And intellectual throne.

And so she throve and prosper'd: so three years
  She prosper'd: on the fourth she fell,
Like Herod, when the shout was in his ears,
    Struck thro' with pangs of hell.

Lest she should fail and perish utterly,
   God, before whom ever lie bare
The abysmal deeps of Personality,
    Plagued her with sore despair.

When she would think, where'er she turn'd her sight
   The airy hand confusion wrought,
Wrote, 'Mene, mene,' and divided quite
    The kingdom of her thought.

Deep dread and loathing of her solitude
   Fell on her, from which mood was born
Scorn of herself; again, from out that mood
    Laughter at her self-scorn.

'What! is not this my place of strength,' she said,
   'My spacious mansion built for me,
Whereof the strong foundation-stones were laid
    Since my first memory?'

But in dark corners of her palace stood
   Uncertain shapes; and unawares
On white-eyed phantasms weeping tears of blood,
    And horrible nightmares,

And hollow shades enclosing hearts of flame,
   And, with dim fretted foreheads all,
On corpses three-months-old at noon she came,
    That stood against the wall.

A spot of dull stagnation, without light
   Or power of movement, seem'd my soul,
'Mid onward-sloping motions infinite
    Making for one sure goal.

A still salt pool, lock'd in with bars of sand,
   Left on the shore; that hears all night
The plunging seas draw backward from the land
   Their moon-led waters white.

A star that with the choral starry dance
   Join'd not, but stood, and standing saw
The hollow orb of moving Circumstance
   Roll'd round by one fix'd law.

Back on herself her serpent pride had curl'd.
   'No voice,' she shriek'd in that lone hall,
'No voice breaks thro' the stillness of this world:
   One deep, deep silence all!'

She, mouldering with the dull earth's mouldering sod,
   Inwrapt tenfold in slothful shame,
Lay there exiled from eternal God,
   Lost to her place and name;

And death and life she hated equally,
   And nothing saw, for her despair,
But dreadful time, dreadful eternity.
   No comfort anywhere;

Remaining utterly confused with fears,
   And ever worse with growing time,
And ever unrelieved by dismal tears,
   And all alone in crime:

Shut up as in a crumbling tomb, girt round
   With blackness as a solid wall,
Far off she seem'd to hear the dully sound
   Of human footsteps fall.

As in strange lands a traveller walking slow,
  In doubt and great perplexity,
A little before moon-rise hears the low
  Moan of an unknown sea;   280

And knows not if it be thunder, or a sound
  Of rocks thrown down, or one deep cry
Of great wild beasts; then thinketh, 'I have found
  A new land, but I die.'

She howl'd aloud, 'I am on fire within.   285
  There comes no murmur of reply.
What is it that will take away my sin,
  And save me lest I die?'

So when four years were wholly finished,
  She threw her royal robes away.   290
'Make me a cottage in the vale,' she said,
  'Where I may mourn and pray.

'Yet pull not down my palace towers, that are
  So lightly, beautifully built:
Perchance I may return with others there   295
  When I have purged my guilt.'

LADY CLARA VERE DE VERE

  Lady Clara Vere de Vere,
    Of me you shall not win renown:
  You thought to break a country heart
    For pastime, ere you went to town.
  At me you smiled, but unbeguiled   5
    I saw the snare, and I retired:
  The daughter of a hundred Earls,
    You are not one to be desired.

Lady Clara Vere de Vere,
   I know you proud to bear your name, 10
Your pride is yet no mate for mine,
   Too proud to care from whence I came.
Nor would I break for your sweet sake
   A heart that doats on truer charms.
A simple maiden in her flower 15
   Is worth a hundred coats-of-arms.

Lady Clara Vere de Vere,
   Some meeker pupil you must find,
For were you queen of all that is,
   I could not stoop to such a mind. 20
You sought to prove how I could love,
   And my disdain is my reply.
The lion on your old stone gates
   Is not more cold to you than I.

Lady Clara Vere de Vere, 25
   You put strange memories in my head.
Not thrice your branching limes have blown
   Since I beheld young Laurence dead.
Oh your sweet eyes, your low replies:
   A great enchantress you may be; 30
But there was that across his throat
   Which you had hardly cared to see.

Lady Clara Vere de Vere,
   When thus he met his mother's view,
She had the passions of her kind, 35
   She spake some certain truths of you.
Indeed I heard one bitter word
   That scarce is fit for you to hear;
Her manners had not that repose
   Which stamps the caste of Vere de Vere. 40

Lady Clara Vere de Vere,
  There stands a spectre in your hall:
The guilt of blood is at your door:
  You changed a wholesome heart to gall.
You held your course without remorse,   45
  To make him trust his modest worth,
And, last, you fix'd a vacant stare,
  And slew him with your noble birth.

Trust me, Clara Vere de Vere,
  From yon blue heavens above us bent   50
The gardener Adam and his wife
  Smile at the claims of long descent.
Howe'er it be, it seems to me,
  'Tis only noble to be good.
Kind hearts are more than coronets,   55
  And simple faith than Norman blood.

I know you, Clara Vere de Vere,
  You pine among your halls and towers:
The languid light of your proud eyes
  Is wearied of the rolling hours.   60
In glowing health, with boundless wealth,
  But sickening of a vague disease,
You know so ill to deal with time,
  You needs must play such pranks as these.

Clara, Clara Vere de Vere,   65
  If time be heavy on your hands,
Are there no beggars at your gate,
  Nor any poor about your lands?
Oh! teach the orphan-boy to read,
  Or teach the orphan-girl to sew,   70
Pray Heaven for a human heart,
  And let the foolish yeoman go.

THE MAY QUEEN

You must wake and call me early, call me early, mother
   dear;
To-morrow 'ill be the happiest time of all the glad
   New-year;
Of all the glad New-year, mother, the maddest merriest
   day;
For I'm to be Queen o' the May, mother, I'm to be
   Queen o' the May.

There's many a black eye, they say, but none so   5
   bright as mine;
There's Margaret and Mary, there's Kate and Caroline:
But none so fair as little Alice in all the land they say,
So I'm to be Queen o' the May, mother, I'm to be
   Queen o' the May.

I sleep so sound all night, mother, that I shall never
   wake,
If you do not call me loud when the day begins to   10
   break:
But I must gather knots of flowers, and buds and
   garlands gay,
For I'm to be Queen o' the May, mother, I'm to be
   Queen o' the May.

As I came up the valley whom think ye should I see,
But Robin leaning on the bridge beneath the hazel-tree?
He thought of that sharp look, mother, I gave him   15
   yesterday,
But I'm to be Queen o' the May, mother, I'm to be
   Queen o' the May.

He thought I was a ghost, mother, for I was all in white,
And I ran by him without speaking, like a flash of light.
They call me cruel-hearted, but I care not what they say,
For I'm to be Queen o' the May, mother, I'm to be   20
    Queen o' the May.

They say he's dying all for love, but that can never be:
They say his heart is breaking, mother—what is that to me?
There's many a bolder lad 'ill woo me any summer day,
And I'm to be Queen o' the May, mother, I'm to be
    Queen o' the May.

Little Effie shall go with me to-morrow to the green,   25
And you'll be there, too, mother, to see me made the
    Queen;
For the shepherd lads on every side 'ill come from far
    away,
And I'm to be Queen o' the May, mother, I'm to be
    Queen o' the May.

The honeysuckle round the porch has wov'n its wavy
    bowers,
And by the meadow-trenches blow the faint sweet   30
    cuckoo-flowers;
And the wild marsh-marigold shines like fire in swamps
    and hollows gray,
And I'm to be Queen o' the May, mother, I'm to be
    Queen o' the May.

The night-winds come and go, mother, upon the
    meadow-grass,
And the happy stars above them seem to brighten as they
    pass;
There will not be a drop of rain the whole of the   35
    livelong day,
And I'm to be Queen o' the May, mother, I'm to be
    Queen o' the May.

All the valley, mother, 'ill be fresh and green and still,
And the cowslip and the crowfoot are over all the hill,
And the rivulet in the flowery dale 'ill merrily glance and
    play,
For I'm to be Queen o' the May, mother, I'm to be   40
    Queen o' the May.

So you must wake and call me early, call me early,
    mother dear,
To-morrow 'ill be the happiest time of all the glad
    New-year:
To-morrow 'ill be of all the year the maddest merriest
    day,
For I'm to be Queen o' the May, mother, I'm to be
    Queen o' the May.

NEW-YEAR'S EVE

IF you're waking call me early, call me early, mother dear,
For I would see the sun rise upon the glad New-year.
It is the last New-year that I shall ever see,
Then you may lay me low i' the mould and think no
    more of me.

To-night I saw the sun set: he set and left behind   5
The good old year, the dear old time, and all my peace
    of mind;
And the New-year's coming up, mother, but I shall
    never see
The blossom on the blackthorn, the leaf upon the tree.

Last May we made a crown of flowers: we had a merry
    day;
Beneath the hawthorn on the green they made me   10
    Queen of May;

And we danced about the may-pole and in the hazel copse,
Till Charles's Wain came out above the tall white
    chimney-tops.

There's not a flower on all the hills: the frost is on the pane:
I only wish to live till the snowdrops come again:
I wish the snow would melt and the sun come out on high:
I long to see a flower so before the day I die.   16

The building rook 'll caw from the windy tall elm-tree,
And the tufted plover pipe along the fallow lea,
And the swallow 'ill come back again with summer o'er
    the wave,
But I shall lie alone, mother, within the mouldering grave.

Upon the chancel-casement, and upon that grave of mine,
In the early early morning the summer sun 'ill shine,   22
Before the red cock crows from the farm upon the hill,
When you are warm-asleep, mother, and all the world is
    still.

When the flowers come again, mother, beneath the   25
    waning light
You'll never see me more in the long gray fields at night;
When from the dry dark wold the summer airs blow cool
On the oat-grass and the sword-grass, and the bulrush
    in the pool.

You'll bury me, my mother, just beneath the hawthorn
    shade,
And you'll come sometimes and see me where I am   30
    lowly laid.
I shall not forget you, mother, I shall hear you when you
    pass,
With your feet above my head in the long and pleasant
    grass.

I have been wild and wayward, but you'll forgive me now;
You'll kiss me, my own mother, and forgive me ere I go;
Nay, nay, you must not weep, nor let your grief be wild, 35
You should not fret for me, mother, you have another child.

If I can I'll come again, mother, from out my resting-
    place;
Tho' you'll not see me, mother, I shall look upon your
    face;
Tho' I cannot speak a word, I shall harken what you say,
And be often, often with you when you think I'm far 40
    away.

Goodnight, goodnight, when I have said goodnight for
    evermore,
And you see me carried out from the threshold of the
    door;
Don't let Effie come to see me till my grave be growing
    green:
She'll be a better child to you than ever I have been.

She'll find my garden-tools upon the granary floor: 45
Let her take 'em: they are hers: I shall never garden
    more:
But tell her, when I'm gone, to train the rosebush that I
    set
About the parlour-window and the box of mignonette.

Goodnight, sweet mother: call me before the day is born.
All night I lie awake, but I fall asleep at morn; 50
But I would see the sun rise upon the glad New-year,
So, if you're waking, call me, call me early, mother dear.

CONCLUSION

I THOUGHT to pass away before, and yet alive I am;
And in the fields all round I hear the bleating of the
    lamb.
How sadly, I remember, rose the morning of the year!
To die before the snowdrop came, and now the violet's
    here.

O sweet is the new violet, that comes beneath the skies,   5
And sweeter is the young lamb's voice to me that cannot
    rise,
And sweet is all the land about, and all the flowers that
    blow,
And sweeter far is death than life to me that long to go.

It seem'd so hard at first, mother, to leave the blessed sun,
And now it seems as hard to stay, and yet His will be   10
    done!
But still I think it can't be long before I find release;
And that good man, the clergyman, has told me words of
    peace.

O blessings on his kindly voice and on his silver hair!
And blessings on his whole life long, until he meet me
    there!
O blessings on his kindly heart and on his silver head!   15
A thousand times I blest him, as he knelt beside my bed.

He taught me all the mercy, for he show'd me all the sin.
Now, tho' my lamp was lighted late, there's One will let
    me in:
Nor would I now be well, mother, again if that could be,
For my desire is but to pass to Him that died for me.   20

I did not hear the dog howl, mother, or the death-watch
    beat,
There came a sweeter token when the night and morning
    meet:
But sit beside my bed, mother, and put your hand in
    mine,
And Effie on the other side, and I will tell the sign.

All in the wild March-morning I heard the angels call; 25
It was when the moon was setting, and the dark was over
    all;
The trees began to whisper, and the wind began to roll,
And in the wild March-morning I heard them call my soul.

For lying broad awake I thought of you and Effie dear;
I saw you sitting in the house, and I no longer here; 30
With all my strength I pray'd for both, and so I felt
    resign'd,
And up the valley came a swell of music on the wind.

I thought that it was fancy, and I listen'd in my bed,
And then did something speak to me—I know not what
    was said;
For great delight and shuddering took hold of all my 35
    mind,
And up the valley came again the music on the wind.

But you were sleeping; and I said, 'It's not for them:
    it's mine.'
And if it come three times, I thought, I take it for a sign.
And once again it came, and close beside the window-bars,
Then seem'd to go right up to Heaven and die among the
    stars. 40

So now I think my time is near. I trust it is. I know
The blessed music went that way my soul will have to go.

And for myself, indeed, I care not if I go to-day.
But, Effie, you must comfort *her* when I am past away.

And say to Robin a kind word, and tell him not to fret; 45
There's many a worthier than I, would make him happy yet.
If I had lived—I cannot tell—I might have been his wife;
But all these things have ceased to be, with my desire of life.

O look! the sun begins to rise, the heavens are in a glow;
He shines upon a hundred fields, and all of them I know. 50
And there I move no longer now, and there his light may shine—
Wild flowers in the valley for other hands than mine.

O sweet and strange it seems to me, that ere this day is done
The voice, that now is speaking, may be beyond the sun—
For ever and for ever with those just souls and true— 55
And what is life, that we should moan? why make we such ado?

For ever and for ever, all in a blessed home—
And there to wait a little while till you and Effie come—
To lie within the light of God, as I lie upon your breast—
And the wicked cease from troubling, and the weary 60
   are at rest.

THE LOTOS-EATERS

'COURAGE!' he said, and pointed toward the land,
'This mounting wave will roll us shoreward soon.'
In the afternoon they came unto a land
In which it seemed always afternoon.
All round the coast the languid air did swoon,   5
Breathing like one that hath a weary dream.
Full-faced above the valley stood the moon;
And like a downward smoke, the slender stream
Along the cliff to fall and pause and fall did seem.

A land of streams! some, like a downward smoke,   10
Slow-dropping veils of thinnest lawn, did go;
And some thro' wavering lights and shadows broke,
Rolling a slumbrous sheet of foam below.
They saw the gleaming river seaward flow
From the inner land: far off, three mountain-tops,   15
Three silent pinnacles of aged snow,
Stood sunset-flush'd: and, dew'd with showery drops,
Up-clomb the shadowy pine above the woven copse.

The charmed sunset linger'd low adown
In the red West: thro' mountain clefts the dale   20
Was seen far inland, and the yellow down
Border'd with palm, and many a winding vale
And meadow, set with slender galingale;
A land where all things always seem'd the same!
And round about the keel with faces pale,   25
Dark faces pale against that rosy flame,
The mild-eyed melancholy Lotos-eaters came.

Branches they bore of that enchanted stem,
Laden with flower and fruit, whereof they gave
To each, but whoso did receive of them,
And taste, to him the gushing of the wave
Far far away did seem to mourn and rave
On alien shores; and if his fellow spake,
His voice was thin, as voices from the grave;
And deep-asleep he seem'd, yet all awake,
And music in his ears his beating heart did make.

They sat them down upon the yellow sand,
Between the sun and moon upon the shore;
And sweet it was to dream of Fatherland,
Of child, and wife, and slave; but evermore
Most weary seem'd the sea, weary the oar,
Weary the wandering fields of barren foam.
Then some one said, 'We will return no more;'
And all at once they sang, 'Our island home
Is far beyond the wave; we will no longer roam.'

CHORIC SONG

I

THERE is sweet music here that softer falls
Than petals from blown roses on the grass,
Or night-dews on still waters between walls
Of shadowy granite, in a gleaming pass;
Music that gentlier on the spirit lies,
Than tir'd eyelids upon tir'd eyes;
Music that brings sweet sleep down from the blissful skies.
Here are cool mosses deep,
And thro' the moss the ivies creep,
And in the stream the long-leaved flowers weep,
And from the craggy ledge the poppy hangs in sleep.

II

Why are we weigh'd upon with heaviness,
And utterly consumed with sharp distress,
While all things else have rest from weariness?
All things have rest: why should we toil alone, 60
We only toil, who are the first of things,
And make perpetual moan,
Still from one sorrow to another thrown:
Nor ever fold our wings,
And cease from wanderings, 65
Nor steep our brows in slumber's holy balm;
Nor harken what the inner spirit sings,
'There is no joy but calm!'
Why should we only toil, the roof and crown of things?

III

Lo! in the middle of the wood, 70
The folded leaf is woo'd from out the bud
With winds upon the branch, and there
Grows green and broad, and takes no care,
Sun-steep'd at noon, and in the moon
Nightly dew-fed; and turning yellow 75
Falls, and floats adown the air.
Lo! sweeten'd with the summer light,
The full-juiced apple, waxing over-mellow,
Drops in a silent autumn night.
All its allotted length of days, 80
The flower ripens in its place,
Ripens and fades, and falls, and hath no toil,
Fast-rooted in the fruitful soil.

IV

Hateful is the dark-blue sky,
Vaulted o'er the dark-blue sea. 85
Death is the end of life; ah, why
Should life all labour be?

Let us alone. Time driveth onward fast,
And in a little while our lips are dumb.
Let us alone. What is it that will last? 90
All things are taken from us, and become
Portions and parcels of the dreadful Past.
Let us alone. What pleasure can we have
To war with evil? Is there any peace
In ever climbing up the climbing wave? 95
All things have rest, and ripen toward the grave
In silence; ripen, fall and cease:
Give us long rest or death, dark death, or dreamful ease.

V

How sweet it were, hearing the downward stream,
With half-shut eyes ever to seem 100
Falling asleep in a half-dream!
To dream and dream, like yonder amber light,
Which will not leave the myrrh-bush on the height;
To hear each other's whisper'd speech;
Eating the Lotos day by day, 105
To watch the crisping ripples on the beach,
And tender curving lines of creamy spray;
To lend our hearts and spirits wholly
To the influence of mild-minded melancholy;
To muse and brood and live again in memory, 110
With those old faces of our infancy
Heap'd over with a mound of grass,
Two handfuls of white dust, shut in an urn of brass!

VI

Dear is the memory of our wedded lives,
And dear the last embraces of our wives 115
And their warm tears: but all hath suffer'd change:
For surely now our household hearths are cold:
Our sons inherit us: our looks are strange:
And we should come like ghosts to trouble joy.

Or else the island princes over-bold 120
Have eat our substance, and the minstrel sings
Before them of the ten years' war in Troy,
And our great deeds, as half-forgotten things.
Is there confusion in the little isle?
Let what is broken so remain. 125
The Gods are hard to reconcile:
'Tis hard to settle order once again.
There *is* confusion worse than death,
Trouble on trouble, pain on pain,
Long labour unto aged breath, 130
Sore task to hearts worn out by many wars
And eyes grown dim with gazing on the pilot-stars.

VII

But, propt on beds of amaranth and moly,
How sweet (while warm airs lull us, blowing lowly)
With half-dropt eyelid still, 135
Beneath a heaven dark and holy,
To watch the long bright river drawing slowly
His waters from the purple hill—
To hear the dewy echoes calling
From cave to cave thro' the thick-twined vine— 140
To watch the emerald-colour'd water falling
Thro' many a wov'n acanthus-wreath divine!
Only to hear and see the far-off sparkling brine,
Only to hear were sweet, stretch'd out beneath the pine.

VIII

The Lotos blooms below the barren peak: 145
The Lotos blows by every winding creek:
All day the wind breathes low with mellower tone:
Thro' every hollow cave and alley lone
Round and round the spicy downs the yellow Lotos-dust
  is blown.

We have had enough of action, and of motion we, 150
Roll'd to starboard, roll'd to larboard, when the surge
    was seething free,
Where the wallowing monster spouted his foam-fountains
    in the sea.
Let us swear an oath, and keep it with an equal mind,
In the hollow Lotos-land to live and lie reclined
On the hills like Gods together, careless of mankind. 155
For they lie beside their nectar, and the bolts are hurl'd
Far below them in the valleys, and the clouds are lightly
    curl'd
Round their golden houses, girdled with the gleaming
    world:
Where they smile in secret, looking over wasted lands,
Blight and famine, plague and earthquake, roaring 160
    deeps and fiery sands,
Clanging fights, and flaming towns, and sinking ships,
    and praying hands.
But they smile, they find a music centred in a doleful song
Steaming up, a lamentation and an ancient tale of wrong,
Like a tale of little meaning tho' the words are strong;
Chanted from an ill-used race of men that cleave the 165
    soil,
Sow the seed, and reap the harvest with enduring toil,
Storing yearly little dues of wheat, and wine and oil;
Till they perish and they suffer—some, 'tis whisper'd—
    down in hell
Suffer endless anguish, others in Elysian valleys dwell,
Resting weary limbs at last on beds of asphodel. 170
Surely, surely, slumber is more sweet than toil, the shore
Than labour in the deep mid-ocean, wind and wave and
    oar;
Oh rest ye, brother mariners, we will not wander more.

A DREAM OF FAIR WOMEN

I READ, before my eyelids dropt their shade,
  'The Legend of Good Women,' long ago
Sung by the morning star of song, who made
  His music heard below;

Dan Chaucer, the first warbler, whose sweet breath
  Preluded those melodious bursts that fill
The spacious times of great Elizabeth
  With sounds that echo still.

And, for a while, the knowledge of his art
  Held me above the subject, as strong gales
Hold swollen clouds from raining, tho' my heart,
  Brimful of those wild tales,

Charged both mine eyes with tears. In every land
  I saw, wherever light illumineth,
Beauty and anguish walking hand in hand
  The downward slope to death.

Those far-renowned brides of ancient song
  Peopled the hollow dark, like burning stars,
And I heard sounds of insult, shame, and wrong,
  And trumpets blown for wars;

And clattering flints batter'd with clanging hoofs;
  And I saw crowds in column'd sanctuaries;
And forms that pass'd at windows and on roofs
  Of marble palaces;

Corpses across the threshold; heroes tall
  Dislodging pinnacle and parapet
Upon the tortoise creeping to the wall;
  Lances in ambush set;

And high shrine-doors burst thro' with heated blasts
  That run before the fluttering tongues of fire;   30
White surf wind-scatter'd over sails and masts,
  And ever climbing higher;

Squadrons and squares of men in brazen plates,
  Scaffolds, still sheets of water, divers woes,
Ranges of glimmering vaults with iron grates,   35
  And hush'd seraglios.

So shape chased shape as swift as, when to land
  Bluster the winds and tides the self-same way,
Crisp foam-flakes scud along the level sand,
  Torn from the fringe of spray.   40

I started once, or seem'd to start in pain,
  Resolved on noble things, and strove to speak,
As when a great thought strikes along the brain,
  And flushes all the cheek.

And once my arm was lifted to hew down   45
  A cavalier from off his saddle-bow,
That bore a lady from a leaguer'd town;
  And then, I know not how,

All those sharp fancies, by down-lapsing thought
  Stream'd onward, lost their edges, and did creep   50
Roll'd on each other, rounded, smooth'd, and brought
  Into the gulfs of sleep.

At last methought that I had wander'd far
  In an old wood: fresh-wash'd in coolest dew
The maiden splendours of the morning star   55
  Shook in the stedfast blue.

36. seraglios: harems

Enormous elm-tree-boles did stoop and lean
   Upon the dusky brushwood underneath
Their broad curved branches, fledged with clearest green,
   New from its silken sheath.   60

The dim red morn had died, her journey done,
   And with dead lips smiled at the twilight plain,
Half-fall'n across the threshold of the sun,
   Never to rise again.

There was no motion in the dumb dead air,   65
   Not any song of bird or sound of rill;
Gross darkness of the inner sepulchre
   Is not so deadly still

As that wide forest. Growths of jasmine turn'd
   Their humid arms festooning tree to tree,   70
And at the root thro' lush green grasses burn'd
   The red anemone.

I knew the flowers, I knew the leaves, I knew
   The tearful glimmer of the languid dawn
On those long, rank, dark wood-walks drench'd in   75
     dew,
   Leading from lawn to lawn.

The smell of violets, hidden in the green,
   Pour'd back into my empty soul and frame
The times when I remember to have been
   Joyful and free from blame.   80

And from within me a clear under-tone
   Thrill'd thro' mine ears in that unblissful clime,
'Pass freely thro': the wood is all thine own,
   Until the end of time.'

At length I saw a lady within call, 85
  Stiller than chisell'd marble, standing there;
A daughter of the gods, divinely tall,
  And most divinely fair.

Her loveliness with shame and with surprise
  Froze my swift speech: she turning on my face 90
The star-like sorrows of immortal eyes,
  Spoke slowly in her place.

'I had great beauty: ask thou not my name:
  No one can be more wise than destiny.
Many drew swords and died. Where'er I came 95
  I brought calamity.'

'No marvel, sovereign lady: in fair field
  Myself for such a face had boldly died,'
I answer'd free; and turning I appeal'd
  To one that stood beside. 100

But she, with sick and scornful looks averse,
  To her full height for stately stature draws;
'My youth,' she said, 'was blasted with a curse:
  This woman was the cause.

'I was cut off from hope in that sad place, 105
  Which men call'd Aulis in those iron years:
My father held his hand upon his face;
  I, blinded with my tears,

'Still strove to speak: my voice was thick with sighs
  As in a dream. Dimly I could descry 110
The stern black-bearded kings with wolfish eyes,
  Waiting to see me die.

'The high masts flicker'd as they lay afloat;
  The crowds, the temples, waver'd, and the shore;
The bright death quiver'd at the victim's throat;   115
  Tou'chd; and I knew no more.'

Whereto the other with a downward brow:
  'I would the white cold heavy-plunging foam,
Whirl'd by the wind, had roll'd me deep below,
  Then when I left my home.'   120

Her slow full words sank thro' the silence drear,
  As thunder-drops fall on a sleeping sea:
Sudden I heard a voice that cried, 'Come here,
  That I may look on thee.'

I turning saw, throned on a flowery rise,   125
  One sitting on a crimson scarf unroll'd;
A queen, with swarthy cheeks and bold black eyes,
  Brow-bound with burning gold.

She, flashing forth a haughty smile, began:
  'I govern'd men by change, and so I sway'd   130
All moods. 'Tis long since I have seen a man.
  Once, like the moon, I made

'The ever-shifting currents of the blood
  According to my humour ebb and flow.
I have no men to govern in this wood: 135
  That makes my only woe.

'Nay—yet it chafes me that I could not bend
  One will; nor tame and tutor with mine eye
That dull cold-blooded Cæsar. Prythee, friend,
  Where is Mark Antony?   140

'The man, my lover, with whom I rode sublime
  On Fortune's neck: we sat as God by God:
The Nilus would have risen before his time
  And flooded at our nod.

'We drank the Libyan Sun to sleep, and lit
  Lamps which out-burn'd Canopus. O my life
In Egypt! O the dalliance and the wit,
  The flattery and the strife,

'And the wild kiss, when fresh from war's alarms,
  My Hercules, my Roman Antony,
My mailed Bacchus leapt into my arms,
  Contented there to die!

'And there he died: and when I heard my name
  Sigh'd forth with life I would not brook my fear
Of the other: with a worm I balk'd his fame.
  What else was left? look here!'

(With that she tore her robe apart, and half
  The polish'd argent of her breast to sight
Laid bare. Thereto she pointed with a laugh,
  Showing the aspick's bite.)

'I died a Queen. The Roman soldier found
  Me lying dead, my crown about my brows,
A name for ever!—lying robed and crown'd,
  Worthy a Roman spouse.'

Her warbling voice, a lyre of widest range
  Struck by all passion, did fall down and glance
From tone to tone, and glided thro' all change
  Of liveliest utterance.

When she made pause I knew not for delight;
   Because with sudden motion from the ground   170
She raised her piercing orbs, and fill'd with light
   The interval of sound.

Still with their fires Love tipt his keenest darts;
   As once they drew into two burning rings
All beams of Love, melting the mighty hearts   175
   Of captains and of kings.

Slowly my sense undazzled. Then I heard
   A noise of some one coming thro' the lawn,
And singing clearer than the crested bird
   That claps his wings at dawn.   180

'The torrent brooks of hallow'd Israel
   From craggy hollows pouring, late and soon,
Sound all night long, in falling thro' the dell,
   Far-heard beneath the moon.

'The balmy moon of blessed Israel   185
   Floods all the deep-blue gloom with beams divine:
All night the splinter'd crags that wall the dell
   With spires of silver shine.'

As one that museth where broad sunshine laves
   The lawn by some cathedral, thro' the door   190
Hearing the holy organ rolling waves
   Of sound on roof and floor

Within, and anthem sung, is charm'd and tied
   To where he stands,—so stood I, when that flow
Of music left the lips of her that died   195
   To save her father's vow;

The daughter of the warrior Gileadite,
   A maiden pure; as when she went along
From Mizpeh's tower'd gate with welcome light,
   With timbrel and with song.   200

My words leapt forth: 'Heaven heads the count of crimes
   With that wild oath.' She render'd answer high:
'Not so, nor once alone; a thousand times
   I would be born and die.

'Single I grew, like some green plant, whose root   205
   Creeps to the garden water-pipes beneath,
Feeding the flower; but ere my flower to fruit
   Changed, I was ripe for death.

'My God, my land, my father—these did move
   Me from my bliss of life, that Nature gave,   210
Lower'd softly with a threefold cord of love
   Down to a silent grave.

'And I went mourning, "No fair Hebrew boy
   Shall smile away my maiden blame among
The Hebrew mothers"—emptied of all joy,   215
   Leaving the dance and song,

'Leaving the olive-gardens far below,
   Leaving the promise of my bridal bower,
The valleys of grape-loaded vines that glow
   Beneath the battled tower.   220

'The light white cloud swam over us. Anon
   We heard the lion roaring from his den;
We saw the large white stars rise one by one,
   Or, from the darken'd glen,

'Saw God divide the night with flying flame, 225
  And thunder on the everlasting hills.
I heard Him, for He spake, and grief became
  A solemn scorn of ills.

'When the next moon was roll'd into the sky,
  Strength came to me that equall'd my desire. 230
How beautiful a thing it was to die
  For God and for my sire!

'It comforts me in this one thought to dwell,
  That I subdued me to my father's will;
Because the kiss he gave me, ere I fell, 235
  Sweetens the spirit still.

'Moreover it is written that my race
  Hew'd Ammon, hip and thigh, from Aroer
On Arnon unto Minneth.' Here her face
  Glow'd, as I look'd at her. 240

She lock'd her lips: she left me where I stood:
  'Glory to God,' she sang, and past afar,
Thridding the sombre boskage of the wood,
  Toward the morning-star.

Losing her carol I stood pensively, 245
  As one that from a casement leans his head,
When midnight bells cease ringing suddenly,
  And the old year is dead.

'Alas! alas!' a low voice, full of care,
  Murmur'd beside me: 'Turn and look on me: 250
I am that Rosamond, whom men call fair,
  If what I was I be.

'Would I had been some maiden coarse and poor!
  O me, that I should ever see the light!
Those dragon eyes of anger'd Eleanor
  Do hunt me, day and night.'

She ceased in tears, fallen from hope and trust:
  To whom the Egyptian: 'O, you tamely died!
You should have clung to Fulvia's waist, and thrust
  The dagger thro' her side.'

With that sharp sound the white dawn's creeping beams,
  Stol'n to my brain, dissolved the mystery
Of folded sleep. The captain of my dreams
  Ruled in the eastern sky.

Morn broaden'd on the borders of the dark,
  Ere I saw her, who clasp'd in her last trance
Her murder'd father's head, or Joan of Arc,
  A light of ancient France;

Or her who knew that Love can vanquish Death,
  Who kneeling, with one arm about her king,
Drew forth the poison with her balmy breath,
  Sweet as new buds in Spring.

No memory labours longer from the deep
  Gold-mines of thought to lift the hidden ore
That glimpses, moving up, than I from sleep
  To gather and tell o'er

Each little sound and sight. With what dull pain
  Compass'd, how eagerly I sought to strike
Into that wondrous track of dreams again!
  But no two dreams are like.

As when a soul laments, which hath been blest,
   Desiring what is mingled with past years,
In yearnings that can never be exprest
   By signs or groans or tears;

Because all words, tho' cull'd with choicest art,   285
   Failing to give the bitter of the sweet,
Wither beneath the palate, and the heart
   Faints, faded by its heat.

MARGARET

I

   O SWEET pale Margaret,
   O rare pale Margaret,
What lit your eyes with tearful power,
Like moonlight on a falling shower?
Who lent you, love, your mortal dower   5
   Of pensive thought and aspect pale,
   Your melancholy sweet and frail
As perfume of the cuckoo-flower?
From the westward-winding flood,
From the evening-lighted wood,   10
   From all things outward you have won
A tearful grace, as tho' you stood
   Between the rainbow and the sun.
The very smile before you speak,
   That dimples your transparent cheek,   15
   Encircles all the heart, and feedeth
The senses with a still delight
   Of dainty sorrow without sound,
   Like the tender amber round,
   Which the moon about her spreadeth,   20
Moving thro' a fleecy night.

II

You love, remaining peacefully,
  To hear the murmur of the strife,
  But enter not the toil of life.
Your spirit is the calmed sea,
  Laid by the tumult of the fight.
You are the evening star, alway
  Remaining betwixt dark and bright:
Lull'd echoes of laborious day
  Come to you, gleams of mellow light
  Float by you on the verge of night.

III

What can it matter, Margaret,
  What songs below the waning stars
The lion-heart, Plantagenet,
  Sang looking thro' his prison bars?
  Exquisite Margaret, who can tell
The last wild thought of Chatelet,
  Just ere the falling axe did part
  The burning brain from the true heart,
  Even in her sight he loved so well?

IV

A fairy shield your Genius made
  And gave you on your natal day.
Your sorrow, only sorrow's shade,
  Keeps real sorrow far away.
You move not in such solitudes,
  You are not less divine,
But more human in your moods,
  Than your twin-sister, Adeline.
Your hair is darker, and your eyes
  Touch'd with a somewhat darker hue,
  And less aërially blue,
  But ever trembling thro' the dew
Of dainty-woeful sympathies.

V

    O sweet pale Margaret,
    O rare pale Margaret, 55
Come down, come down, and hear me speak:
Tie up the ringlets on your cheek:
    The sun is just about to set,
The arching limes are tall and shady,
    And faint, rainy lights are seen, 60
      Moving in the leavy beech.
Rise from the feast of sorrow, lady,
    Where all day long you sit between
      Joy and woe, and whisper each.
Or only look across the lawn, 65
    Look out below your bower-eaves,
Look down, and let your blue eyes dawn
    Upon me thro' the jasmine-leaves.

THE BLACKBIRD

O BLACKBIRD! sing me something well:
    While all the neighbours shoot thee round,
    I keep smooth plats of fruitful ground,
Where thou may'st warble, eat and dwell.

The espaliers and the standards all 5
    Are thine; the range of lawn and park:
    The unnetted black-hearts ripen dark
All thine, against the garden wall.

Yet, tho' I spared thee all the spring,
    Thy sole delight is, sitting still, 10
    With that gold dagger of thy bill
To fret the summer jenneting.

A golden bill! the silver tongue,
  Cold February loved, is dry:
  Plenty corrupts the melody 15
That made thee famous once, when young:

And in the sultry garden-squares,
  Now thy flute-notes are changed to coarse,
  I hear thee not at all, or hoarse
As when a hawker hawks his wares. 20

Take warning! he that will not sing
  While yon sun prospers in the blue,
  Shall sing for want, ere leaves are new,
Caught in the frozen palms of Spring.

THE DEATH OF THE OLD YEAR

FULL knee-deep lies the winter snow,
  And the winter winds are wearily sighing:
Toll ye the church-bell sad and slow,
And tread softly and speak low,
For the old year lies a-dying. 5
    Old year, you must not die;
    You came to us so readily,
    You lived with us so steadily,
    Old year, you shall not die.

He lieth still: he doth not move: 10
He will not see the dawn of day.
He hath no other life above.
He gave me a friend, and a true true-love,
And the New-year will take 'em away.

Old year, you must not go; 15
So long as you have been with us,
Such joy as you have seen with us,
Old year, you shall not go.

He froth'd his bumpers to the brim;
A jollier year we shall not see. 20
But tho' his eyes are waxing dim,
And tho' his foes speak ill of him,
He was a friend to me.
    Old year, you shall not die;
    We did so laugh and cry with you, 25
    I've half a mind to die with you,
    Old year, if you must die.

He was full of joke and jest,
But all his merry quips are o'er.
To see him die, across the waste 30
His son and heir doth ride post-haste,
But he'll be dead before.
    Every one for his own.
    The night is starry and cold, my friend,
    And the New-year blithe and bold, my friend,
    Comes up to take his own. 36

How hard he breathes! over the snow
I heard just now the crowing cock.
The shadows flicker to and fro:
The cricket chirps: the light burns low: 40
'Tis nearly twelve o'clock.
    Shake hands, before you die.
    Old year, we'll dearly rue for you:
    What is it we can do for you?
    Speak out before you die. 45

His face is growing sharp and thin.
Alack! our friend is gone.
Close up his eyes: tie up his chin:
Step from the corpse, and let him in
That standeth there alone, 50
    And waiteth at the door.
    There's a new foot on the floor, my friend,
    And a new face at the door, my friend,
    A new face at the door.

TO J. S.

THE wind, that beats the mountain, blows
    More softly round the open wold,
And gently comes the world to those
    That are cast in gentle mould.

And me this knowledge bolder made, 5
    Or else I had not dared to flow
In these words toward you, and invade
    Even with a verse your holy woe.

'Tis strange that those we lean on most,
    Those in whose laps our limbs are nursed, 10
Fall into shadow, soonest lost:
    Those we love first are taken first.

God gives us love. Something to love
    He lends us; but, when love is grown
To ripeness, that on which it throve 15
    Falls off, and love is left alone.

This is the curse of time. Alas!
    In grief I am not all unlearn'd;

Once thro' mine own doors Death did pass;
    One went, who never hath return'd.   20

He will not smile—not speak to me
    Once more. Two years his chair is seen
Empty before us. That was he
    Without whose life I had not been.

Your loss is rarer; for this star   25
    Rose with you thro' a little arc
Of heaven, nor having wander'd far
    Shot on the sudden into dark.

I knew your brother: his mute dust
    I honour and his living worth: 30
A man more pure and bold and just
    Was never born into the earth.

I have not look'd upon you nigh,
    Since that dear soul hath fall'n asleep.
Great Nature is more wise than I: 35
    I will not tell you not to weep.

And tho' mine own eyes fill with dew,
    Drawn from the spirit thro' the brain,
I will not even preach to you,
    'Weep, weeping dulls the inward pain.'   40

Let Grief be her own mistress still.
    She loveth her own anguish deep
More than much pleasure. Let her will
    Be done—to weep or not to weep.

I will not say, 'God's ordinance   45
    Of Death is blown in every wind;'
For that is not a common chance
    That takes away a noble mind.

His memory long will live alone
    In all our hearts, as mournful light
That broods above the fallen sun,
    And dwells in heaven half the night.

Vain solace! Memory standing near
    Cast down her eyes, and in her throat
Her voice seem'd distant, and a tear
    Dropt on the letters as I wrote.

I wrote I know not what. In truth,
    How *should* I soothe you anyway,
Who miss the brother of your youth?
    Yet something I did wish to say:

For he too was a friend to me:
    Both are my friends, and my true breast
Bleedeth for both; yet it may be
    That only silence suiteth best.

Words weaker than your grief would make
    Grief more. 'Twere better I should cease
Although myself could almost take
    The place of him that sleeps in peace.

Sleep sweetly, tender heart, in peace:
    Sleep, holy spirit, blessed soul,
While the stars burn, the moons increase,
    And the great ages onward roll.

Sleep till the end, true soul and sweet.
    Nothing comes to thee new or strange.
Sleep full of rest from head to feet;
    Lie still, dry dust, secure of change.

'YOU ASK ME, WHY, THO' ILL AT EASE'

You ask me, why, tho' ill at ease,
    Within this region I subsist,
    Whose spirits falter in the mist,
And languish for the purple seas.

It is the land that freemen till,   5
    That sober-suited Freedom chose,
    The land, where girt with friends or foes
A man may speak the thing he will;

A land of settled government,
    A land of just and old renown,   10
    Where Freedom slowly broadens down
From precedent to precedent:

Where faction seldom gathers head,
    But by degrees to fullness wrought,
    The strength of some diffusive thought   15
Hath time and space to work and spread.

Should banded unions persecute
    Opinion, and induce a time
    When single thought is civil crime,
And individual freedom mute;   20

Tho' Power should make from land to land
    The name of Britain trebly great—
    Tho' every channel of the State
Should fill and choke with golden sand—

Yet waft me from the harbour-mouth,   25
    Wild wind! I seek a warmer sky,
    And I will see before I die
The palms and temples of the South.

'OF OLD SAT FREEDOM ON THE HEIGHTS'

Of old sat Freedom on the heights,
    The thunders breaking at her feet:
Above her shook the starry lights:
    She heard the torrents meet.

There in her place she did rejoice,
    Self-gather'd in her prophet-mind,
But fragments of her mighty voice
    Came rolling on the wind.

Then stept she down thro' town and field
    To mingle with the human race,
And part by part to men reveal'd
    The fullness of her face—

Grave mother of majestic works,
    From her isle-altar gazing down,
Who, God-like, grasps the triple forks,
    And, King-like, wears the crown:

Her open eyes desire the truth.
    The wisdom of a thousand years
Is in them. May perpetual youth
    Keep dry their light from tears;

That her fair form may stand and shine,
    Make bright our days and light our dreams,
Turning to scorn with lips divine
    The falsehood of extremes!

'LOVE THOU THY LAND, WITH LOVE FAR-BROUGHT'

Love thou thy land, with love far-brought
   From out the storied Past, and used
   Within the Present, but transfused
Thro' future time by power of thought.

True love turn'd round on fixed poles,   5
   Love, that endures not sordid ends,
   For English natures, freemen, friends,
Thy brothers and immortal souls.

But pamper not a hasty time,
   Nor feed with crude imaginings   10
   The herd, wild hearts and feeble wings
That every sophister can lime.

Deliver not the tasks of might
   To weakness, neither hide the ray
   From those, not blind, who wait for day,   15
Tho' sitting girt with doubtful light.

Make knowledge circle with the winds;
   But let her herald, Reverence, fly
   Before her to whatever sky
Bear seed of men and growth of minds.   20

Watch what main-currents draw the years:
   Cut Prejudice against the grain:
   But gentle words are always gain:
Regard the weakness of thy peers:

Nor toil for title, place, or touch   25
   Of pension, neither count on praise:

It grows to guerdon after-days:
Nor deal in watch-words overmuch:

Not clinging to some ancient saw;
  Not master'd by some modern term;
  Not swift nor slow to change, but firm:
And in its season bring the law;

That from Discussion's lip may fall
  With Life, that, working strongly, binds—
  Set in all lights by many minds,
To close the interests of all.

For Nature also, cold and warm,
  And moist and dry, devising long,
  Thro' many agents making strong,
Matures the individual form.

Meet is it changes should control
  Our being, lest we rust in ease.
  We all are changed by still degrees,
All but the basis of the soul.

So let the change which comes be free
  To ingroove itself with that which flies,
  And work, a joint of state, that plies
Its office, moved with sympathy.

A saying, hard to shape in act;
  For all the past of Time reveals
  A bridal dawn of thunder-peals,
Wherever Thought hath wedded Fact.

Ev'n now we hear with inward strife
  A motion toiling in the gloom—
  The Spirit of the years to come
Yearning to mix himself with Life.

    40. *individual:* indivisible

A slow-develop'd strength awaits
   Completion in a painful school;
   Phantoms of other forms of rule,
New Majesties of mighty States—

The warders of the growing hour,
   But vague in vapour, hard to mark;
   And round them sea and air are dark
With great contrivances of Power.

Of many changes, aptly join'd,
   Is bodied forth the second whole.
   Regard gradation, lest the soul
Of Discord race the rising wind;

A wind to puff your idol-fires,
   And heap their ashes on the head;
   To shame the boast so often made,
That we are wiser than our sires.

Oh yet, if Nature's evil star
   Drive men in manhood, as in youth,
   To follow flying steps of Truth
Across the brazen bridge of war—

If New and Old, disastrous feud,
   Must ever shock, like armed foes,
   And this be true, till Time shall close,
That Principles are rain'd in blood;

Not yet the wise of heart would cease
   To hold his hope thro' shame and guilt,
   But with his hand against the hilt,
Would pace the troubled land, like Peace;

Not less, tho' dogs of Faction bay,
   Would serve his kind in deed and word,

Certain, if knowledge bring the sword,
That knowledge takes the sword away—

Would love the gleams of good that broke
  From either side, nor veil his eyes:
  And if some dreadful need should rise
Would strike, and firmly, and one stroke:

To-morrow yet would reap to-day,
  As we bear blossom of the dead;
  Earn well the thrifty months, nor wed
Raw Haste, half-sister to Delay.

THE GOOSE

I KNEW an old wife lean and poor,
  Her rags scarce held together;
There strode a stranger to the door,
  And it was windy weather.

He held a goose upon his arm,
  He utter'd rhyme and reason,
'Here, take the goose, and keep you warm.
  It is a stormy season.'

She caught the white goose by the leg,
  A goose—'twas no great matter.
The goose let fall a golden egg
  With cackle and with clatter.

She dropt the goose, and caught the pelf,
  And ran to tell her neighbours;
And bless'd herself, and cursed herself,
  And rested from her labours.

And feeding high, and living soft,
   Grew plump and able-bodied;
Until the grave churchwarden doff'd,
   The parson smirk'd and nodded.   20

So sitting, served by man and maid,
   She felt her heart grow prouder:
But ah! the more the white goose laid
   It clack'd and cackled louder.

It clutter'd here, it chuckled there;   25
   It stirr'd the old wife's mettle:
She shifted in her elbow-chair,
   And hurl'd the pan and kettle.

'A quinsy choke thy cursed note!'
   Then wax'd her anger stronger.   30
'Go, take the goose, and wring her throat,
   I will not bear it longer.'

Then yelp'd the cur, and yawl'd the cat;
   Ran Gaffer, stumbled Gammer.
The goose flew this way and flew that,   35
   And fill'd the house with clamour.

As head and heels upon the floor
   They flounder'd all together,
There strode a stranger to the door,
   And it was windy weather: 40

He took the goose upon his arm,
   He utter'd words of scorning;
'So keep you cold, or keep you warm,
   It is a stormy morning.'

The wild wind rang from park and plain, 45
 And round the attics rumbled,
Till all the tables danced again,
 And half the chimneys tumbled.

The glass blew in, the fire blew out,
 The blast was hard and harder. 50
Her cap blew off, her gown blew up,
 And a whirlwind clear'd the larder:

And while on all sides breaking loose
 Her household fled the danger,
Quoth she, 'The Devil take the goose, 55
 And God forget the stranger!'

THE EPIC

At Francis Allen's on the Christmas-eve,—
The game of forfeits done—the girls all kiss'd
Beneath the sacred bush and past away—
The parson Holmes, the poet Everard Hall,
The host, and I sat round the wassail-bowl, 5
Then half-way ebb'd: and there we held a talk,
How all the old honour had from Christmas gone,
Or gone, or dwindled down to some odd games
In some odd nooks like this; till I, tired out
With cutting eights that day upon the pond, 10
Where, three times slipping from the outer edge,
I bump'd the ice into three several stars,
Fell in a doze; and half-awake I heard
The parson taking wide and wider sweeps,
Now harping on the church-commissioners, 15
Now hawking at Geology and schism;

Until I woke, and found him settled down
Upon the general decay of faith
Right thro' the world, 'at home was little left,
And none abroad: there was no anchor, none, 20
To hold by.' Francis, laughing, clapt his hand
On Everard's shoulder, with 'I hold by him.'
'And I,' quoth Everard, 'by the wassail-bowl.'
'Why yes,' I said, 'we knew your gift that way
At college: but another which you had, 25
I mean of verse (for so we held it then),
What came of that?' 'You know,' said Frank,
    'he burnt
His epic, his King Arthur, some twelve books'—
And then to me demanding why? 'Oh, sir,
He thought that nothing new was said, or else 30
Something so said 'twas nothing—that a truth
Looks freshest in the fashion of the day:
God knows: he has a mint of reasons: ask.
It pleased *me* well enough.' 'Nay, nay,' said Hall,
'Why take the style of those heroic times? 35
For nature brings not back the Mastodon,
Nor we those times; and why should any man
Remodel models? these twelve books of mine
Were faint Homeric echoes, nothing-worth,
Mere chaff and draff, much better burnt.' 'But I,' 40
Said Francis, 'pick'd the eleventh from this hearth
And have it: keep a thing, its use will come.
I hoard it as a sugar-plum for Holmes.'
He laugh'd, and I, tho' sleepy, like a horse
That hears the corn-bin open, prick'd my ears; 45
For I remember'd Everard's college fame
When we were Freshmen: then at my request
He brought it; and the poet little urged,
But with some prelude of disparagement,
Read, mouthing out his hollow oes and aes, 50
Deep-chested music, and to this result.

MORTE D'ARTHUR

So all day long the noise of battle roll'd
Among the mountains by the winter sea;
Until King Arthur's table, man by man,
Had fallen in Lyonnesse about their Lord,
King Arthur: then, because his wound was deep, 5
The bold Sir Bedivere uplifted him,
Sir Bedivere, the last of all his knights,
And bore him to a chapel nigh the field,
A broken chancel with a broken cross,
That stood on a dark strait of barren land. 10
On one side lay the Ocean, and on one
Lay a great water, and the moon was full.

Then spake King Arthur to Sir Bedivere:
'The sequel of to-day unsolders all
The goodliest fellowship of famous knights 15
Whereof this world holds record. Such a sleep
They sleep—the men I loved. I think that we
Shall never more, at any future time,
Delight our souls with talk of knightly deeds,
Walking about the gardens and the halls 20
Of Camelot, as in the days that were.
I perish by this people which I made,—
Tho' Merlin sware that I should come again
To rule once more—but let what will be, be,
I am so deeply smitten thro' the helm 25
That without help I cannot last till morn.
Thou therefore take my brand Excalibur,
Which was my pride: for thou rememberest how
In those old days, one summer noon, an arm
Rose up from out the bosom of the lake, 30
Clothed in white samite, mystic, wonderful,
Holding the sword—and how I row'd across
And took it, and have worn it, like a king:

And, wheresoever I am sung or told
In aftertime, this also shall be known: 35
But now delay not: take Excalibur,
And fling him far into the middle mere:
Watch what thou seëst, and lightly bring me word.'

To him replied the bold Sir Bedivere:
'It is not meet, Sir King, to leave thee thus, 40
Aidless, alone, and smitten thro' the helm.
A little thing may harm a wounded man.
Yet I thy hest will all perform at full,
Watch what I see, and lightly bring thee word.'

So saying, from the ruin'd shrine he stept 45
And in the moon athwart the place of tombs,
Where lay the mighty bones of ancient men,
Old knights, and over them the sea-wind sang
Shrill, chill, with flakes of foam. He, stepping down
By zig-zag paths, and juts of pointed rock, 50
Came on the shining levels of the lake.

There drew he forth the brand Excalibur,
And o'er him, drawing it, the winter moon,
Brightening the skirts of a long cloud, ran forth
And sparkled keen with frost against the hilt: 55
For all the haft twinkled with diamond sparks,
Myriads of topaz-lights, and jacinth-work
Of subtlest jewellery. He gazed so long
That both his eyes were dazzled, as he stood,
This way and that dividing the swift mind, 60
In act to throw: but at the last it seem'd
Better to leave Excalibur conceal'd
There in the many-knotted waterflags,
That whistled stiff and dry about the marge.
So strode he back slow to the wounded King. 65

Then spake King Arthur to Sir Bedivere:
'Hast thou perform'd my mission which I gave?
What is it thou hast seen? or what hast heard?'

And answer made the bold Sir Bedivere:
'I heard the ripple washing in the reeds, 70
And the wild water lapping on the crag.'

To whom replied King Arthur, faint and pale:
'Thou hast betray'd thy nature and thy name,
Not rendering true answer, as beseem'd
Thy fëalty, nor like a noble knight: 75
For surer sign had follow'd, either hand,
Or voice, or else a motion of the mere.
This is a shameful thing for men to lie.
Yet now, I charge thee, quickly go again
As thou art lief and dear, and do the thing 80
I bad thee, watch, and lightly bring me word.'

Then went Sir Bedivere the second time
Across the ridge, and paced beside the mere,
Counting the dewy pebbles, fix'd in thought;
But when he saw the wonder of the hilt, 85
How curiously and strangely chased, he smote
His palms together, and he cried aloud,

'And if indeed I cast the brand away,
Surely a precious thing, one worthy note,
Should thus be lost for ever from the earth, 90
Which might have pleased the eyes of many men.
What good should follow this, if this were done?
What harm, undone? deep harm to disobey,
Seeing obedience is the bond of rule.
Were it well to obey then, if a king demand 95
An act unprofitable, against himself?

The King is sick, and knows not what he does.
What record, or what relic of my lord
Should be to aftertime, but empty breath
And rumours of a doubt? but were this kept, 100
Stored in some treasure-house of mighty kings,
Some one might show it at a joust of arms,
Saying, "King Arthur's sword, Excalibur,
Wrought by the lonely maiden of the Lake.
Nine years she wrought it, sitting in the deeps 105
Upon the hidden bases of the hills."
So might some old man speak in the aftertime
To all the people, winning reverence.
But now much honour and much fame were lost.'

So spake he, clouded with his own conceit, 110
And hid Excalibur the second time,
And so strode back slow to the wounded King.

Then spoke King Arthur, breathing heavily:
'What is it thou hast seen? or what hast heard?'

And answer made the bold Sir Bedivere: 115
'I heard the water lapping on the crag,
And the long ripple washing in the reeds.'

To whom replied King Arthur, much in wrath:
'Ah, miserable and unkind, untrue,
Unknightly, traitor-hearted! Woe is me! 120
Authority forgets a dying king,
Laid widow'd of the power in his eye
That bow'd the will. I see thee what thou art,
For thou, the latest-left of all my knights,
In whom should meet the offices of all, 125
Thou wouldst betray me for the precious hilt;
Either from lust of gold, or like a girl
Valuing the giddy pleasure of the eyes.
Yet, for a man may fail in duty twice,

110. *conceit:* fancy

And the third time may prosper, get thee hence: 130
But, if thou spare to fling Excalibur,
I will arise and slay thee with my hands.'

Then quickly rose Sir Bedivere, and ran,
And, leaping down the ridges lightly, plunged
Among the bulrush-beds, and clutch'd the sword, 135
And strongly wheel'd and threw it. The great brand
Made lightnings in the splendour of the moon,
And flashing round and round, and whirl'd in an arch,
Shot like a streamer of the northern morn,
Seen where the moving isles of winter shock 140
By night, with noises of the northern sea.
So flash'd and fell the brand Excalibur:
But ere he dipt the surface, rose an arm
Clothed in white samite, mystic, wonderful,
And caught him by the hilt, and brandish'd him 145
Three times, and drew him under in the mere.
And lightly went the other to the King.

Then spoke King Arthur, drawing thicker breath:
'Now see I by thine eyes that this is done.
Speak out: what is it thou hast heard, or seen?' 150

And answer made the bold Sir Bedivere:
'Sir King, I closed mine eyelids, lest the gems
Should blind my purpose, for I never saw,
Nor shall see, here or elsewhere, till I die,
Not tho' I live three lives of mortal men, 155
So great a miracle as yonder hilt.
Then with both hands I flung him, wheeling him;
But when I look'd again, behold an arm,
Clothed in white samite, mystic, wonderful,
That caught him by the hilt, and brandish'd him 160
Three times, and drew him under in the mere.'

And answer made King Arthur, breathing hard:
'My end draws nigh; 'tis time that I were gone.
Make broad thy shoulders to receive my weight,
And bear me to the margin; yet I fear   165
My wound hath taken cold, and I shall die.'

So saying, from the pavement he half rose,
Slowly, with pain, reclining on his arm,
And looking wistfully with wide blue eyes
As in a picture. Him Sir Bedivere   170
Remorsefully regarded thro' his tears,
And would have spoken, but he found not words,
Then took with care, and kneeling on one knee,
O'er both his shoulders drew the languid hands,
And rising bore him thro' the place of tombs. 175

But, as he walk'd, King Arthur panted hard,
Like one that feels a nightmare on his bed
When all the house is mute. So sigh'd the King,
Muttering and murmuring at his ear, 'Quick, quick!
I fear it is too late, and I shall die.'   180
But the other swiftly strode from ridge to ridge,
Clothed with his breath, and looking, as he walk'd,
Larger than human on the frozen hills.
He heard the deep behind him, and a cry
Before. His own thought drove him, like a goad. 185
Dry clash'd his harness in the icy caves
And barren chasms, and all to left and right
The bare black cliff clang'd round him, as he based
His feet on juts of slippery crag that rang
Sharp-smitten with the dint of armed heels—   190
And on a sudden, lo! the level lake,
And the long glories of the winter moon.

Then saw they how there hove a dusky barge,
Dark as a funeral scarf from stem to stern,

POEMS OF 1842

Beneath them; and descending they were ware   195
That all the decks were dense with stately forms
Black-stoled, black-hooded, like a dream—by these
Three Queens with crowns of gold—and from them
    rose
A cry that shiver'd to the tingling stars,
And, as it were one voice, an agony   200
Of lamentation, like a wind, that shrills
All night in a waste land, where no one comes,
Or hath come, since the making of the world.

Then murmur'd Arthur, 'Place me in the barge,'
And to the barge they came. There those three   205
    Queens
Put forth their hands, and took the King, and wept.
But she, that rose the tallest of them all
And fairest, laid his head upon her lap,
And loosed the shatter'd casque, and chafed his
    hands,
And call'd him by his name, complaining loud,   210
And dropping bitter tears against his brow
Striped with dark blood: for all his face was white
And colourless, and like the wither'd moon
Smote by the fresh beam of the springing east;
And all his greaves and cuisses dash'd with drops   215
Of onset; and the light and lustrous curls—
That made his forehead like a rising sun
High from the daïs-throne—were parch'd with dust;
Or, clotted into points and hanging loose,
Mix'd with the knightly growth that fringed his   220
    lips.
So like a shatter'd column lay the King;
Not like that Arthur who, with lance in rest,
From spur to plume a star of tournament,
Shot thro' the lists at Camelot, and charged
Before the eyes of ladies and of kings.   225

Then loudly cried the bold Sir Bedivere,
'Ah! my Lord Arthur, whither shall I go?
Where shall I hide my forehead and my eyes?
For now I see the true old times are dead,
When every morning brought a noble chance, 230
And every chance brought out a noble knight.
Such times have been not since the light that led
The holy Elders with the gift of myrrh.
But now the whole ROUND TABLE is dissolved
Which was an image of the mighty world; 235
And I, the last, go forth companionless,
And the days darken round me, and the years,
Among new men, strange faces, other minds.'

And slowly answered Arthur from the barge:
'The old order changeth, yielding place to new, 240
And God fulfils Himself in many ways,
Lest one good custom should corrupt the world.
Comfort thyself: what comfort is in me?
I have lived my life, and that which I have done
May He within Himself make pure! but thou, 245
If thou shouldst never see my face again,
Pray for my soul. More things are wrought by
    prayer
Than this world dreams of. Wherefore, let thy voice
Rise like a fountain for me night and day.
For what are men better than sheep or goats 250
That nourish a blind life within the brain,
If, knowing God, they lift not hands of prayer
Both for themselves and those who call them friend?
For so the whole round earth is every way
Bound by gold chains about the feet of God. 255
But now farewell. I am going a long way
With these thou seëst—if indeed I go—
(For all my mind is clouded with a doubt)
To the island-valley of Avilion;

Where falls not hail, or rain, or any snow,   260
Nor ever wind blows loudly; but it lies
Deep-meadow'd, happy, fair with orchard-lawns
And bowery hollows crown'd with summer sea,
Where I will heal me of my grievous wound.'

So said he, and the barge with oar and sail   265
Moved from the brink, like some full-breasted swan
That, fluting a wild carol ere her death,
Ruffles her pure cold plume, and takes the flood
With swarthy webs. Long stood Sir Bedivere
Revolving many memories, till the hull   270
Look'd one black dot against the verge of dawn,
And on the mere the wailing died away.

HERE ended Hall, and our last light, that long
Had wink'd and threaten'd darkness, flared and fell:
At which the Parson, sent to sleep with sound,   275
And waked with silence, grunted 'Good!' but we
Sat rapt: it was the tone with which he read—
Perhaps some modern touches here and there
Redeem'd it from the charge of nothingness—
Or else we loved the man, and prized his work;   280
I know not: but we sitting, as I said,
The cock crew loud; as at that time of year
The lusty bird takes every hour for dawn:
Then Francis, muttering, like a man ill-used,
'There now—that's nothing!' drew a little back,   285
And drove his heel into the smoulder'd log,
That sent a blast of sparkles up the flue:
And so to bed; where yet in sleep I seem'd
To sail with Arthur under looming shores,
Point after point; till on to dawn, when dreams   290

Begin to feel the truth and stir of day,
To me, methought, who waited with a crowd,
There came a bark that, blowing forward, bore
King Arthur, like a modern gentleman
Of stateliest port; and all the people cried, 295
'Arthur is come again: he cannot die.'
Then those that stood upon the hills behind
Repeated—'Come again, and thrice as fair;'
And, further inland, voices echo'd—'Come
With all good things, and war shall be no more.' 300
At this a hundred bells began to peal,
That with the sound I woke, and heard indeed
The clear church-bells ring in the Christmas-morn.

THE GARDENER'S DAUGHTER;

OR, THE PICTURES

THIS morning is the morning of the day,
When I and Eustace from the city went
To see the Gardener's Daughter; I and he,
Brothers in Art; a friendship so complete
Portion'd in halves between us, that we grew 5
The fable of the city where we dwelt.

My Eustace might have sat for Hercules;
So muscular he spread, so broad of breast.
He, by some law that holds in love, and draws
The greater to the lesser, long desired 10
A certain miracle of symmetry,
A miniature of loveliness, all grace
Summ'd up and closed in little;—Juliet, she

So light of foot, so light of spirit—oh, she
To me myself, for some three careless moons, 15
The summer pilot of an empty heart
Unto the shores of nothing! Know you not
Such touches are but embassies of love,
To tamper with the feelings, ere he found
Empire for life? but Eustace painted her, 20
And said to me, she sitting with us then,
'When will *you* paint like this?' and I replied,
(My words were half in earnest, half in jest,)
' 'Tis not your work, but Love's. Love, unperceived,
A more ideal Artist he than all, 25
Came, drew your pencil from you, made those eyes
Darker than darkest pansies, and that hair
More black than ashbuds in the front of March.'
And Juliet answer'd laughing, 'Go and see
The Gardener's daughter: trust me, after that, 30
You scarce can fail to match his masterpiece.'
And up we rose, and on the spur we went.

  Not wholly in the busy world, nor quite
Beyond it, blooms the garden that I love.
News from the humming city comes to it 35
In sound of funeral or of marriage bells;
And, sitting muffled in dark leaves, you hear
The windy clanging of the minster clock;
Although between it and the garden lies
A league of grass, wash'd by a slow broad stream, 40
That, stirr'd with languid pulses of the oar,
Waves all its lazy lilies, and creeps on,
Barge-laden, to three arches of a bridge
Crown'd with the minster-towers.
                              The fields between
Are dewy-fresh, browsed by deep-udder'd kine, 45
And all about the large lime feathers low,
The lime a summer home of murmurous wings.

In that still place she, hoarded in herself,
Grew, seldom seen; not less among us lived
Her fame from lip to lip. Who had not heard   50
Of Rose, the Gardener's daughter? Where was he,
So blunt in memory, so old at heart,
At such a distance from his youth in grief,
That, having seen, forgot? The common mouth,
So gross to express delight, in praise of her   55
Grew oratory. Such a lord is Love,
And Beauty such a mistress of the world.

And if I said that Fancy, led by Love,
Would play with flying forms and images,
Yet this is also true, that, long before   60
I look'd upon her, when I heard her name
My heart was like a prophet to my heart,
And told me I should love. A crowd of hopes,
That sought to sow themselves like winged seeds,
Born out of everything I heard and saw,   65
Flutter'd about my senses and my soul;
And vague desires, like fitful blasts of balm
To one that travels quickly, made the air
Of Life delicious, and all kinds of thought,
That verged upon them, sweeter than the dream   70
Dream'd by a happy man, when the dark East,
Unseen, is brightening to his bridal morn.

And sure this orbit of the memory folds
For ever in itself the day we went
To see her. All the land in flowery squares,   75
Beneath a broad and equal-blowing wind,
Smelt of the coming summer, as one large cloud
Drew downward: but all else of heaven was pure
Up to the Sun, and May from verge to verge,
And May with me from head to heel. And now,   80
As tho' 'twere yesterday, as tho' it were

The hour just flown, that morn with all its sound,
(For those old Mays had thrice the life of these,)
Rings in mine ears. The steer forgot to graze,
And, where the hedge-row cuts the pathway, stood, 85
Leaning his horns into the neighbour field,
And lowing to his fellows. From the woods
Came voices of the well-contented doves.
The lark could scarce get out his notes for joy,
But shook his song together as he near'd 90
His happy home, the ground. To left and right,
The cuckoo told his name to all the hills;
The mellow ouzel fluted in the elm;
The redcap whistled; and the nightingale
Sang loud, as tho' he were the bird of day. 95

And Eustace turn'd, and smiling said to me,
'Hear how the bushes echo! by my life,
These birds have joyful thoughts. Think you they sing
Like poets, from the vanity of song?
Or have they any sense of why they sing? 100
And would they praise the heavens for what they have?'
And I made answer, 'Were there nothing else
For which to praise the heavens but only love,
That only love were cause enough for praise.'

Lightly he laugh'd, as one that read my thought,
And on we went; but ere an hour had pass'd, 106
We reach'd a meadow slanting to the North;
Down which a well-worn pathway courted us
To one green wicket in a privet hedge;
This, yielding, gave into a grassy walk 110
Thro' crowded lilac-ambush trimly pruned;
And one warm gust, full-fed with perfume, blew

Beyond us, as we enter'd in the cool.
The garden stretches southward. In the midst
A cedar spread his dark-green layers of shade. 115
The garden-glasses glanced, and momently
The twinkling laurel scatter'd silver lights.

  'Eustace,' I said, 'this wonder keeps the house.'
He nodded, but a moment afterwards
He cried, 'Look! look!' Before he ceased I turn'd, 120
And, ere a star can wink, beheld her there.

  For up the porch there grew an Eastern rose,
That, flowering high, the last night's gale had caught,
And blown across the walk. One arm aloft—
Gown'd in pure white, that fitted to the shape— 125
Holding the bush, to fix it back, she stood,
A single stream of all her soft brown hair
Pour'd on one side: the shadow of the flowers
Stole all the golden gloss, and, wavering
Lovingly lower, trembled on her waist— 130
Ah, happy shade—and still went wavering down,
But, ere it touch'd a foot, that might have danced
The greensward into greener circles, dipt,
And mix'd with shadows of the common ground!
But the full day dwelt on her brows, and sunn'd 135
Her violet eyes, and all her Hebe bloom,
And doubled his own warmth against her lips,
And on the bounteous wave of such a breast
As never pencil drew. Half light, half shade,
She stood, a sight to make an old man young. 140

  So rapt, we near'd the house; but she, a Rose
In roses, mingled with her fragrant toil,
Nor heard us come, nor from her tendance turn'd
Into the world without; till close at hand,
And almost ere I knew mine own intent, 145

This murmur broke the stillness of that air
Which brooded round about her:
                      'Ah, one rose,
One rose, but one, by those fair fingers cull'd,
Were worth a hundred kisses press'd on lips
Less exquisite than thine.'
                      She look'd: but all
Suffused with blushes—neither self-possess'd
Nor startled, but betwixt this mood and that,
Divided in a graceful quiet—paused,
And dropt the branch she held, and turning, wound
Her looser hair in braid, and stirr'd her lips
For some sweet answer, tho' no answer came,
Nor yet refused the rose, but granted it,
And moved away, and left me, statue-like,
In act to render thanks.
                      I, that whole day,
Saw her no more, altho' I linger'd there
Till every daisy slept, and Love's white star
Beam'd thro' the thicken'd cedar in the dusk.

So home we went, and all the livelong way
With solemn gibe did Eustace banter me.
'Now,' said he, 'will you climb the top of Art.
You cannot fail but work in hues to dim
The Titianic Flora. Will you match
My Juliet? you, not you,—the Master, Love,
A more ideal Artist he than all.'

So home I went, but could not sleep for joy,
Reading her perfect features in the gloom,
Kissing the rose she gave me o'er and o'er,
And shaping faithful record of the glance
That graced the giving—such a noise of life
Swarm'd in the golden present, such a voice
Call'd to me from the years to come, and such

A length of bright horizon rimm'd the dark.
And all that night I heard the watchman peal
The sliding season: all that night I heard
The heavy clocks knolling the drowsy hours.   180
The drowsy hours, dispensers of all good,
O'er the mute city stole with folded wings,
Distilling odours on me as they went
To greet their fairer sisters of the East.

  Love at first sight, first-born, and heir to all,   185
Made this night thus. Henceforward squall nor storm
Could keep me from that Eden where she dwelt.
Light pretexts drew me; sometimes a Dutch love
For tulips; then for roses, moss or musk,
To grace my city rooms; or fruits and cream   190
Served in the weeping elm; and more and more
A word could bring the colour to my cheek;
A thought would fill my eyes with happy dew;
Love trebled life within me, and with each
The year increased.
                  The daughters of the year,   195
One after one, thro' that still garden pass'd;
Each garlanded with her peculiar flower
Danced into light, and died into the shade;
And each in passing touch'd with some new grace
Or seem'd to touch her, so that day by day,   200
Like one that never can be wholly known,
Her beauty grew; till Autumn brought an hour
For Eustace, when I heard his deep 'I will,'
Breathed, like the covenant of a God, to hold
From thence thro' all the worlds: but I rose up   205
Full of his bliss, and following her dark eyes
Felt earth as air beneath me, till I reach'd
The wicket-gate, and found her standing there.

There sat we down upon a garden mound,
Two mutually enfolded; Love, the third, 210
Between us, in the circle of his arms
Enwound us both; and over many a range
Of waning lime the gray cathedral towers,
Across a hazy glimmer of the west,
Reveal'd their shining windows: from them clash'd 215
The bells; we listen'd; with the time we play'd,
We spoke of other things; we coursed about
The subject most at heart, more near and near,
Like doves about a dovecote, wheeling round
The central wish, until we settled there. 220

Then, in that time and place, I spoke to her,
Requiring, tho' I knew it was mine own,
Yet for the pleasure that I took to hear,
Requiring at her hand the greatest gift,
A woman's heart, the heart of her I loved; 225
And in that time and place she answer'd me,
And in the compass of three little words,
More musical than ever came in one,
The silver fragments of a broken voice,
Made me most happy, faltering, 'I am thine.' 230

Shall I cease here? Is this enough to say
That my desire, like all strongest hopes,
By its own energy fulfill'd itself,
Merged in completion? Would you learn at full
How passion rose thro' circumstantial grades 235
Beyond all grades develop'd? and indeed
I had not stay'd so long to tell you all,
But while I mused came Memory with sad eyes,
Holding the folded annals of my youth;
And while I mused, Love with knit brows went by,
And with a flying finger swept my lips, 241

And spake, 'Be wise: not easily forgiven
Are those, who setting wide the doors that bar
The secret bridal chambers of the heart,
Let in the day.' Here, then, my words have end.   245

   Yet might I tell of meetings, of farewells—
Of that which came between, more sweet than each,
In whispers, like the whispers of the leaves
That tremble round a nightingale—in sighs
Which perfect Joy, perplex'd for utterance,   250
Stole from her sister Sorrow. Might I not tell
Of difference, reconcilement, pledges given,
And vows, where there was never need of vows,
And kisses, where the heart on one wild leap
Hung tranced from all pulsation, as above   255
The heavens between their fairy fleeces pale
Sow'd all their mystic gulfs with fleeting stars;
Or while the balmy glooming, crescent-lit,
Spread the light haze along the river-shores,
And in the hollows; or as once we met   260
Unheedful, tho' beneath a whispering rain
Night slid down one long stream of sighing wind,
And in her bosom bore the baby, Sleep.

   But this whole hour your eyes have been intent
On that veil'd picture—veil'd, for what it holds   265
May not be dwelt on by the common day.
This prelude has prepared thee. Raise thy soul;
Make thine heart ready with thine eyes: the time
Is come to raise the veil.
                        Behold her there,
As I beheld her ere she knew my heart,   270
My first, last love; the idol of my youth,
The darling of my manhood, and, alas!
Now the most blessed memory of mine age.

DORA

WITH farmer Allan at the farm abode
William and Dora. William was his son,
And she his niece. He often look'd at them,
And often thought, 'I'll make them man and wife.'
Now Dora felt her uncle's will in all, 5
And yearn'd towards William; but the youth, because
He had been always with her in the house,
Thought not of Dora.
          Then there came a day
When Allan call'd his son, and said, 'My son:
I married late, but I would wish to see 10
My grandchild on my knees before I die:
And I have set my heart upon a match.
Now therefore look to Dora; she is well
To look to; thrifty too beyond her age.
She is my brother's daughter: he and I 15
Had once hard words, and parted, and he died
In foreign lands; but for his sake I bred
His daughter Dora: take her for your wife;
For I have wish'd this marriage, night and day,
For many years.' But William answer'd short; 20
'I cannot marry Dora; by my life,
I will not marry Dora.' Then the old man
Was wroth, and doubled up his hands, and said:
'You will not, boy! you dare to answer thus!
But in my time a father's word was law, 25
And so it shall be now for me. Look to it;
Consider, William: take a month to think,
And let me have an answer to my wish;
Or, by the Lord that made me, you shall pack,
And never more darken my doors again.' 30
But William answer'd madly; bit his lips,
And broke away. The more he look'd at her

The less he liked her; and his ways were harsh;
But Dora bore them meekly. Then before
The month was out he left his father's house,   35
And hired himself to work within the fields;
And half in love, half spite, he woo'd and wed
A labourer's daughter, Mary Morrison.

   Then, when the bells were ringing, Allan call'd
His niece and said: 'My girl, I love you well;   40
But if you speak with him that was my son,
Or change a word with her he calls his wife,
My home is none of yours. My will is law.'
And Dora promised, being meek. She thought
'It cannot be: my uncle's mind will change!'   45

   And days went on, and there was born a boy
To William; then distresses came on him;
And day by day he pass'd his father's gate,
Heart-broken, and his father help'd him not.
But Dora stored what little she could save,   50
And sent it them by stealth, nor did they know
Who sent it; till at last a fever seized
On William, and in harvest time he died.

   Then Dora went to Mary. Mary sat
And look'd with tears upon her boy, and thought   55
Hard things of Dora. Dora came and said:

   'I have obey'd my uncle until now,
And I have sinn'd, for it was all thro' me
This evil came on William at the first.
But, Mary, for the sake of him that's gone,   60
And for your sake, the woman that he chose,
And for this orphan, I am come to you:
You know there has not been for these five years
So full a harvest: let me take the boy,

And I will set him in my uncle's eye 65
Among the wheat; that when his heart is glad
Of the full harvest, he may see the boy,
And bless him for the sake of him that's gone.'

And Dora took the child, and went her way
Across the wheat, and sat upon a mound 70
That was unsown, where many poppies grew.
Far off the farmer came into the field
And spied her not; for none of all his men
Dare tell him Dora waited with the child;
And Dora would have risen and gone to him, 75
But her heart fail'd her; and the reapers reap'd,
And the sun fell, and all the land was dark.

But when the morrow came, she rose and took
The child once more, and sat upon the mound;
And made a little wreath of all the flowers 80
That grew about, and tied it round his hat
To make him pleasing in her uncle's eye.
Then when the farmer pass'd into the field
He spied her, and he left his men at work,
And came and said: 'Where were you yesterday? 85
Whose child is that? What are you doing here?'
So Dora cast her eyes upon the ground,
And answer'd softly, 'This is William's child!'
'And did I not,' said Allan, 'did I not
Forbid you, Dora?' Dora said again: 90
'Do with me as you will, but take the child,
And bless him for the sake of him that's gone!'
And Allan said, 'I see it is a trick
Got up betwixt you and the woman there.
I must be taught my duty, and by you! 95
You knew my word was law, and yet you dared
To slight it. Well—for I will take the boy;
But go you hence, and never see me more.'

So saying, he took the boy that cried aloud
And struggled hard. The wreath of flowers fell   100
At Dora's feet. She bow'd upon her hands,
And the boy's cry came to her from the field,
More and more distant. She bow'd down her head,
Remembering the day when first she came,
And all the things that had been. She bow'd down   105
And wept in secret; and the reapers reap'd,
And the sun fell, and all the land was dark.

Then Dora went to Mary's house, and stood
Upon the threshold. Mary saw the boy
Was not with Dora. She broke out in praise   110
To God, that help'd her in her widowhood.
And Dora said, 'My uncle took the boy;
But, Mary, let me live and work with you:
He says that he will never see me more.'
Then answer'd Mary, 'This shall never be,   115
That thou shouldst take my trouble on thyself:
And, now I think, he shall not have the boy,
For he will teach him hardness, and to slight
His mother; therefore thou and I will go,
And I will have my boy, and bring him home;   120
And I will beg of him to take thee back:
But if he will not take thee back again,
Then thou and I will live within one house,
And work for William's child, until he grows
Of age to help us.'
              So the women kiss'd   125
Each other, and set out, and reach'd the farm.
The door was off the latch: they peep'd, and saw
The boy set up betwixt his grandsire's knees,
Who thrust him in the hollows of his arm,
And clapt him on the hands and on the cheeks,   130
Like one that loved him: and the lad stretch'd out
And babbled for the golden seal, that hung

From Allan's watch, and sparkled by the fire.
Then they came in: but when the boy beheld
His mother, he cried out to come to her: 135
And Allan set him down, and Mary said:

'O Father!—if you let me call you so—
I never came a-begging for myself,
Or William, or this child; but now I come
For Dora: take her back; she loves you well. 140
O Sir, when William died, he died at peace
With all men; for I ask'd him, and he said,
He could not ever rue his marrying me—
I had been a patient wife: but, Sir, he said
That he was wrong to cross his father thus: 145
"God bless him!" he said, "and may he never know
The troubles I have gone thro'!" Then he turn'd
His face and pass'd—unhappy that I am!
But now, Sir, let me have my boy, for you
Will make him hard, and he will learn to slight 150
His father's memory; and take Dora back,
And let all this be as it was before.'

So Mary said, and Dora hid her face
By Mary. There was silence in the room;
And all at once the old man burst in sobs:— 155

'I have been to blame—to blame. I have kill'd my son.
I have kill'd him—but I loved him—my dear son.
May God forgive me!—I have been to blame.
Kiss me, my children.'
      Then they clung about
The old man's neck, and kiss'd him many times. 160
And all the man was broken with remorse;
And all his love came back a hundredfold;
And for three hours he sobb'd o'er William's child
Thinking of William.

                    So those four abode
Within one house together; and as years   165
Went forward, Mary took another mate;
But Dora lived unmarried till her death.

AUDLEY COURT

'THE Bull, the Fleece are cramm'd, and not a room
For love or money. Let us picnic there
At Audley Court.'
                    I spoke, while Audley feast
Humm'd like a hive all round the narrow quay,
To Francis, with a basket on his arm,   5
To Francis just alighted from the boat,
And breathing of the sea. 'With all my heart,'
Said Francis. Then we shoulder'd thro' the swarm,
And rounded by the stillness of the beach
To where the bay runs up its latest horn.   10

  We left the dying ebb that faintly lipp'd
The flat red granite; so by many a sweep
Of meadow smooth from aftermath we reach'd
The griffin-guarded gates, and pass'd thro' all
The pillar'd dusk of sounding sycamores,   15
And cross'd the garden to the gardener's lodge,
With all its casements bedded, and its walls
And chimneys muffled in the leafy vine.

  There, on a slope of orchard, Francis laid
A damask napkin wrought with horse and hound,   20
Brought out a dusky loaf that smelt of home,
And, half-cut-down, a pasty costly-made,
Where quail and pigeon, lark and leveret lay,
Like fossils of the rock, with golden yolks

Imbedded and injellied; last, with these, 25
A flask of cider from his father's vats,
Prime, which I knew; and so we sat and eat
And talk'd old matters over; who was dead,
Who married, who was like to be, and how
The races went, and who would rent the hall: 30
Then touch'd upon the game, how scarce it was
This season; glancing thence, discuss'd the farm,
The four-field system, and the price of grain;
And struck upon the corn-laws, where we split,
And came again together on the king 35
With heated faces; till he laugh'd aloud;
And, while the blackbird on the pippin hung
To hear him, clapt his hand in mine and sang—

'Oh! who would fight and march and countermarch,
Be shot for sixpence in a battle-field, 40
And shovell'd up into some bloody trench
Where no one knows? but let me live my life.
  'Oh! who would cast and balance at a desk,
Perch'd like a crow upon a three-legg'd stool,
Till all his juice is dried, and all his joints 45
Are full of chalk? but let me live my life.
  'Who'd serve the state? for if I carved my name
Upon the cliffs that guard my native land,
I might as well have traced it in the sands;
The sea wastes all: but let me live my life. 50
  'Oh! who would love? I woo'd a woman once,
But she was sharper than an eastern wind,
And all my heart turn'd from her, as a thorn
Turns from the sea; but let me live my life.'
  He sang his song, and I replied with mine: 55
I found it in a volume, all of songs,
Knock'd down to me, when old Sir Robert's pride,
His books—the more the pity, so I said—

Came to the hammer here in March—and this—
I set the words, and added names I knew. 60

'Sleep, Ellen Aubrey, sleep, and dream of me:
Sleep, Ellen, folded in thy sister's arm,
And sleeping, haply dream her arm is mine.
  'Sleep, Ellen folded in Emilia's arm;
Emilia, fairer than all else but thou, 65
For thou art fairer than all else that is.
  'Sleep, breathing health and peace upon her breast:
Sleep, breathing love and trust against her lip:
I go to-night: I come to-morrow morn.
  'I go, but I return: I would I were 70
The pilot of the darkness and the dream.
Sleep, Ellen Aubrey, love, and dream of me.'

So sang we each to either, Francis Hale,
The farmer's son, who lived across the bay,
My friend; and I, that having wherewithal, 75
And in the fallow leisure of my life
A rolling stone of here and everywhere,
Did what I would; but ere the night we rose
And saunter'd home beneath a moon, that, just
In crescent, dimly rain'd about the leaf 80
Twilights of airy silver, till we reach'd
The limit of the hills; and as we sank
From rock to rock upon the glooming quay,
The town was hush'd beneath us: lower down
The bay was oily calm; the harbour-buoy, 85
Sole star of phosphorescence in the calm,
With one green sparkle ever and anon
Dipt by itself, and we were glad at heart.

WALKING TO THE MAIL

JOHN. I'M glad I walk'd. How fresh the meadows look
Above the river, and, but a month ago,
The whole hill-side was redder than a fox.
Is yon plantation where this byway joins
The turnpike?
    JAMES. Yes.
    JOHN.   And when does this come by?   5
    JAMES. The mail? At one o'clock.
    JOHN.   What is it now?
    JAMES. A quarter to.
    JOHN.   Whose house is that I see?
No, not the County Member's with the vane:
Up higher with the yew-tree by it, and half
A score of gables.
    JAMES.   That? Sir Edward Head's: 10
But he's abroad: the place is to be sold.
    JOHN. Oh, his. He was not broken.
    JAMES.   No, sir, he,
Vex'd with a morbid devil in his blood
That veil'd the world with jaundice, hid his face
From all men, and commercing with himself,   15
He lost the sense that handles daily life—
That keeps us all in order more or less—
And sick of home went overseas for change.
    JOHN. And whither?
    JAMES. Nay, who knows? he's here and there.
But let him go; his devil goes with him,   20
As well as with his tenant, Jocky Dawes.
    JOHN. What's that?
    JAMES. You saw the man—on Monday, was it?—
There by the humpback'd willow; half stands up
And bristles; half has fall'n and made a bridge;
And there he caught the younker tickling trout—   25

12. *broken:* bankrupt.   25. *younker:* youngsters

Caught *in flagrante*—what's the Latin word?—
Delicto: but his house, for so they say,
Was haunted with a jolly ghost, that shook
The curtains, whined in lobbies, tapt at doors,
And rummaged like a rat: no servant stay'd: 30
The farmer vext packs up his beds and chairs,
And all his household stuff; and with his boy
Betwixt his knees, his wife upon the tilt,
Sets out, and meets a friend who hails him, 'What!
You're flitting!' 'Yes, we're flitting,' says the ghost 35
(For they had pack'd the thing among the beds,)
'Oh well,' says he, 'you flitting with us too—
Jack, turn the horses' heads and home again.'

   JOHN. *He* left *his* wife behind; for so I heard.

   JAMES. He left her, yes. I met my lady once: 40
A woman like a butt, and harsh as crabs.

   JOHN. Oh yet but I remember, ten years back—
'Tis now at least ten years—and then she was—
You could not light upon a sweeter thing:
A body slight and round, and like a pear 45
In growing, modest eyes, a hand, a foot
Lessening in perfect cadence, and a skin
As clean and white as privet when it flowers.

   JAMES. Ay, ay, the blossom fades, and they that loved
At first like dove and dove were cat and dog. 50
She was the daughter of a cottager,
Out of her sphere. What betwixt shame and pride,
New things and old, himself and her, she sour'd
To what she is: a nature never kind!
Like men, like manners: like breeds like, they say: 55
Kind nature is the best: those manners next
That fit us like a nature second-hand;
Which are indeed the manners of the great.

   JOHN. But I had heard it was this bill that past,
And fear of change at home, that drove him hence. 60

   JAMES. That was the last drop in the cup of gall.

I once was near him, when his bailiff brought
A Chartist pike. You should have seen him wince
As from a venomous thing: he thought himself
A mark for all, and shudder'd, lest a cry   65
Should break his sleep by night, and his nice eyes
Should see the raw mechanic's bloody thumbs
Sweat on his blazon'd chairs; but, sir, you know
That these two parties still divide the world—
Of those that want, and those that have: and still   70
The same old sore breaks out from age to age
With much the same result. Now I myself,
A Tory to the quick, was as a boy
Destructive, when I had not what I would.
I was at school—a college in the South: 75
There lived a flayflint near; we stole his fruit,
His hens, his eggs; but there was law for *us*;
We paid in person. He had a sow, sir. She,
With meditative grunts of much content,
Lay great with pig, wallowing in sun and mud.   80
By night we dragg'd her to the college tower
From her warm bed, and up the cork-screw stair
With hand and rope we haled the groaning sow,
And on the leads we kept her till she pigg'd.
Large range of prospect had the mother sow,   85
And but for daily loss of one she loved
As one by one we took them—but for this—
As never sow was higher in this world—
Might have been happy: but what lot is pure?
We took them all, till she was left alone   90
Upon her tower, the Niobe of swine,
And so return'd unfarrow'd to her sty.
    JOHN.   They found you out?
    JAMES.   Not they.
    JOHN.   Well—after all—
What know we of the secret of a man?
His nerves were wrong. What ails us, who are sound,   95

That we should mimic this raw fool the world,
Which charts us all in its coarse blacks or whites,
As ruthless as a baby with a worm,
As cruel as a schoolboy ere he grows
To Pity—more from ignorance than will.   100

   But put your best foot forward, or I fear
That we shall miss the mail: and here it comes
With five at top: as quaint a four-in-hand
As you shall see—three pyebalds and a roan.

ST. SIMEON STYLITES

ALTHO' I be the basest of mankind,
From scalp to sole one slough and crust of sin,
Unfit for earth, unfit for heaven, scarce meet
For troops of devils, mad with blasphemy,
I will not cease to grasp the hope I hold   5
Of saintdom, and to clamour, mourn and sob,
Battering the gates of heaven with storms of prayer,
Have mercy, Lord, and take away my sin.

   Let this avail, just, dreadful, mighty God,
This not be all in vain, that thrice ten years,   10
Thrice multiplied by superhuman pangs,
In hungers and in thirsts, fevers and cold,
In coughs, aches, stitches, ulcerous throes and cramps,
A sign betwixt the meadow and the cloud,
Patient on this tall pillar I have borne   15
Rain, wind, frost, heat, hail, damp, and sleet, and snow;
And I had hoped that ere this period closed
Thou wouldst have caught me up into thy rest,

Denying not these weather-beaten limbs
The meed of saints, the white robe and the palm. 20

   O take the meaning, Lord: I do not breathe,
Not whisper, any murmur of complaint.
Pain heap'd ten-hundred-fold to this, were still
Less burthen, by ten-hundred-fold, to bear,
Than were those lead-like tons of sin that crush'd 25
My spirit flat before thee.
                O Lord, Lord,
Thou knowest I bore this better at the first,
For I was strong and hale of body then;
And tho' my teeth, which now are dropt away,
Would chatter with the cold, and all my beard 30
Was tagg'd with icy fringes in the moon,
I drown'd the whoopings of the owl with sound
Of pious hymns and psalms, and sometimes saw
An angel stand and watch me, as I sang.
Now am I feeble grown; my end draws nigh; 35
I hope my end draws nigh: half deaf I am,
So that I scarce can hear the people hum
About the column's base, and almost blind,
And scarce can recognise the fields I know;
And both my thighs are rotted with the dew; 40
Yet cease I not to clamour and to cry,
While my stiff spine can hold my weary head,
Till all my limbs drop piecemeal from the stone,
Have mercy, mercy: take away my sin.

   O Jesus, if thou wilt not save my soul, 45
Who may be saved? who is it may be saved?
Who may be made a saint, if I fail here?
Show me the man hath suffer'd more than I.
For did not all thy martyrs die one death?
For either they were stoned, or crucified, 50
Or burn'd in fire, or boil'd in oil, or sawn

In twain beneath the ribs; but I die here
To-day, and whole years long, a life of death.
Bear witness, if I could have found a way
(And heedfully I sifted all my thought) 55
More slowly-painful to subdue this home
Of sin, my flesh, which I despise and hate,
I had not stinted practice, O my God.

For not alone this pillar-punishment,
Not this alone I bore: but while I lived 60
In the white convent down the valley there,
For many weeks about my loins I wore
The rope that haled the buckets from the well,
Twisted as tight as I could knot the noose;
And spake not of it to a single soul, 65
Until the ulcer, eating thro' my skin,
Betray'd my secret penance, so that all
My brethren marvell'd greatly. More than this
I bore, whereof, O God, thou knowest all.

Three winters, that my soul might grow to thee, 70
I lived up there on yonder mountain side.
My right leg chain'd into the crag, I lay
Pent in a roofless close of ragged stones;
Inswathed sometimes in wandering mist, and twice
Black'd with thy branding thunder, and sometimes 75
Sucking the damps for drink, and eating not,
Except the spare chance-gift of those that came
To touch my body and be heal'd, and live:
And they say then that I work'd miracles,
Whereof my fame is loud amongst mankind, 80
Cured lameness, palsies, cancers. Thou, O God,
Knowest alone whether this was or no.
Have mercy, mercy! cover all my sin.

Then, that I might be more alone with thee,
Three years I lived upon a pillar, high 85

Six cubits, and three years on one of twelve;
And twice three years I crouch'd on one that rose
Twenty by measure; last of all, I grew
Twice ten long weary weary years to this,
That numbers forty cubits from the soil.

I think that I have borne as much as this—
Or else I dream—and for so long a time,
If I may measure time by yon slow light,
And this high dial, which my sorrow crowns—
So much—even so.

                      And yet I know not well,
For that the evil ones come here, and say,
'Fall down, O Simeon: thou hast suffer'd long
For ages and for ages!' then they prate
Of penances I cannot have gone thro',
Perplexing me with lies; and oft I fall,
Maybe for months, in such blind lethargies
That Heaven, and Earth, and Time are choked.

                                                    But yet
Bethink thee, Lord, while thou and all the saints
Enjoy themselves in heaven, and men on earth
House in the shade of comfortable roofs,
Sit with their wives by fires, eat wholesome food,
And wear warm clothes, and even beasts have stalls,
I, 'tween the spring and downfall of the light,
Bow down one thousand and two hundred times,
To Christ, the Virgin Mother, and the saints;
Or in the night, after a little sleep,
I wake: the chill stars sparkle; I am wet
With drenching dews, or stiff with crackling frost.
I wear an undress'd goatskin on my back;
A grazing iron collar grinds my neck;
And in my weak, lean arms I lift the cross,
And strive and wrestle with thee till I die:
O mercy, mercy! wash away my sin.

O Lord, thou knowest what a man I am;
A sinful man, conceived and born in sin: 120
'Tis their own doing; this is none of mine;
Lay it not to me. Am I to blame for this,
That here come those that worship me? Ha! ha!
They think that I am somewhat. What am I?
The silly people take me for a saint, 125
And bring me offerings of fruit and flowers:
And I, in truth (thou wilt bear witness here)
Have all in all endured as much, and more
Than many just and holy men, whose names
Are register'd and calendar'd for saints. 130

Good people, you do ill to kneel to me.
What is it I can have done to merit this?
I am a sinner viler than you all.
It may be I have wrought some miracles,
And cured some halt and maim'd; but what of that? 135
It may be, no one, even among the saints,
May match his pains with mine; but what of that?
Yet do not rise; for you may look on me,
And in your looking you may kneel to God.
Speak! is there any of you halt or maim'd? 140
I think you know I have some power with Heaven
From my long penance: let him speak his wish.

Yes, I can heal him. Power goes forth from me.
They say that they are heal'd. Ah, hark! they shout
'St. Simeon Stylites.' Why, if so, 145
God reaps a harvest in me. O my soul,
God reaps a harvest in thee. If this be,
Can I work miracles and not be saved?
This is not told of any. They were saints.
It cannot be but that I shall be saved; 150
Yea, crown'd a saint. They shout, 'Behold a saint!'
And lower voices saint me from above.

Courage, St. Simeon! This dull chrysalis
Cracks into shining wings, and hope ere death
Spreads more and more and more, that God that now
Sponged and made blank of crimeful record all   156
My mortal archives.
                   O my sons, my sons,
I, Simeon of the pillar, by surname
Stylites, among men; I, Simeon,
The watcher on the column till the end;   160
I, Simeon, whose brain the sunshine bakes;
I, whose bald brows in silent hours become
Unnaturally hoar with rime, do now
From my high nest of penance here proclaim
That Pontius and Iscariot by my side   165
Show'd like fair seraphs. On the coals I lay,
A vessel full of sin: all hell beneath
Made me boil over. Devils pluck'd my sleeve,
Abaddon and Asmodeus caught at me.
I smote them with the cross; they swarm'd again. 170
In bed like monstrous apes they crush'd my chest:
They flapp'd my light out as I read: I saw
Their faces grow between me and my book;
With colt-like whinny and with hoggish whine
They burst my prayer. Yet this way was left,   175
And by this way I 'scaped them. Mortify
Your flesh, like me, with scourges and with thorns;
Smite, shrink not, spare not. If it may be, fast
Whole Lents, and pray. I hardly, with slow steps,
With slow, faint steps, and much exceeding pain, 180
Have scrambled past those pits of fire, that still
Sing in mine ears. But yield not me the praise:
God only thro' his bounty hath thought fit,
Among the powers and princes of this world,
To make me an example to mankind,   185
Which few can reach to. Yet I do not say
But that a time may come—yea, even now,

Now, now, his footsteps smite the threshold stairs
Of life—I say, that time is at the doors
When you may worship me without reproach;   190
For I will leave my relics in your land,
And you may carve a shrine about my dust,
And burn a fragrant lamp before my bones,
When I am gather'd to the glorious saints.

   While I spake then, a sting of shrewdest pain   195
Ran shrivelling thro' me, and a cloudlike change,
In passing, with a grosser film made thick
These heavy, horny eyes. The end! the end!
Surely the end! What's here? a shape, a shade,
A flash of light. Is that the angel there   200
That holds a crown? Come, blessed brother, come.
I know thy glittering face. I waited long;
My brows are ready. What! deny it now?
Nay, draw, draw, draw nigh. So I clutch it. Christ!
'Tis gone: 'tis here again; the crown! the crown!   205
So now 'tis fitted on and grows to me,
And from it melt the dews of Paradise,
Sweet! sweet! spikenard, and balm, and frankincense.
Ah! let me not be fool'd, sweet saints: I trust
That I am whole, and clean, and meet for Heaven.   210

   Speak, if there be a priest, a man of God,
Among you there, and let him presently
Approach, and lean a ladder on the shaft,
And climbing up into my airy home,
Deliver me the blessed sacrament;   215
For by the warning of the Holy Ghost,
I prophesy that I shall die to-night,
A quarter before twelve.
                    But thou, O Lord,
Aid all this foolish people; let them take
Example, pattern: lead them to thy light.   220

THE TALKING OAK

Once more the gate behind me falls;
   Once more before my face
I see the moulder'd Abbey-walls,
   That stand within the chace.

Beyond the lodge the city lies,
   Beneath its drift of smoke;
And ah! with what delighted eyes
   I turn to yonder oak.

For when my passion first began,
   Ere that, which in me burn'd,
The love, that makes me thrice a man,
   Could hope itself return'd;

To yonder oak within the field
   I spoke without restraint,
And with a larger faith appeal'd
   Than Papist unto Saint.

For oft I talk'd with him apart,
   And told him of my choice,
Until he plagiarised a heart,
   And answer'd with a voice.

Tho' what he whisper'd under Heaven
   None else could understand;
I found him garrulously given,
   A babbler in the land.

But since I heard him make reply
   Is many a weary hour;
'Twere well to question him, and try
   If yet he keeps the power.

Hail, hidden to the knees in fern,
    Broad Oak of Sumner-chace,
Whose topmost branches can discern
    The roofs of Sumner-place!

Say thou, whereon I carved her name,
    If ever maid or spouse,
As fair as my Olivia, came
    To rest beneath thy boughs.—

'O Walter, I have shelter'd here
    Whatever maiden grace
The good old Summers, year by year
    Made ripe in Sumner-chace:

'Old Summers, when the monk was fat,
    And, issuing shorn and sleek,
Would twist his girdle tight, and pat
    The girls upon the cheek,

'Ere yet, in scorn of Peter's-pence,
    And number'd bead, and shrift,
Bluff Harry broke into the spence
    And turn'd the cowls adrift:

'And I have seen some score of those
    Fresh faces, that would thrive
When his man-minded offset rose
    To chase the deer at five;

'And all that from the town would stroll,
    Till that wild wind made work
In which the gloomy brewer's soul
    Went by me, like a stork:

'The slight she-slips of loyal blood,
    And others, passing praise,

Strait-laced, but all-too-full in bud
  For puritanic stays: 60

'And I have shadow'd many a group
  Of beauties, that were born
In teacup-times of hood and hoop,
  Or while the patch was worn;

'And leg and arm with love-knots gay,   65
  About me leap'd and laugh'd
The modish Cupid of the day,
  And shrill'd his tinsel shaft.

'I swear (and else may insects prick
  Each leaf into a gall)   70
This girl, for whom your heart is sick,
  Is three times worth them all;

'For those and theirs, by Nature's law,
  Have faded long ago;
But in these latter springs I saw   75
  Your own Olivia blow,

'From when she gamboll'd on the greens
  A baby-germ, to when
The maiden blossoms of her teens
  Could number five from ten.   80

'I swear, by leaf, and wind, and rain,
  (And hear me with thine ears,)
That, tho' I circle in the grain
  Five hundred rings of years—

'Yet, since I first could cast a shade,   85
  Did never creature pass
So slightly, musically made,
  So light upon the grass:

'For as to fairies, that will flit
    To make the greensward fresh,   90
I hold them exquisitely knit,
    But far too spare of flesh.'

Oh, hide thy knotted knees in fern,
    And overlook the chace;
And from thy topmost branch discern   95
    The roofs of Sumner-place.

But thou, whereon I carved her name,
    That oft hast heard my vows,
Declare when last Olivia came
    To sport beneath thy boughs.   100

'O yesterday, you know, the fair
    Was holden at the town;
Her father left his good arm-chair,
    And rode his hunter down.

'And with him Albert came on his.   105
    I look'd at him with joy:
As cowslip unto oxlip is,
    So seems she to the boy.

'An hour had past—and, sitting straight
    Within the low-wheel'd chaise,   110
Her mother trundled to the gate
    Behind the dappled grays.

'But as for her, she stay'd at home,
    And on the roof she went,
And down the way you use to come,   115
    She look'd with discontent.

'She left the novel half-uncut
    Upon the rosewood shelf;

She left the new piano shut:
   She could not please herself.   120

'Then ran she, gamesome as the colt,
   And livelier than a lark
She sent her voice thro' all the holt
   Before her, and the park.

'A light wind chased her on the wing,   125
   And in the chase grew wild,
As close as might be would he cling
   About the darling child:

'But light as any wind that blows
   So fleetly did she stir,   130
The flower, she touch'd on, dipt and rose,
   And turn'd to look at her.

'And here she came, and round me play'd,
   And sang to me the whole
Of those three stanzas that you made   135
   About my "giant bole;"

'And in a fit of frolic mirth
   She strove to span my waist:
Alas, I was so broad of girth,
   I could not be embraced.   140

'I wish'd myself the fair young beech
   That here beside me stands,
That round me, clasping each in each,
   She might have lock'd her hands.

'Yet seem'd the pressure thrice as sweet   145
   As woodbine's fragile hold,
Or when I feel about my feet
   The berried briony fold.'

O muffle round thy knees with fern,
   And shadow Sumner-chace! 150
Long may thy topmost branch discern
   The roofs of Sumner-place!

But tell me, did she read the name
   I carved with many vows
When last with throbbing heart I came 155
   To rest beneath thy boughs?

'O yes, she wander'd round and round
   These knotted knees of mine,
And found, and kiss'd the name she found,
   And sweetly murmur'd thine. 160

'A teardrop trembled from its source,
   And down my surface crept.
My sense of touch is something coarse,
   But I believe she wept.

'Then flush'd her cheek with rosy light, 165
   She glanced across the plain;
But not a creature was in sight:
   She kiss'd me once again.

'Her kisses were so close and kind,
   That, trust me on my word, 170
Hard wood I am, and wrinkled rind,
   But yet my sap was stirr'd:

'And even into my inmost ring
   A pleasure I discern'd,
Like those blind motions of the Spring, 175
   That show the year is turn'd.

'Thrice-happy he that may caress
   The ringlet's waving balm—

The cushions of whose touch may press
   The maiden's tender palm.   180

'I, rooted here among the groves
   But languidly adjust
My vapid vegetable loves
   With anthers and with dust:

'For ah! my friend, the days were brief   185
   Whereof the poets talk,
When that, which breathes within the leaf,
   Could slip its bark and walk.

'But could I, as in times foregone,
   From spray, and branch, and stem,   190
Have suck'd and gather'd into one
   The life that spreads in them,

'She had not found me so remiss;
   But lightly issuing thro',
I would have paid her kiss for kiss,   195
   With usury thereto.'

O flourish high, with leafy towers,
   And overlook the lea,
Pursue thy loves among the bowers
   But leave thou mine to me.   200

O flourish, hidden deep in fern,
   Old oak, I love thee well;
A thousand thanks for what I learn
   And what remains to tell.

' 'Tis little more: the day was warm;   205
   At last, tired out with play,
She sank her head upon her arm
   And at my feet she lay.

'Her eyelids dropp'd their silken eaves.
　　I breathed upon her eyes 210
Thro' all the summer of my leaves
　　A welcome mix'd with sighs.

'I took the swarming sound of life—
　　The music from the town—
The murmurs of the drum and fife 215
　　And lull'd them in my own.

'Sometimes I let a sunbeam slip,
　　To light her shaded eye;
A second flutter'd round her lip
　　Like a golden butterfly; 220

'A third would glimmer on her neck
　　To make the necklace shine;
Another slid, a sunny fleck,
　　From head to ancle fine,

'Then close and dark my arms I spread, 225
　　And shadow'd all her rest—
Dropt dews upon her golden head,
　　An acorn in her breast.

'But in a pet she started up,
　　And pluck'd it out, and drew 230
My little oakling from the cup,
　　And flung him in the dew.

'And yet it was a graceful gift—
　　I felt a pang within
As when I see the woodman lift 235
　　His axe to slay my kin.

'I shook him down because he was
    The finest on the tree.
He lies beside thee on the grass.
    O kiss him once for me.   240

'O kiss him twice and thrice for me,
    That have no lips to kiss,
For never yet was oak on lea
    Shall grow so fair as this.'

Step deeper yet in herb and fern,   245
    Look further thro' the chace,
Spread upward till thy boughs discern
    The front of Sumner-place.

This fruit of thine by Love is blest,
    That but a moment lay   250
Where fairer fruit of Love may rest
    Some happy future day.

I kiss it twice, I kiss it thrice,
    The warmth it thence shall win
To riper life may magnetise   255
    The baby-oak within.

But thou, while kingdoms overset,
    Or lapse from hand to hand,
Thy leaf shall never fail, nor yet
    Thine acorn in the land.   260

May never saw dismember thee,
    Nor wielded axe disjoint,
That art the fairest-spoken tree
    From here to Lizard-point.

O rock upon thy tower-top 265
  All throats that gurgle sweet!
All starry culmination drop
  Balm-dews to bathe thy feet!

All grass of silky feather grow—
  And while he sinks or swells 270
The full south-breeze around thee blow
  The sound of minster bells.

The fat earth feed thy branchy root,
  That under deeply strikes!
The northern morning o'er thee shoot, 275
  High up, in silver spikes!

Nor ever lightning char thy grain,
  But, rolling as in sleep,
Low thunders bring the mellow rain,
  That makes thee broad and deep! 280

And hear me swear a solemn oath,
  That only by thy side
Will I to Olive plight my troth,
  And gain her for my bride.

And when my marriage morn may fall, 285
  She, Dryad-like, shall wear
Alternate leaf and acorn-ball
  In wreath about her hair.

And I will work in prose and rhyme,
  And praise thee more in both 290
Than bard has honour'd beech or lime,
  Or that Thessalian growth,

In which the swarthy ringdove sat,
    And mystic sentence spoke;
And more than England honours that,
    Thy famous brother-oak,

Wherein the younger Charles abode
    Till all the paths were dim,
And far below the Roundhead rode,
    And humm'd a surly hymn.

LOVE AND DUTY

Of love that never found his earthly close,
What sequel? Streaming eyes and breaking hearts?
Or all the same as if he had not been?

  Not so. Shall Error in the round of time
Still father Truth? O shall the braggart shout
For some blind glimpse of freedom work itself
Thro' madness, hated by the wise, to law
System and empire? Sin itself be found
The cloudy porch oft opening on the Sun?
And only he, this wonder, dead, become
Mere highway dust? or year by year alone
Sit brooding in the ruins of a life,
Nightmare of youth, the spectre of himself?

  If this were thus, if this, indeed, were all,
Better the narrow brain, the stony heart,
The staring eye glazed o'er with sapless days,
The long mechanic pacings to and fro,
The set gray life, and apathetic end.
But am not I the nobler thro' thy love?

O three times less unworthy! likewise thou 20
Art more thro' Love, and greater than thy years
The Sun will run his orbit, and the Moon
Her circle. Wait, and Love himself will bring
The drooping flower of knowledge changed to fruit
Of wisdom. Wait: my faith is large in Time, 25
And that which shapes it to some perfect end.

  Will some one say, Then why not ill for good?
Why took ye not your pastime? To that man
My work shall answer, since I knew the right
And did it; for a man is not as God, 30
But then most Godlike being most a man.
—So let me think 'tis well for thee and me—
Ill-fated that I am, what lot is mine
Whose foresight preaches peace, my heart so slow
To feel it! For how hard it seem'd to me, 35
When eyes, love-languid thro' half tears would dwell
One earnest, earnest moment upon mine,
Then not to dare to see! when thy low voice,
Faltering, would break its syllables, to keep
My own full-tuned,—hold passion in a leash, 40
And not leap forth and fall about thy neck,
And on thy bosom (deep desired relief!)
Rain out the heavy mist of tears, that weigh'd
Upon my brain, my senses and my soul!

  For Love himself took part against himself 45
To warn us off, and Duty loved of Love—
O this world's curse,—beloved but hated—came
Like Death betwixt thy dear embrace and mine,
And crying, 'Who is this? behold thy bride,'
She push'd me from thee.
                If the sense is hard 50
To alien ears, I did not speak to these—
No, not to thee, but to thyself in me:
Hard is my doom and thine: thou knowest it all.

    Could Love part thus? was it not well to speak,
To have spoken once? It could not but be well. 55
The slow sweet hours that bring us all things good,
The slow sad hours that bring us all things ill,
And all good things from evil, brought the night
In which we sat together and alone,
And to the want, that hollow'd all the heart, 60
Gave utterance by the yearning of an eye,
That burn'd upon its object thro' such tears
As flow but once a life.
                        The trance gave way
To those caresses, when a hundred times
In that last kiss, which never was the last, 65
Farewell, like endless welcome, lived and died.
Then follow'd counsel, comfort, and the words
That make a man feel strong in speaking truth;
Till now the dark was worn, and overhead
The lights of sunset and of sunrise mix'd 70
In that brief night; the summer night, that paused
Among her stars to hear us; stars that hung
Love-charm'd to listen: all the wheels of Time
Spun round in station, but the end had come.

  O then like those, who clench their nerves to rush 75
Upon their dissolution, we two rose,
There—closing like an individual life—
In one blind cry of passion and of pain,
Like bitter accusation ev'n to death,
Caught up the whole of love and utter'd it, 80
And bade adieu for ever.
                        Live—yet live—
Shall sharpest pathos blight us, knowing all
Life needs for life is possible to will—
Live happy; tend thy flowers; be tended oy
My blessing! Should my Shadow cross thy thoughts 85
Too sadly for their peace, remand it thou

For calmer hours to Memory's darkest hold,
If not to be forgotten—not at once—
Not all forgotten. Should it cross thy dreams,
O might it come like one that looks content,   90
With quiet eyes unfaithful to the truth,
And point thee forward to a distant light,
Or seem to lift a burthen from thy heart
And leave thee freër, till thou wake refresh'd
Then when the first low matin-chirp hath grown   95
Full quire, and morning driv'n her plow of pearl
Far furrowing into light the mounded rack,
Beyond the fair green field and eastern sea.

ULYSSES

It little profits that an idle king,
By this still hearth, among these barren crags,
Match'd with an aged wife, I mete and dole
Unequal laws unto a savage race,
That hoard, and sleep, and feed, and know not me.   5

I cannot rest from travel: I will drink
Life to the lees: all times I have enjoy'd
Greatly, have suffer'd greatly, both with those
That loved me, and alone; on shore, and when
Thro' scudding drifts the rainy Hyades   10
Vext the dim sea: I am become a name;
For always roaming with a hungry heart
Much have I seen and known; cities of men
And manners, climates, councils, governments,
Myself not least, but honour'd of them all;   15
And drunk delight of battle with my peers,
Far on the ringing plains of windy Troy.

I am a part of all that I have met;
Yet all experience is an arch wherethro'
Gleams that untravell'd world, whose margin fades   20
For ever and for ever when I move.
How dull it is to pause, to make an end,
To rust unburnish'd, not to shine in use!
As tho' to breathe were life. Life piled on life
Were all too little, and of one to me   25
Little remains: but every hour is saved
From that eternal silence, something more,
A bringer of new things; and vile it were
For some three suns to store and hoard myself,
And this gray spirit yearning in desire   30
To follow knowledge like a sinking star,
Beyond the utmost bound of human thought.

This is my son, mine own Telemachus,
To whom I leave the sceptre and the isle—
Well-loved of me, discerning to fulfil   35
This labour, by slow prudence to make mild
A rugged people, and thro' soft degrees
Subdue them to the useful and the good.
Most blameless is he, centred in the sphere
Of common duties, decent not to fail   40
In offices of tenderness, and pay
Meet adoration to my household gods,
When I am gone. He works his work, I mine.

There lies the port; the vessel puffs her sail:
There gloom the dark broad seas. My mariners,   45
Souls that have toil'd, and wrought, and thought with me—
That ever with a frolic welcome took
The thunder and the sunshine, and opposed
Free hearts, free foreheads—you and I are old;
Old age hath yet his honour and his toil;   50

Death closes all: but something ere the end,
Some work of noble note, may yet be done,
Not unbecoming men that strove with Gods.
The lights begin to twinkle from the rocks:
The long day wanes: the slow moon climbs: the deep 55
Moans round with many voices. Come, my friends,
'Tis not too late to seek a newer world.
Push off, and sitting well in order smite
The sounding furrows; for my purpose holds
To sail beyond the sunset, and the baths 60
Of all the western stars, until I die.
It may be that the gulfs will wash us down:
It may be we shall touch the Happy Isles,
And see the great Achilles, whom we knew.
Tho' much is taken, much abides; and tho' 65
We are not now that strength which in old days
Moved earth and heaven; that which we are, we are;
One equal temper of heroic hearts,
Made weak by time and fate, but strong in will
To strive, to seek, to find, and not to yield. 70

LOCKSLEY HALL

Comrades, leave me here a little, while as yet 'tis early morn:
Leave me here, and when you want me, sound upon the bugle-horn.

'Tis the place, and all around it, as of old, the curlews call,
Dreary gleams about the moorland flying over Locksley Hall;

Locksley Hall, that in the distance overlooks the sandy 5
    tracts,
And the hollow ocean-ridges roaring into cataracts.

Many a night from yonder ivied casement, ere I went
    to rest,
Did I look on great Orion sloping slowly to the West.

Many a night I saw the Pleiads, rising thro' the mellow
    shade,
Glitter like a swarm of fire-flies tangled in a silver braid. 10

Here about the beach I wander'd, nourishing a youth
    sublime
With the fairy tales of science, and the long result of Time;

When the centuries behind me like a fruitful land reposed;
When I clung to all the present for the promise that it
    closed:

When I dipt into the future far as human eye could see; 15
Saw the Vision of the world, and all the wonder that
    would be.——

In the Spring a fuller crimson comes upon the robin's
    breast;
In the Spring the wanton lapwing gets himself another
    crest;

In the Spring a livelier iris changes on the burnish'd dove;
In the Spring a young man's fancy lightly turns to
    thoughts of love.   20

Then her cheek was pale and thinner than should be for
    one so young,
And her eyes on all my motions with a mute observance
    hung.

And I said, 'My cousin Amy, speak, and speak the truth to me,
Trust me, cousin, all the current of my being sets to thee.'

On her pallid cheek and forehead came a colour and a light, 25
As I have seen the rosy red flushing in the northern night.

And she turn'd—her bosom shaken with a sudden storm of sighs—
All the spirit deeply dawning in the dark of hazel eyes—

Saying, 'I have hid my feelings, fearing they should do me wrong;'
Saying, 'Dost thou love me, cousin?' weeping, 'I have loved thee long.' 30

Love took up the glass of Time, and turn'd it in his glowing hands;
Every moment, lightly shaken, ran itself in golden sands.

Love took up the harp of Life, and smote on all the chords with might;
Smote the chord of Self, that, trembling, pass'd in music out of sight.

Many a morning on the moorland did we hear the copses ring, 35
And her whisper throng'd my pulses with the fullness of the Spring.

Many an evening by the waters did we watch the stately ships,
And our spirits rush'd together at the touching of the lips.

O my cousin, shallow-hearted! O my Amy, mine no more!
O the dreary, dreary moorland! O the barren, barren shore! 40

Falser than all fancy fathoms, falser than all songs have sung,
Puppet to a father's threat, and servile to a shrewish tongue!

Is it well to wish thee happy?—having known me—to decline
On a range of lower feelings and a narrower heart than mine!

Yet it shall be: thou shalt lower to his level day by day, 45
What is fine within thee growing coarse to sympathise with clay.

As the husband is, the wife is: thou art mated with a clown,
And the grossness of his nature will have weight to drag thee down.

He will hold thee, when his passion shall have spent its novel force,
Something better than his dog, a little dearer than his horse. 50

What is this? his eyes are heavy: think not they are glazed with wine.
Go to him: it is thy duty: kiss him: take his hand in thine.

It may be my lord is weary, that his brain is overwrought:
Soothe him with thy finer fancies, touch him with thy lighter thought.

He will answer to the purpose, easy things to 55
    understand—
Better thou wert dead before me, tho' I slew thee with
    my hand!

Better thou and I were lying, hidden from the heart's
    disgrace,
Roll'd in one another's arms, and silent in a last embrace.

Cursed be the social wants that sin against the strength
    of youth!
Cursed be the social lies that warp us from the living 60
    truth!

Cursed be the sickly forms that err from honest Nature's
    rule!
Cursed be the gold that gilds the straiten'd forehead of
    the fool!

Well—'tis well that I should bluster!—Hadst thou less
    unworthy proved—
Would to God—for I had loved thee more than ever
    wife was loved.

Am I mad, that I should cherish that which bears but 65
    bitter fruit?
I will pluck it from my bosom, tho' my heart be at the
    root.

Never, tho' my mortal summers to such length of years
    should come
As the many-winter'd crow that leads the clanging
    rookery home.

Where is comfort? in division of the records of the mind?
Can I part her from herself, and love her, as I knew 70
    her, kind?

I remember one that perish'd: sweetly did she speak and
    move:
Such a one do I remember, whom to look at was to love.

Can I think of her as dead, and love her for the love she
    bore?
No—she never loved me truly: love is love for evermore.

Comfort? comfort scorn'd of devils! this is truth the   75
    poet sings,
That a sorrow's crown of sorrow is remembering happier
    things.

Drug thy memories, lest thou learn it, lest thy heart be
    put to proof,
In the dead unhappy night, and when the rain is on the
    roof.

Like a dog, he hunts in dreams, and thou art staring at
    the wall,
Where the dying night-lamp flickers, and the shadows   80
    rise and fall.

Then a hand shall pass before thee, pointing to his
    drunken sleep,
To thy widow'd marriage-pillows, to the tears that thou
    wilt weep.

Thou shalt hear the 'Never never,' whisper'd by the
    phantom years,
And a song from out the distance in the ringing of thine
    ears;

And an eye shall vex thee, looking ancient kindness on   85
    thy pain.
Turn thee, turn thee on thy pillow: get thee to thy rest
    again.

Nay, but Nature brings thee solace; for a tender voice
  will cry.
'Tis a purer life than thine; a lip to drain thy trouble dry.

Baby lips will laugh me down: my latest rival brings thee
  rest.
Baby fingers, waxen touches, press me from the 90
  mother's breast.

O, the child too clothes the father with a dearness not
  his due.
Half is thine and half is his: it will be worthy of the two.

O, I see thee old and formal, fitted to thy petty part,
With a little hoard of maxims preaching down a
  daughter's heart.

'They were dangerous guides the feelings—she herself 95
  was not exempt—
Truly, she herself had suffer'd'—Perish in thy self-
  contempt!

Overlive it—lower yet—be happy! wherefore should I
  care?
I myself must mix with action, lest I wither by despair.

What is that which I should turn to, lighting upon days
  like these?
Every door is barr'd with gold, and opens but to 100
  golden keys.

Every gate is throng'd with suitors, all the markets
  overflow.
I have but an angry fancy: what is that which I should
  do?

I had been content to perish, falling on the foeman's
    ground,
When the ranks are roll'd in vapour, and the winds are
    laid with sound.

But the jingling of the guinea helps the hurt that   105
    Honour feels,
And the nations do but murmur, snarling at each other's
    heels.

Can I but relive in sadness? I will turn that earlier page.
Hide me from my deep emotion, O thou wondrous
    Mother-Age!

Make me feel the wild pulsation that I felt before the
    strife,
When I heard my days before me, and the tumult of   110
    my life;

Yearning for the large excitement that the coming years
    would yield,
Eager-hearted as a boy when first he leaves his father's
    field,

And at night along the dusky highway near and nearer
    drawn,
Sees in heaven the light of London flaring like a dreary
    dawn;

And his spirit leaps within him to be gone before him   115
    then,
Underneath the light he looks at, in among the throngs
    of men:

Men, my brothers, men the workers, ever reaping
    something new:

That which they have done but earnest of the things
    that they shall do:

For I dipt into the future, far as human eye could see,
Saw the Vision of the world, and all the wonder that   120
    would be;

Saw the heavens fill with commerce, argosies of magic
    sails,
Pilots of the purple twilight, dropping down with costly
    bales;

Heard the heavens fill with shouting, and there rain'd a
    ghastly dew
From the nations' airy navies grappling in the central
    blue;

Far along the world-wide whisper of the south-wind   125
    rushing warm,
With the standards of the peoples plunging thro' the
    thunder-storm;

Till the war-drum throbb'd no longer, and the battle-flags
    were furl'd
In the Parliament of man, the Federation of the world.

There the common sense of most shall hold a fretful
    realm in awe,
And the kindly earth shall slumber, lapt in universal   130
    law.

So I triumph'd ere my passion sweeping thro' me left
    me dry,
Left me with the palsied heart, and left me with the
    jaundiced eye;

Eye, to which all order festers, all things here are out of joint:
Science moves, but slowly slowly, creeping on from point to point:

Slowly comes a hungry people, as a lion creeping nigher, 135
Glares at one that nods and winks behind a slowly-dying fire.

Yet I doubt not thro' the ages one increasing purpose runs,
And the thoughts of men are widen'd with the process of the suns.

What is that to him that reaps not harvest of his youthful joys,
Tho' the deep heart of existence beat for ever like a 140 boy's?

Knowledge comes, but wisdom lingers, and I linger on the shore,
And the individual withers, and the world is more and more.

Knowledge comes, but wisdom lingers, and he bears a laden breast,
Full of sad experience, moving toward the stillness of his rest.

Hark, my merry comrades call me, sounding on the 145 bugle-horn,
They to whom my foolish passion were a target for their scorn:

Shall it not be scorn to me to harp on such a moulder'd string?

I am shamed thro' all my nature to have loved so slight a thing.

Weakness to be wroth with weakness! woman's pleasure, woman's pain—
Nature made them blinder motions bounded in a shallower brain: 150

Woman is the lesser man, and all thy passions, match'd with mine,
Are as moonlight unto sunlight, and as water unto wine—

Here at least, where nature sickens, nothing. Ah, for some retreat
Deep in yonder shining Orient, where my life began to beat;

Where in wild Mahratta-battle fell my father evil- 155
starr'd;—
I was left a trampled orphan, and a selfish uncle's ward.

Or to burst all links of habit—there to wander far away,
On from island unto island at the gateways of the day.

Larger constellations burning, mellow moons and happy skies,
Breadths of tropic shade and palms in cluster, knots 160
of Paradise.

Never comes the trader, never floats an European flag,
Slides the bird o'er lustrous woodland, swings the trailer from the crag;

Droops the heavy-blossom'd bower, hangs the heavy-fruited tree—
Summer isles of Eden lying in dark-purple spheres of sea.

There methinks would be enjoyment more than in   165
    this march of mind,
In the steamship, in the railway, in the thoughts that
    shake mankind.

There the passions cramp'd no longer shall have scope
    and breathing space;
I will take some savage woman, she shall rear my dusky
    race.

Iron jointed, supple-sinew'd, they shall dive, and they
    shall run,
Catch the wild goat by the hair, and hurl their lances   170
    in the sun;

Whistle back the parrot's call, and leap the rainbows of
    the brooks,
Not with blinded eyesight poring over miserable books—

Fool, again the dream, the fancy! but I *know* my words
    are wild,
But I count the gray barbarian lower than the Christian
    child.

I, to herd with narrow foreheads, vacant of our   175
    glorious gains,
Like a beast with lower pleasures, like a beast with lower
    pains!

Mated with a squalid savage—what to me were sun or
    clime?
I the heir of all the ages, in the foremost files of time—

I that rather held it better men should perish one by one,
Than that earth should stand at gaze like Joshua's   180
    moon in Ajalon!

Not in vain the distance beacons. Forward, forward let
  us range,
Let the great world spin for ever down the ringing
  grooves of change.

Thro' the shadow of the globe we sweep into the
  younger day:
Better fifty years of Europe than a cycle of Cathay.

Mother-Age (for mine I knew not) help me as when   185
  life begun:
Rift the hills, and roll the waters, flash the lightnings,
  weigh the Sun.

O, I see the crescent promise of my spirit hath not set.
Ancient founts of inspiration well thro' all my fancy yet.

Howsoever these things be, a long farewell to Locksley
  Hall!
Now for me the woods may wither, now for me the   190
  roof-tree fall.

Comes a vapour from the margin, blackening over heath
  and holt,
Cramming all the blast before it, in its breast a thunderbolt.

Let it fall on Locksley Hall, with rain or hail, or fire or
  snow;
For the mighty wind arises, roaring seaward, and I go.

184. *Cathay:* China

GODIVA

I waited for the train at Coventry;
I hung with grooms and porters on the bridge,
To watch the three tall spires; and there I shaped
The city's ancient legend into this:—

  Not only we, the latest seed of Time, 5
New men, that in the flying of a wheel
Cry down the past, not only we, that prate
Of rights and wrongs, have loved the people well,
And loathed to see them overtax'd; but she
Did more, and underwent, and overcame, 10
The woman of a thousand summers back,
Godiva, wife to that grim Earl, who ruled
In Coventry: for when he laid a tax
Upon his town, and all the mothers brought
Their children, clamouring, 'If we pay, we starve!' 15
She sought her lord, and found him, where he strode
About the hall, among his dogs, alone,
His beard a foot before him, and his hair
A yard behind. She told him of their tears,
And pray'd him, 'If they pay this tax, they starve.' 20
Whereat he stared, replying, half-amazed,
'You would not let your little finger ache
For such as *these*?'—'But I would die,' said she.
He laugh'd, and swore by Peter and by Paul:
Then fillip'd at the diamond in her ear; 25
'Oh ay, ay, ay, you talk!'—'Alas!' she said,
'But prove me what it is I would not do.'
And from a heart as rough as Esau's hand,
He answer'd, 'Ride you naked thro' the town,
And I repeal it;' and nodding, as in scorn, 30
He parted, with great strides among his dogs.

So left alone, the passions of her mind,
As winds from all the compass shift and blow,
Made war upon each other for an hour,
Till pity won. She sent a herald forth, 35
And bade him cry, with sound of trumpet, all
The hard condition; but that she would loose
The people: therefore, as they loved her well,
From then till noon no foot should pace the street,
No eye look down, she passing; but that all 40
Should keep within, door shut, and window barr'd.

Then fled she to her inmost bower, and there
Unclasp'd the wedded eagles of her belt,
The grim Earl's gift; but ever at a breath
She linger'd, looking like a summer moon 45
Half-dipt in cloud: anon she shook her head,
And shower'd the rippled ringlets to her knee;
Unclad herself in haste; adown the stair
Stole on; and, like a creeping sunbeam, slid
From pillar unto pillar, until she reach'd 50
The gateway; there she found her palfrey trapt
In purple blazon'd with armorial gold.

Then she rode forth, clothed on with chastity:
The deep air listen'd round her as she rode,
And all the low wind hardly breathed for fear. 55
The little wide-mouth'd heads upon the spout
Had cunning eyes to see: the barking cur
Made her cheek flame: her palfrey's footfall shot
Light horrors thro' her pulses: the blind walls
Were full of chinks and holes; and overhead 60
Fantastic gables, crowding, stared: but she
Not less thro' all bore up, till, last, she saw
The white-flower'd elder-thicket from the field
Gleam thro' the Gothic archway in the wall.

Then she rode back, clothed on with chastity: 65
And one low churl, compact of thankless earth,
The fatal byword of all years to come,
Boring a little auger-hole in fear,
Peep'd—but his eyes, before they had their will,
Were shrivell'd into darkness in his head, 70
And dropt before him. So the Powers, who wait
On noble deeds, cancell'd a sense misused;
And she, that knew not, pass'd: and all at once,
With twelve great shocks of sound, the shameless noon
Was clash'd and hammer'd from a hundred towers, 75
One after one: but even then she gain'd
Her bower; whence reissuing, robed and crown'd,
To meet her lord, she took the tax away
And built herself an everlasting name.

THE TWO VOICES

A STILL small voice spake unto me,
'Thou art so full of misery,
Were it not better not to be?'

Then to the still small voice I said;
'Let me not cast in endless shade 5
What is so wonderfully made.'

To which the voice did urge reply;
'To-day I saw the dragon-fly
Come from the wells where he did lie.

'An inner impulse rent the veil 10
Of his old husk: from head to tail
Came out clear plates of sapphire mail.

'He dried his wings: like gauze they grew;
Thro' crofts and pastures wet with dew
A living flash of light he flew.' 15

I said, 'When first the world began,
Young Nature thro' five cycles ran,
And in the sixth she moulded man.

'She gave him mind, the lordliest
Proportion, and, above the rest, 20
Dominion in the head and breast.'

Thereto the silent voice replied;
'Self-blinded are you by your pride:
Look up thro' night: the world is wide.

'This truth within thy mind rehearse, 25
That in a boundless universe
Is boundless better, boundless worse.

'Think you this mould of hopes and fears
Could find no statelier than his peers
In yonder hundred million spheres?' 30

It spake, moreover, in my mind:
'Tho' thou wert scatter'd to the wind,
Yet is there plenty of the kind.'

Then did my response clearer fall:
'No compound of this earthly ball 35
Is like another, all in all.'

To which he answer'd scoffingly;
'Good soul! suppose I grant it thee,
Who'll weep for thy deficiency?

'Or will one beam be less intense, 40
When thy peculiar difference
Is cancell'd in the world of sense?'

I would have said, 'Thou canst not know,'
But my full heart, that work'd below,
Rain'd thro' my sight its overflow. 45

Again the voice spake unto me:
'Thou art so steep'd in misery,
Surely 'twere better not to be.

'Thine anguish will not let thee sleep,
Nor any train of reason keep: 50
Thou canst not think, but thou wilt weep.'

I said, 'The years with change advance:
If I make dark my countenance,
I shut my life from happier chance.

'Some turn this sickness yet might take, 55
Ev'n yet.' But he: 'What drug can make
A wither'd palsy cease to shake?'

I wept, 'Tho' I should die, I know
That all about the thorn will blow
In tufts of rosy-tinted snow; 60

'And men, thro' novel spheres of thought
Still moving after truth long sought,
Will learn new things when I am not.'

'Yet,' said the secret voice, 'some time,
Sooner or later, will gray prime 65
Make thy grass hoar with early rime.

'Not less swift souls that yearn for light,
Rapt after heaven's starry flight,
Would sweep the tracts of day and night.

'Not less the bee would range her cells, 70
The furzy prickle fire the dells,
The foxglove cluster dappled bells.'

I said that 'all the years invent;
Each month is various to present
The world with some development. 75

'Were this not well, to bide mine hour,
Tho' watching from a ruin'd tower
How grows the day of human power?'

'The highest-mounted mind,' he said,
'Still sees the sacred morning spread 80
The silent summit overhead.

'Will thirty seasons render plain
Those lonely lights that still remain,
Just breaking over land and main?

'Or make that morn, from his cold crown 85
And crystal silence creeping down,
Flood with full daylight glebe and town?

'Forerun thy peers, thy time, and let
Thy feet, millenniums hence, be set
In midst of knowledge, dream'd not yet, 90

'Thou hast not gain'd a real height,
Nor art thou nearer to the light,
Because the scale is infinite.

' 'Twere better not to breathe or speak,
Than cry for strength, remaining weak, 95
And seem to find, but still to seek.

'Moreover, but to seem to find
Asks what thou lackest, thought resign'd,
A healthy frame, a quiet mind.'

I said, 'When I am gone away, 100
"He dared not tarry," men will say,
Doing dishonour to my clay.'

'This is more vile,' he made reply,
'To breathe and loathe, to live and sigh,
Than once from dread of pain to die. 105

'Sick art thou—a divided will
Still heaping on the fear of ill
The fear of men, a coward still.

'Do men love thee? Art thou so bound
To men, that how thy name may sound 110
Will vex thee lying underground?

'The memory of the wither'd leaf
In endless time is scarce more brief
Than of the garner'd Autumn-sheaf.

'Go vexed Spirit, sleep in trust; 115
The right ear, that is fill'd with dust,
Hears little of the false or just.'

'Hard task, to pluck resolve,' I cried,
'From emptiness and the waste wide
Of that abyss, or scornful pride! 120

'Nay—rather yet that I could raise
One hope that warm'd me in the days
While still I yearn'd for human praise.

'When, wide in soul and bold of tongue,
Among the tents I paused and sung,   125
The distant battle flash'd and rung.

'I sung the joyful Pæan clear,
And, sitting, burnish'd without fear
The brand, the buckler, and the spear—

'Waiting to strive a happy strife,   130
To war with falsehood to the knife,
And not to lose the good of life—

'Some hidden principle to move,
To put together, part and prove,
And mete the bounds of hate and love—   135

'As far as might be, to carve out
Free space for every human doubt,
That the whole mind might orb about—

'To search thro' all I felt or saw,
The springs of life, the depths of awe,   140
And reach the law within the law:

'At least, not rotting like a weed,
But, having sown some generous seed,
Fruitful of further thought and deed,

'To pass, when Life her light withdraws,   145
Not void of righteous self-applause,
Nor in a merely selfish cause—

'In some good cause, not in mine own,
To perish, wept for, honour'd, known,
And like a warrior overthrown;   150

'Whose eyes are dim with glorious tears,
When, soil'd with noble dust, he hears
His country's war-song thrill his ears:

'Then dying of a mortal stroke,
What time the foeman's line is broke,   155
And all the war is roll'd in smoke.'

'Yea!' said the voice, 'thy dream was good,
While thou abodest in the bud.
It was the stirring of the blood.

'If Nature put not forth her power   160
About the opening of the flower,
Who is it that could live an hour?

'Then comes the check, the change, the fall,
Pain rises up, old pleasures pall.
There is one remedy for all.   165

'Yet hadst thou, thro' enduring pain,
Link'd month to month with such a chain
Of knitted purport, all were vain.

'Thou hadst not between death and birth
Dissolved the riddle of the earth.   170
So were thy labour little-worth.

'That men with knowledge merely play'd
I told thee—hardly nigher made,
Tho' scaling slow from grade to grade;

'Much less this dreamer, deaf and blind, 175
Named man, may hope some truth to find,
That bears relation to the mind.

'For every worm beneath the moon
Draws different threads, and late and soon
Spins, toiling out his own cocoon. 180

'Cry, faint not: either Truth is born
Beyond the polar gleam forlorn,
Or in the gateways of the morn.

'Cry, faint not, climb: the summits slope
Beyond the furthest flights of hope, 185
Wrapt in dense cloud from base to cope.

'Sometimes a little corner shines,
As over rainy mist inclines
A gleaming crag with belts of pines.

'I will go forward, sayest thou, 190
I shall not fail to find her now.
Look up, the fold is on her brow.

'If straight thy track, or if oblique,
Thou know'st not. Shadows thou dost strike,
Embracing cloud, Ixion-like; 195

'And owning but a little more
Than beasts, abidest lame and poor,
Calling thyself a little lower

'Than angels. Cease to wail and brawl!
Why inch by inch to darkness crawl? 200
There is one remedy for all.'

'O dull, one-sided voice,' said I,
'Wilt thou make everything a lie,
To flatter me that I may die?

'I know that age to age succeeds, 205
Blowing a noise of tongues and deeds,
A dust of systems and of creeds.

'I cannot hide that some have striven,
Achieving calm, to whom was given
The joy that mixes man with Heaven: 210

'Who, rowing hard against the stream,
Saw distant gates of Eden gleam,
And did not dream it was a dream;

'But heard, by secret transport led,
Ev'n in the charnels of the dead, 215
The murmur of the fountain-head—

'Which did accomplish their desire,
Bore and forebore, and did not tire,
Like Stephen, an unquenched fire.

'He heeded not reviling tones, 220
Nor sold his heart to idle moans,
Tho' cursed and scorn'd, and bruised with stones:

'But looking upward, full of grace,
He pray'd, and from a happy place
God's glory smote him on the face.' 225

The sullen answer slid betwixt:
'Not that the grounds of hope were fix'd,
The elements were kindlier mix'd.'

I said, 'I toil beneath the curse,
But, knowing not the universe, 230
I fear to slide from bad to worse.

'And that, in seeking to undo
One riddle, and to find the true,
I knit a hundred others new:

'Or that this anguish fleeting hence, 235
Unmanacled from bonds of sense,
Be fix'd and froz'n to permanence:

'For I go, weak from suffering here:
Naked I go, and void of cheer:
What is it that I may not fear?' 240

'Consider well,' the voice replied,
'His face, that two hours since hath died;
Wilt thou find passion, pain or pride?

'Will he obey when one commands?
Or answer should one press his hands? 245
He answers not, nor understands.

'His palms are folded on his breast:
There is no other thing express'd
But long disquiet merged in rest.

'His lips are very mild and meek: 250
Tho' one should smite him on the cheek,
And on the mouth, he will not speak.

'His little daughter, whose sweet face
He kiss'd, taking his last embrace,
Becomes dishonour to her race— 255

'His sons grow up that bear his name,
Some grow to honour, some to shame,—
But he is chill to praise or blame.

'He will not hear the north-wind rave,
Nor, moaning, household shelter crave   260
From winter rains that beat his grave.

'High up the vapours fold and swim:
About him broods the twilight dim:
The place he knew forgetteth him.'

'If all be dark, vague voice,' I said,   265
'These things are wrapt in doubt and dread,
Nor canst thou show the dead are dead.

'The sap dries up: the plant declines.
A deeper tale my heart divines.
Know I not Death? the outward signs?   270

'I found him when my years were few;
A shadow on the graves I knew,
And darkness in the village yew.

'From grave to grave the shadow crept:
In her still place the morning wept: 275
Touch'd by his feet the daisy slept.

'The simple senses crown'd his head:
"Omega! thou art Lord," they said,
"We find no motion in the dead."

'Why, if man rot in dreamless ease,   280
Should that plain fact, as taught by these,
Not make him sure that he shall cease?

'Who forged that other influence,
The heat of inward evidence,
By which he doubts against the sense? 285

'He owns the fatal gift of eyes,
That read his spirit blindly wise,
Not simple as a thing that dies.

'Here sits he shaping wings to fly:
His heart forebodes a mystery: 290
He names the name Eternity.

'That type of Perfect in his mind
In Nature can he nowhere find.
He sows himself on every wind.

'He seems to hear a Heavenly Friend, 295
And thro' thick veils to apprehend
A labour working to an end.

'The end and the beginning vex
His reason: many things perplex,
With motions, checks, and counterchecks. 300

'He knows a baseness in his blood
At such strange war with something good,
He may not do the thing he would.

'Heaven opens inward, chasms yawn,
Vast images in glimmering dawn, 305
Half shown, are broken and withdrawn.

'Ah! sure within him and without,
Could his dark wisdom find it out,
There must be answer to his doubt,

'But thou canst answer not again. 310
With thine own weapon art thou slain,
Or thou wilt answer but in vain.

'The doubt would rest, I dare not solve.
In the same circle we revolve.
Assurance only breeds resolve.' 315

As when a billow, blown against,
Falls back, the voice with which I fenced
A little ceased, but recommenced.

'Where wert thou when thy father play'd
In his free field, and pastime made, 320
A merry boy in sun and shade?

'A merry boy they call'd him then,
He sat upon the knees of men
In days that never come again.

'Before the little ducts began 325
To feed thy bones with lime, and ran
Their course, till thou wert also man:

'Who took a wife, who rear'd his race,
Whose wrinkles gather'd on his face,
Whose troubles number with his days: 330

'A life of nothings, nothing-worth,
From that first nothing ere his birth
To that last nothing under earth!'

'These words,' I said, 'are like the rest;
No certain clearness, but at best 335
A vague suspicion of the breast:

'But if I grant, thou mightst defend
The thesis which thy words intend—
That to begin implies to end;

'Yet how should I for certain hold, 340
Because my memory is so cold,
That I first was in human mould?

'I cannot make this matter plain,
But I would shoot, howe'er in vain,
A random arrow from the brain. 345

'It may be that no life is found,
Which only to one engine bound
Falls off, but cycles always round.

'As old mythologies relate,
Some draught of Lethe might await 350
The slipping thro' from state to state.

'As here we find in trances, men
Forget the dream that happens then,
Until they fall in trance again.

'So might we, if our state were such 355
As one before, remember much,
For those two likes might meet and touch.

'But, if I lapsed from nobler place,
Some legend of a fallen race
Alone might hint of my disgrace; 360

'Some vague emotion of delight
In gazing up an Alpine height,
Some yearning toward the lamps of night;

'Or if thro' lower lives I came—
Tho' all experience past became 365
Consolidate in mind and frame—

'I might forget my weaker lot;
For is not our first year forgot?
The haunts of memory echo not.

'And men, whose reason long was blind, 370
From cells of madness unconfined,
Oft lose whole years of darker mind.

'Much more, if first I floated free,
As naked essence, must I be
Incompetent of memory: 375

'For memory dealing but with time,
And he with matter, could she climb
Beyond her own material prime?

'Moreover, something is or seems,
That touches me with mystic gleams, 380
Like glimpses of forgotten dreams—

'Of something felt, like something here;
Of something done, I know not where;
Such as no language may declare.'

The still voice laugh'd. 'I talk,' said he, 385
'Not with thy dreams. Suffice it thee
Thy pain is a reality.'

'But thou,' said I, 'hast missed thy mark,
Who sought'st to wreck my mortal ark,
By making all the horizon dark. 390

'Why not set forth, if I should do
This rashness, that which might ensue
With this old soul in organs new?

'Whatever crazy sorrow saith,
No life that breathes with human breath   395
Has ever truly long'd for death.

' 'Tis life, whereof our nerves are scant,
Oh life, not death, for which we pant;
More life, and fuller, that I want.'

I ceased, and sat as one forlorn.   400
Then said the voice, in quiet scorn,
'Behold, it is the Sabbath morn.'

And I arose, and I released
The casement, and the light increased
With freshness in the dawning east.   405

Like soften'd airs that blowing steal,
When meres begin to uncongeal,
The sweet church bells began to peal.

On to God's house the people prest:
Passing the place where each must rest,   410
Each enter'd like a welcome guest.

One walk'd between his wife and child,
With measured footfall firm and mild,
And now and then he gravely smiled.

The prudent partner of his blood   415
Lean'd on him, faithful, gentle, good,
Wearing the rose of womanhood.

And in their double love secure,
The little maiden walk'd demure,
Pacing with downward eyelids pure. 420

These three made unity so sweet,
My frozen heart began to beat,
Remembering its ancient heat.

I blest them, and they wander'd on:
I spoke, but answer came there none: 425
The dull and bitter voice was gone.

A second voice was at mine ear,
A little whisper silver-clear,
A murmur, 'Be of better cheer.'

As from some blissful neighbourhood, 430
A notice faintly understood,
'I see the end, and know the good.'

A little hint to solace woe,
A hint, a whisper breathing low,
'I may not speak of what I know.' 435

Like an Æolian harp that wakes
No certain air, but overtakes
Far thought with music that it makes:

Such seem'd the whisper at my side:
'What is it thou knowest, sweet voice?' I cried. 440
'A hidden hope,' the voice replied:

So heavenly-toned, that in that hour
From out my sullen heart a power
Broke, like the rainbow from the shower,

To feel, altho' no tongue can prove, 445
That every cloud, that spreads above
And veileth love, itself is love.

And forth into the fields I went,
And Nature's living motion lent
The pulse of hope to discontent. 450

I wonder'd at the bounteous hours,
The slow result of winter showers:
You scarce could see the grass for flowers.

I wonder'd, while I paced along:
The woods were fill'd so full with song, 455
There seem'd no room for sense of wrong;

And all so variously wrought,
I marvell'd how the mind was brought
To anchor by one gloomy thought;

And wherefore rather I made choice 460
To commune with that barren voice,
Than him that said, 'Rejoice! Rejoice!'

THE DAY-DREAM

PROLOGUE

O Lady Flora, let me speak:
   A pleasant hour has passed away
While, dreaming on your damask cheek,
   The dewy sister-eyelids lay.
As by the lattice you reclined, 5
   I went thro' many wayward moods

To see you dreaming—and, behind,
  A summer crisp with shining woods.
And I too dream'd, until at last
  Across my fancy, brooding warm,
The reflex of a legend past,
  And loosely settled into form.
And would you have the thought I had,
  And see the vision that I saw,
Then take the broidery-frame, and add
  A crimson to the quaint Macaw,
And I will tell it. Turn your face,
  Nor look with that too-earnest eye—
The rhymes are dazzled from their place
  And order'd words asunder fly.

THE SLEEPING PALACE

I

The varying year with blade and sheaf
  Clothes and reclothes the happy plains,
Here rests the sap within the leaf,
  Here stays the blood along the veins.
Faint shadows, vapours lightly curl'd,
  Faint murmurs from the meadows come.
Like hints and echoes of the world
  To spirits folded in the womb.

II

Soft lustre bathes the range of urns
  On every slanting terrace-lawn.
The fountain to his place returns
  Deep in the garden lake withdrawn.
Here droops the banner on the tower,
  On the hall-hearths the festal fires,
The peacock in his laurel bower,
  The parrot in his gilded wires.

III

Roof-haunting martins warm their eggs:
  In these, in those the life is stay'd.
The mantles from the golden pegs
  Droop sleepily: no sound is made,   20
Not even of a gnat that sings.
  More like a picture seemeth all
Than those old portraits of old kings,
  That watch the sleepers from the wall.

IV

Here sits the Butler with a flask   25
  Between his knees, half-drain'd; and there
The wrinkled steward at his task,
  The maid-of-honour blooming fair;
The page has caught her hand in his:
  Her lips are sever'd as to speak: 30
His own are pouted to a kiss:
  The blush is fix'd upon her cheek.

V

Till all the hundred summers pass,
  The beams, that thro' the Oriel shine,
Make prisms in every carven glass,   35
  And beaker brimm'd with noble wine.
Each baron at the banquet sleeps,
  Grave faces gather'd in a ring.
His state the king reposing keeps.
  He must have been a jovial king.   40

VI

All round a hedge upshoots, and shows
  At distance like a little wood;
Thorns, ivies, woodbine, mistletoes,
  And grapes with bunches red as blood;

All creeping plants, a wall of green 45
  Close-matted, bur and brake and briar,
And glimpsing over these, just seen,
  High up, the topmost palace spire.

VII

When will the hundred summers die,
  And thought and time be born again, 50
And newer knowledge, drawing nigh,
  Bring truth that sways the soul of men?
Here all things in their place remain,
  As all were order'd, ages since.
Come, Care and Pleasure, Hope and Pain, 55
  And bring the fated fairy Prince.

THE SLEEPING BEAUTY

I

YEAR after year unto her feet,
  She lying on her couch alone,
Across the purple coverlet,
  The maiden's jet-black hair has grown,
On either side her tranced form 5
  Forth streaming from a braid of pearl:
The slumbrous light is rich and warm,
  And moves not on the rounded curl.

II

The silk star-broider'd coverlid
  Unto her limbs itself doth mould 10
Languidly ever; and, amid
  Her full black ringlets downward roll'd,
Glows forth each softly-shadow'd arm
  With bracelets of the diamond bright:
Her constant beauty doth inform 15
  Stillness with love, and day with light.

III

She sleeps: her breathings are not heard
　In palace chambers far apart.
The fragrant tresses are not stirr'd
　That lie upon her charmed heart.　　　　　　　　20
She sleeps: on either hand upswells
　The gold-fringed pillow lightly prest:
She sleeps, nor dreams, but ever dwells
　A perfect form in perfect rest.

THE ARRIVAL

I

ALL precious things, discover'd late,
　To those that seek them issue forth;
For love in sequel works with fate,
　And draws the veil from hidden worth.
He travels far from other skies—　　　　　　　　5
　His mantle glitters on the rocks—
A fairy Prince, with joyful eyes,
　And lighter-footed than the fox.

II

The bodies and the bones of those
　That strove in other days to pass,　　　　　　　10
Are wither'd in the thorny close
　Or scatter'd blanching on the grass.
He gazes on the silent dead:
　'They perish'd in their daring deeds.'
This proverb flashes thro' his head,　　　　　　　15
　'The many fail: the one succeeds.'

III

He comes, scarce knowing what he seeks:
   He breaks the hedge: he enters there:
The colour flies into his cheeks:
   He trusts to light on something fair;   20
For all his life the charm did talk
   About his path, and hover near
With words of promise in his walk,
   And whisper'd voices at his ear.

IV

More close and close his footsteps wind: 25
   The Magic Music in his heart
Beats quick and quicker, till he find
   The quiet chamber far apart.
His spirit flutters like a lark,
   He stoops—to kiss her—on his knee.   30
'Love, if thy tresses be so dark,
   How dark those hidden eyes must be!'

THE REVIVAL

I

A TOUCH, a kiss! the charm was snapt.
   There rose a noise of striking clocks,
And feet that ran, and doors that clapt,
   And barking dogs, and crowing cocks;
A fuller light illumined all,   5
   A breeze thro' all the garden swept,
A sudden hubbub shook the hall,
   And sixty feet the fountain leapt.

II

The hedge broke in, the banner blew,
   The butler drank, the steward scrawl'd,   10
The fire shot up, the martin flew,
   The parrot scream'd, the peacock squall'd,

The maid and page renew'd their strife,
   The palace bang'd, and buzz'd and clackt,
And all the long-pent stream of life   15
   Dash'd downward in a cataract.

III

And last with these the king awoke,
   And in his chair himself uprear'd,
And yawn'd, and rubb'd his face, and spoke,
   'By holy rood, a royal beard!   20
How say you? we have slept, my lords.
   My beard has grown into my lap.'
The barons swore, with many words,
   'Twas but an after-dinner's nap.

IV

'Pardy,' return'd the king, 'but still   25
   My joints are somewhat stiff or so.
My lord, and shall we pass the bill
   I mention'd half an hour ago?'
The chancellor, sedate and vain,
   In courteous words return'd reply: 30
But dallied with his golden chain,
   And, smiling, put the question by.

THE DEPARTURE

I

AND on her lover's arm she leant,
   And round her waist she felt it fold,
And far across the hills they went
   In that new world which is the old:
Across the hills, and far away   5
   Beyond their utmost purple rim,
And deep into the dying day
   The happy princess follow'd him.

II

'I'd sleep another hundred years,
  O love, for such another kiss;'
'O wake for ever, love,' she hears,
  'O love, 'twas such as this and this.'
And o'er them many a sliding star,
  And many a merry wind was borne,
And, stream'd thro' many a golden bar,
  The twilight melted into morn.

III

'O eyes long laid in happy sleep!'
  'O happy sleep, that lightly fled!'
'O happy kiss, that woke thy sleep!'
  'O love, thy kiss would wake the dead!'
And o'er them many a flowing range
  Of vapour buoy'd the crescent-bark,
And, rapt thro' many a rosy change,
  The twilight died into the dark.

IV

'A hundred summers! can it be?
  And whither goest thou, tell me where?'
'O seek my father's court with me,
  For there are greater wonders there.'
And o'er the hills, and far away
  Beyond their utmost purple rim,
Beyond the night, across the day,
  Thro' all the world she follow'd him.

MORAL

I

So, Lady Flora, take my lay,
  And if you find no moral there,
Go, look in any glass and say,
  What moral is in being fair.

Oh, to what uses shall we put
    The wildweed-flower that simply blows?
And is there any moral shut
    Within the bosom of the rose?

II

But any man that walks the mead,
    In bud or blade, or bloom, may find,
According as his humours lead,
    A meaning suited to his mind.
And liberal applications lie
    In Art like Nature, dearest friend;
So 'twere to cramp its use, if I
    Should hook it to some useful end.

L'ENVOI

I

You shake your head. A random string
    Your finer female sense offends.
Well—were it not a pleasant thing
    To fall asleep with all one's friends;
To pass with all our social ties
    To silence from the paths of men;
And every hundred years to rise
    And learn the world, and sleep again;
To sleep thro' terms of mighty wars,
    And wake on science grown to more,
On secrets of the brain, the stars,
    As wild as aught of fairy lore;
And all that else the years will show,
    The Poet-forms of stronger hours,
The vast Republics that may grow,
    The Federations and the Powers;
Titanic forces taking birth

In divers seasons, divers climes;
For we are Ancients of the earth,
    And in the morning of the times.   20

II

So sleeping, so aroused from sleep
    Thro' sunny decads new and strange,
Or gay quinquenniads would we reap
    The flower and quintessence of change.

III

Ah, yet would I—and would I might!   25
    So much your eyes my fancy take—
Be still the first to leap to light
    That I might kiss those eyes awake!
For, am I right, or am I wrong,
    To choose your own you did not care;   30
You'd have *my* moral from the song,
    And I will take my pleasure there:
And, am I right or am I wrong,
    My fancy, ranging thro' and thro',
To search a meaning for the song,   35
    Perforce will still revert to you;
Nor finds a closer truth than this
    All-graceful head, so richly curl'd,
And evermore a costly kiss
    The prelude to some brighter world.   40

IV

For since the time when Adam first
    Embraced his Eve in happy hour,
And every bird of Eden burst
    In carol, every bud to flower,
What eyes, like thine, have waken'd hopes,   45
    What lips, like thine, so sweetly join'd?
Where on the double rosebud droops
    The fullness of the pensive mind;

Which all too dearly self-involved,
    Yet sleeps a dreamless sleep to me;   50
A sleep by kisses undissolved,
    That lets thee neither hear nor see:
But break it. In the name of wife,
    And in the rights that name may give,
Are clasp'd the moral of thy life,   55
    And that for which I care to live.

EPILOGUE

So, Lady Flora, take my lay,
    And, if you find a meaning there,
O whisper to your glass, and say,
    'What wonder, if he thinks me fair?'
What wonder I was all unwise,   5
    To shape the song for your delight
Like long-tail'd birds of Paradise
    That float thro' Heaven, and cannot light?
Or old-world trains, upheld at court
    By Cupid-boys of blooming hue—   10
But take it—earnest wed with sport,
    And either sacred unto you.

AMPHION

My father left a park to me,
    But it is wild and barren,
A garden too with scarce a tree,
    And waster than a warren:
Yet say the neighbours when they call,   5
    It is not bad but good land,
And in it is the germ of all
    That grows within the woodland.

O had I lived when song was great
  In days of old Amphion,
And ta'en my fiddle to the gate,
  Nor cared for seed or scion!
And had I lived when song was great,
  And legs of trees were limber,
And ta'en my fiddle to the gate,
  And fiddled in the timber!

'Tis said he had a tuneful tongue,
  Such happy intonation,
Wherever he sat down and sung
  He left a small plantation;
Wherever in a lonely grove
  He sat up his forlorn pipes,
The gouty oak began to move,
  And flounder into hornpipes.

The mountain stirr'd its bushy crown,
  And, as tradition teaches,
Young ashes pirouetted down
  Coquetting with young beeches;
And briony-vine and ivy-wreath
  Ran forward to his rhyming,
And from the valleys underneath
  Came little copses climbing.

The linden broke her ranks and rent
  The woodbine wreaths that bind her,
And down the middle, buzz! she went
  With all her bees behind her:
The poplars, in long order due,
  With cypress promenaded,
The shock-head willows two and two
  By rivers gallopaded.

40. gallopade: a quick dance

Came wet-shod alder from the wave,
    Came yews, a dismal coterie;
Each pluck'd his one foot from the grave,
    Poussetting with a sloe-tree:
Old elms came breaking from the vine,   45
    The vine stream'd out to follow,
And, sweating rosin, plump'd the pine
    From many a cloudy hollow.

And wasn't it a sight to see,
    When, ere his song was ended,   50
Like some great landslip, tree by tree,
    The country-side descended;
And shepherds from the mountain-eaves
    Look'd down, half-pleased, half-frighten'd,
As dash'd about the drunken leaves   55
    The random sunshine lighten'd!

Oh, nature first was fresh to men,
    And wanton without measure;
So youthful and so flexile then,
    You moved her at your pleasure.   60
Twang out, my fiddle! shake the twigs!
    And make her dance attendance;
Blow, flute, and stir the stiff-set sprigs,
    And scirrhous roots and tendons.

'Tis vain! in such a brassy age   65
    I could not move a thistle;
The very sparrows in the hedge
    Scarce answer to my whistle;
Or at the most, when three-parts-sick
    With strumming and with scraping,   70
A jackass heehaws from the rick,
    The passive oxen gaping.

    44. *poussette*: a movement in a country dance

But what is that I hear? a sound
  Like sleepy counsel pleading;
O Lord!—'tis in my neighbour's ground,
  The modern Muses reading.
They read Botanic Treatises,
  And Works on Gardening thro' there,
And Methods of transplanting trees
  To look as if they grew there.

The wither'd Misses! how they prose
  O'er books of travell'd seamen,
And show you slips of all that grows
  From England to Van Diemen.
They read in arbours clipt and cut,
  And alleys, faded places,
By squares of tropic summer shut
  And warm'd in crystal cases.

But these, tho' fed with careful dirt,
  Are neither green nor sappy;
Half-conscious of the garden-squirt,
  The spindlings look unhappy.
Better to me the meanest weed
  That blows upon its mountain,
The vilest herb that runs to seed
  Beside its native fountain.

And I must work thro' months of toil,
  And years of cultivation,
Upon my proper patch of soil
  To grow my own plantation.
I'll take the showers as they fall,
  I will not vex my bosom:
Enough if at the end of all
  A little garden blossom.

ST. AGNES' EVE

Deep on the convent-roof the snows
  Are sparkling to the moon:
My breath to heaven like vapour goes:
  May my soul follow soon!
The shadows of the convent-towers
  Slant down the snowy sward,
Still creeping with the creeping hours
  That lead me to my Lord:
Make Thou my spirit pure and clear
  As are the frosty skies,
Or this first snowdrop of the year
  That in my bosom lies.

As these white robes are soil'd and dark,
  To yonder shining ground;
As this pale taper's earthly spark,
  To yonder argent round;
So shows my soul before the Lamb,
  My spirit before Thee;
So in mine earthly house I am,
  To that I hope to be.
Break up the heavens, O Lord! and far,
  Thro' all yon starlight keen,
Draw me, thy bride, a glittering star,
  In raiment white and clean.

He lifts me to the golden doors;
  The flashes come and go;
All heaven bursts her starry floors,
  And strows her lights below,
And deepens on and up! the gates
  Roll back, and far within
For me the Heavenly Bridegroom waits,
  To make me pure of sin.

The sabbaths of Eternity,
  One sabbath deep and wide—
A light upon the shining sea—
  The Bridegroom with his bride!

SIR GALAHAD

My good blade carves the casques of men,
  My tough lance thrusteth sure,
My strength is as the strength of ten,
  Because my heart is pure.
The shattering trumpet shrilleth high,
  The hard brands shiver on the steel,
The splinter'd spear-shafts crack and fly,
  The horse and rider reel:
They reel, they roll in clanging lists,
  And when the tide of combat stands,
Perfume and flowers fall in showers,
  That lightly rain from ladies' hands.

How sweet are looks that ladies bend
  On whom their favours fall!
For them I battle till the end,
  To save from shame and thrall:
But all my heart is drawn above,
  My knees are bow'd in crypt and shrine:
I never felt the kiss of love,
  Nor maiden's hand in mine.
More bounteous aspects on me beam,
  Me mightier transports move and thrill;
So keep I fair thro' faith and prayer
  A virgin heart in work and will.

When down the stormy crescent goes, 25
  A light before me swims,
Between dark stems the forest glows,
  I hear a noise of hymns:
Then by some secret shrine I ride;
  I hear a voice but none are there; 30
The stalls are void, the doors are wide,
  The tapers burning fair.
Fair gleams the snowy altar-cloth,
  The silver vessels sparkle clean,
The shrill bell rings, the censer swings, 35
  And solemn chaunts resound between.

Sometimes on lonely mountain-meres
  I find a magic bark;
I leap on board: no helmsman steers;
  I float till all is dark. 40
A gentle sound, an awful light!
  Three angels bear the holy Grail:
With folded feet, in stoles of white,
  On sleeping wings they sail.
Ah, blessed vision! blood of God! 45
  My spirit beats her mortal bars,
As down dark tides the glory slides,
  And star-like mingles with the stars.

When on my goodly charger borne
  Thro' dreaming towns I go, 50
The cock crows ere the Christmas morn,
  The streets are dumb with snow.
The tempest crackles on the leads,
  And, ringing, springs from brand and mail;
But o'er the dark a glory spreads, 55
  And gilds the driving hail.

I leave the plain, I climb the height;
  No branchy thicket shelter yields;
But blessed forms in whistling storms
  Fly o'er waste fens and windy fields.   60

A maiden knight—to me is given
  Such hope, I know not fear;
I yearn to breathe the airs of heaven
  That often meet me here.
I muse on joy that will not cease,   65
  Pure spaces clothed in living beams,
Pure lilies of eternal peace,
  Whose odours haunt my dreams;
And, stricken by an angel's hand,
  This mortal armour that I wear,   70
This weight and size, this heart and eyes,
  Are touch'd, are turn'd to finest air.

The clouds are broken in the sky,
  And thro' the mountain-walls
A rolling organ-harmony   75
  Swells up, and shakes and falls.
Then move the trees, the copses nod,
  Wings flutter, voices hover clear:
'O just and faithful knight of God!
  Ride on! the prize is near.'   80
So pass I hostel, hall, and grange;
  By bridge and ford, by park and pale,
All-arm'd I ride, whate'er betide,
  Until I find the holy Grail.

EDWARD GRAY

Sweet Emma Moreland of yonder town
  Met me walking on yonder way,
'And have you lost your heart?' she said;
  'And are you married yet, Edward Gray?'

Sweet Emma Moreland spoke to me:
  Bitterly weeping I turn'd away:
'Sweet Emma Moreland, love no more
  Can touch the heart of Edward Gray.

'Ellen Adair she loved me well,
  Against her father's and mother's will:
To-day I sat for an hour and wept,
  By Ellen's grave, on the windy hill.

'Shy she was, and I thought her cold;
  Thought her proud, and fled over the sea;
Fill'd I was with folly and spite,
  When Ellen Adair was dying for me.

'Cruel, cruel the words I said!
  Cruelly came they back to-day:
"You're too slight and fickle," I said,
  "To trouble the heart of Edward Gray."

'There I put my face in the grass—
  Whisper'd, "Listen to my despair:
I repent me of all I did:
  Speak a little, Ellen Adair!"

'Then I took a pencil, and wrote
  On the mossy stone, as I lay,
"Here lies the body of Ellen Adair;
  And here the heart of Edward Gray!"

'Love may come, and love may go,
    And fly, like a bird, from tree to tree: 30
But I will love no more, no more,
    Till Ellen Adair come back to me.

'Bitterly wept I over the stone:
    Bitterly weeping I turn'd away:
There lies the body of Ellen Adair!   35
    And there the heart of Edward Gray!'

WILL WATERPROOF'S
LYRICAL MONOLOGUE

MADE AT THE COCK

O PLUMP head-waiter at The Cock,
    To which I most resort,
How goes the time? 'Tis five o'clock.
    Go fetch a pint of port:
But let it not be such as that   5
    You set before chance-comers,
But such whose father-grape grew fat
    On Lusitanian summers.

No vain libation to the Muse,
    But may she still be kind,   10
And whisper lovely words, and use
    Her influence on the mind,
To make me write my random rhymes,
    Ere they be half-forgotten;
Nor add and alter, many times,   15
    Till all be ripe and rotten.

I pledge her, and she comes and dips
   Her laurel in the wine,
And lays it thrice upon my lips,
   These favour'd lips of mine;					20
Until the charm have power to make
   New lifeblood warm the bosom,
And barren commonplaces break
   In full and kindly blossom.

I pledge her silent at the board;					25
   Her gradual fingers steal
And touch upon the master-chord
   Of all I felt and feel.
Old wishes, ghosts of broken plans,
   And phantom hopes assemble;					30
And that child's heart within the man's
   Begins to move and tremble.

Thro' many an hour of summer suns,
   By many pleasant ways,
Against its fountain upward runs					35
   The current of my days:
I kiss the lips I once have kiss'd;
   The gas-light wavers dimmer;
And softly, thro' a vinous mist,
   My college friendships glimmer.					40

I grow in worth, and wit, and sense,
   Unboding critic-pen,
Or that eternal want of pence,
   Which vexes public men,
Who hold their hands to all, and cry					45
   For that which all deny them—
Who sweep the crossings, wet or dry,
   And all the world go by them.

Ah yet, tho' all the world forsake,
  Tho' fortune clip my wings,
I will not cramp my heart, nor take
  Half-views of men and things.
Let Whig and Tory stir their blood;
  There must be stormy weather;
But for some true result of good
  All parties work together.

Let there be thistles, there are grapes;
  If old things, there are new;
Ten thousand broken lights and shapes,
  Yet glimpses of the true.
Let raffs be rife in prose and rhyme,
  We lack not rhymes and reasons,
As on this whirligig of Time
  We circle with the seasons.

This earth is rich in man and maid;
  With fair horizons bound:
This whole wide earth of light and shade
  Comes out a perfect round.
High over roaring Temple-bar,
  And set in Heaven's third story,
I look at all things as they are,
  But thro' a kind of glory.

———

Head-waiter, honour'd by the guest
  Half-mused, or reeling ripe,
The pint, you brought me, was the best
  That ever came from pipe.

61. *raffs:* scraps

But tho' the port surpasses praise,
  My nerves have dealt with stiffer.
Is there some magic in the place?
  Or do my peptics differ?

For since I came to live and learn,
  No pint of white or red
Had ever half the power to turn
  This wheel within my head,
Which bears a season'd brain about,
  Unsubject to confusion,
Tho' soak'd and saturate, out and out,
  Thro' every convolution.

For I am of a numerous house,
  With many kinsmen gay,
Where long and largely we carouse
  As who shall say me nay:
Each month, a birth-day coming on,
  We drink defying trouble,
Or sometimes two would meet in one,
  And then we drank it double;

Whether the vintage, yet unkept,
  Had relish fiery-new,
Or elbow-deep in sawdust, slept,
  As old as Waterloo;
Or stow'd, when classic Canning died,
  In musty bins and chambers,
Had cast upon its crusty side
  The gloom of ten Decembers.

The Muse, the jolly Muse, it is!
  She answer'd to my call,
She changes with that mood or this,
  Is all-in-all to all:

She lit the spark within my throat,
   To make my blood run quicker, 110
Used all her fiery will, and smote
   Her life into the liquor.

And hence this halo lives about
   The waiter's hands, that reach
To each his perfect pint of stout, 115
   His proper chop to each.
He looks not like the common breed
   That with the napkin dally;
I think he came like Ganymede,
   From some delightful valley. 120

The Cock was of a larger egg
   Than modern poultry drop,
Stept forward on a firmer leg,
   And cramm'd a plumper crop;
Upon an ampler dunghill trod, 125
   Crow'd lustier late and early,
Sipt wine from silver, praising God,
   And raked in golden barley.

A private life was all his joy,
   Till in a court he saw 130
A something-pottle-bodied boy
   That knuckled at the taw:
He stoop'd and clutch'd him, fair and good,
   Flew over roof and casement:
His brothers of the weather stood 135
   Stock-still for sheer amazement.

      131. *pottle-bodied:* pot-bellied

But he, by farmstead, thorpe and spire,
    And follow'd with acclaims,
A sign to many a staring shire
    Came crowing over Thames.   140
Right down by smoky Paul's they bore,
    Till, where the street grows straiter,
One fix'd for ever at the door,
    And one became head-waiter.

———

But whither would my fancy go?   145
    How out of place she makes
The violet of a legend blow
    Among the chops and steaks!
'Tis but a steward of the can,
    One shade more plump than common;   150
As just and mere a serving-man
    As any born of woman.

I ranged too high: what draws me down
    Into the common day?
Is it the weight of that half-crown,   155
    Which I shall have to pay?
For, something duller than at first,
    Nor wholly comfortable,
I sit, my empty glass reversed,
    And thrumming on the table: 160

Half fearful that, with self at strife,
    I take myself to task;
Lest of the fullness of my life
    I leave an empty flask:
For I had hope, by something rare,   165
    To prove myself a poet:
But, while I plan and plan, my hair
    Is gray before I know it.

So fares it since the years began,
  Till they be gather'd up;
The truth, that flies the flowing can,
  Will haunt the vacant cup:
And others' follies teach us not,
  Nor much their wisdom teaches;
And most, of sterling worth, is what
  Our own experience preaches.

Ah, let the rusty theme alone!
  We know not what we know.
But for my pleasant hour, 'tis gone;
  'Tis gone, and let it go.
'Tis gone: a thousand such have slipt
  Away from my embraces,
And fall'n into the dusty crypt
  Of darken'd forms and faces.

Go, therefore, thou! thy betters went
  Long since, and came no more;
With peals of genial clamour sent
  From many a tavern-door,
With twisted quirks and happy hits,
  From misty men of letters;
The tavern-hours of mighty wits—
  Thine elders and thy betters.

Hours, when the Poet's words and looks
  Had yet their native glow:
Nor yet the fear of little books
  Had made him talk for show;
But, all his vast heart sherris-warm'd,
  He flash'd his random speeches,
Ere days, that deal in ana, swarm'd
  His literary leeches.

So mix for ever with the past,
  Like all good things on earth!
For should I prize thee, couldst thou last,
  At half thy real worth?
I hold it good, good things should pass: 205
  With time I will not quarrel:
It is but yonder empty glass
  That makes me maudlin-moral.

Head-waiter of the chop-house here,
  To which I most resort, 210
I too must part: I hold thee dear
  For this good pint of port.
For this, thou shalt from all things suck
  Marrow of mirth and laughter;
And wheresoe'er thou move, good luck 215
  Shall fling her old shoe after.

But thou wilt never move from hence,
  The sphere thy fate allots:
Thy latter days increased with pence
  Go down among the pots: 220
Thou battenest by the greasy gleam
  In haunts of hungry sinners,
Old boxes, larded with the steam
  Of thirty thousand dinners.

We fret, we fume, would shift our skins, 225
  Would quarrel with our lot;
Thy care is, under polish'd tins,
  To serve the hot-and-hot;
To come and go, and come again,
  Returning like the pewit, 230
And watch'd by silent gentlemen,
  That trifle with the cruet.

Live long, ere from thy topmost head
  The thick-set hazel dies;
Long, ere the hateful crow shall tread   235
  The corners of thine eyes:
Live long, nor feel in head or chest
  Our changeful equinoxes,
Till mellow Death, like some late guest,
  Shall call thee from the boxes.   240

But when he calls, and thou shalt cease
  To pace the gritted floor,
And, laying down an unctuous lease
  Of life, shalt earn no more;
No carved cross-bones, the types of Death,   245
  Shall show thee past to Heaven:
But carved cross-pipes, and, underneath,
  A pint-pot neatly graven.

LADY CLARE

It was the time when lilies blow,
   And clouds are highest up in air,
Lord Ronald brought a lily-white doe
   To give his cousin, Lady Clare.

I trow they did not part in scorn:
   Lovers long-betroth'd were they:
They two will wed the morrow morn:
   God's blessing on the day!

'He does not love me for my birth,
   Nor for my lands so broad and fair;
He loves me for my own true worth,
   And that is well,' said Lady Clare.

In there came old Alice the nurse,
   Said, 'Who was this that went from thee?'
'It was my cousin,' said Lady Clare,
   'To-morrow he weds with me.'

'O God be thank'd!' said Alice the nurse,
   'That all comes round so just and fair:
Lord Ronald is heir of all your lands,
   And you are *not* the Lady Clare.'

'Are ye out of your mind, my nurse, my nurse?'
   Said Lady Clare, 'that ye speak so wild?'
'As God's above,' said Alice the nurse,
   'I speak the truth: you are my child.

'The old Earl's daughter died at my breast;
   I speak the truth, as I live by bread!
I buried her like my own sweet child,
   And put my child in her stead.'

'Falsely, falsely have ye done,
  O mother,' she said, 'if this be true, 30
To keep the best man under the sun
  So many years from his due.'

'Nay now, my child,' said Alice the nurse,
  'But keep the secret for your life,
And all you have will be Lord Ronald's, 35
  When you are man and wife.'

'If I'm a beggar born,' she said,
  'I will speak out, for I dare not lie.
Pull off, pull off, the brooch of gold,
  And fling the diamond necklace by.' 40

'Nay now, my child,' said Alice the nurse,
  'But keep the secret all ye can.'
She said, 'Not so: but I will know
  If there be any faith in man.'

'Nay now, what faith?' said Alice the nurse, 45
  'The man will cleave unto his right.'
'And he shall have it,' the lady replied,
  'Tho' I should die to-night.'

'Yet give one kiss to your mother dear!
  Alas, my child, I sinn'd for thee.' 50
'O mother, mother, mother,' she said,
  'So strange it seems to me.

'Yet here's a kiss for my mother dear,
  My mother dear, if this be so,
And lay your hand upon my head, 55
  And bless me, mother, ere I go.'

She clad herself in a russet gown,
  She was no longer Lady Clare:

She went by dale, and she went by down,
    With a single rose in her hair.   60

The lily-white doe Lord Ronald had brought
    Leapt up from where she lay,
Dropt her head in the maiden's hand,
    And follow'd her all the way.

Down stept Lord Ronald from his tower: 65
    'O Lady Clare, you shame your worth!
Why come you drest like a village maid,
    That are the flower of the earth?'

'If I come drest like a village maid,
    I am but as my fortunes are: 70
I am a beggar born,' she said,
    'And not the Lady Clare.'

'Play me no tricks,' said Lord Ronald,
    'For I am yours in word and in deed.
Play me no tricks,' said Lord Ronald,   75
    'Your riddle is hard to read.'

O and proudly stood she up!
    Her heart within her did not fail:
She look'd into Lord Ronald's eyes,
    And told him all her nurse's tale.   80

He laugh'd a laugh of merry scorn:
    He turn'd and kiss'd her where she stood:
'If you are not the heiress born,
    And I,' said he, 'the next in blood—

'If you are not the heiress born,   85
    And I,' said he, 'the lawful heir,
We two will wed to-morrow morn,
    And you shall still be Lady Clare.'

THE LORD OF BURLEIGH

In her ear he whispers gaily,
  'If my heart by signs can tell,
Maiden, I have watch'd thee daily,
  And I think thou lov'st me well.'
She replies, in accents fainter,　　　　　　　　5
  'There is none I love like thee.'
He is but a landscape-painter,
  And a village maiden she.
He to lips, that fondly falter,
  Presses his without reproof:　　　　　　　　10
Leads her to the village altar,
  And they leave her father's roof.
'I can make no marriage present:
  Little can I give my wife.
Love will make our cottage pleasant,　　　　　15
  And I love thee more than life.'
They by parks and lodges going
  See the lordly castles stand:
Summer woods, about them blowing,
  Made a murmur in the land.　　　　　　　　20
From deep thought himself he rouses,
  Says to her that loves him well,
'Let us see these handsome houses
  Where the wealthy nobles dwell.'
So she goes by him attended,　　　　　　　　25
  Hears him lovingly converse,
Sees whatever fair and splendid
  Lay betwixt his home and hers;
Parks with oak and chestnut shady,
  Parks and order'd gardens great,　　　　　　30
Ancient homes of lord and lady,
  Built for pleasure and for state.

All he shows her makes him dearer:
   Evermore she seems to gaze
On that cottage growing nearer, 35
   Where they twain will spend their days.
O but she will love him truly!
   He shall have a cheerful home;
She will order all things duly,
   When beneath his roof they come. 40
Thus her heart rejoices greatly,
   Till a gateway she discerns
With armorial bearings stately,
   And beneath the gate she turns;
Sees a mansion more majestic 45
   Than all those she saw before:
Many a gallant gay domestic
   Bows before him at the door.
And they speak in gentle murmur,
   When they answer to his call, 50
While he treads with footstep firmer,
   Leading on from hall to hall.
And, while now she wonders blindly,
   Nor the meaning can divine,
Proudly turns he round and kindly, 55
   'All of this is mine and thine.'
Here he lives in state and bounty,
   Lord of Burleigh, fair and free,
Not a lord in all the county
   Is so great a lord as he. 60
All at once the colour flushes
   Her sweet face from brow to chin:
As it were with shame she blushes,
   And her spirit changed within.
Then her countenance all over 65
   Pale again as death did prove:
But he clasp'd her like a lover,
   And he cheer'd her soul with love.

So she strove against her weakness,
    Tho' at times her spirit sank: 70
Shaped her heart with woman's meekness
    To all duties of her rank:
And a gentle consort made he,
    And her gentle mind was such
That she grew a noble lady,   75
    And the people loved her much.
But a trouble weigh'd upon her,
    And perplex'd her, night and morn,
With the burthen of an honour
    Unto which she was not born.   80
Faint she grew, and ever fainter,
    And she murmur'd, 'Oh, that he
Were once more that landscape-painter,
    Which did win my heart from me!'
So she droop'd and droop'd before him,   85
    Fading slowly from his side:
Three fair children first she bore him,
    Then before her time she died.
Weeping, weeping late and early,
    Walking up and pacing down,   90
Deeply mourn'd the Lord of Burleigh,
    Burleigh-house by Stamford-town.
And he came to look upon her,
    And he look'd at her and said,
'Bring the dress and put it on her,   95
    That she wore when she was wed.'
Then her people, softly treading,
    Bore to earth her body, drest
In the dress that she was wed in,
    That her spirit might have rest.   100

SIR LAUNCELOT AND QUEEN GUINEVERE

A FRAGMENT

LIKE souls that balance joy and pain,
With tears and smiles from heaven again
The maiden Spring upon the plain
Came in a sun-lit fall of rain.
  In crystal vapour everywhere
Blue isles of heaven laugh'd between,
And far, in forest-deeps unseen,
The topmost elm-tree gather'd green
  From draughts of balmy air.

Sometimes the linnet piped his song:
Sometimes the throstle whistled strong:
Sometimes the sparhawk, wheel'd along,
Hush'd all the groves from fear of wrong:
  By grassy capes with fuller sound
In curves the yellowing river ran,
And drooping chestnut-buds began
To spread into the perfect fan,
  Above the teeming ground.

Then, in the boyhood of the year,
Sir Launcelot and Queen Guinevere
Rode thro' the coverts of the deer,
With blissful treble ringing clear.
  She seem'd a part of joyous Spring:
A gown of grass-green silk she wore,
Buckled with golden clasps before;
A light-green tuft of plumes she bore
  Closed in a golden ring.

Now on some twisted ivy-net,
Now by some tinkling rivulet,
In mosses mixt with violet
Her cream-white mule his pastern set:
    And fleeter now she skimm'd the plains
Than she whose elfin prancer springs
By night to eery warblings,
When all the glimmering moorland rings
    With jingling bridle-reins.

As fast she fled thro' sun and shade,
The happy winds upon her play'd,
Blowing the ringlet from the braid:
She look'd so lovely, as she sway'd
    The rein with dainty finger-tips,
A man had given all other bliss,
And all his worldly worth for this,
To waste his whole heart in one kiss
    Upon her perfect lips.

A FAREWELL

Flow down, cold rivulet, to the sea,
    Thy tribute wave deliver:
No more by thee my steps shall be,
    For ever and for ever.

Flow, softly flow, by lawn and lea,
    A rivulet then a river:
No where by thee my steps shall be,
    For ever and for ever.

But here will sigh thine alder tree,
  And here thine aspen shiver;   10
And here by thee will hum the bee,
  For ever and for ever.

A thousand suns will stream on thee,
  A thousand moons will quiver;
But not by thee my steps shall be,   15
  For ever and for ever.

THE BEGGAR MAID

HER arms across her breast she laid;
  She was more fair than words can say
Bare-footed came the beggar maid
  Before the king Cophetua.
In robe and crown the king stept down,   5
  To meet and greet her on her way;
'It is no wonder,' said the lords,
  'She is more beautiful than day.'

As shines the moon in clouded skies,
  She in her poor attire was seen: 10
One praised her ancles, one her eyes,
  One her dark hair and lovesome mien.
So sweet a face, such angel grace,
  In all that land had never been:
Cophetua sware a royal oath: 15
  'This beggar maid shall be my queen!'

THE VISION OF SIN

I

I HAD a vision when the night was late:
A youth came riding toward a palace-gate.
He rode a horse with wings, that would have flown,
But that his heavy rider kept him down.
And from the palace came a child of sin, 5
And took him by the curls, and led him in,
Where sat a company with heated eyes,
Expecting when a fountain should arise:
A sleepy light upon their brows and lips—
As when the sun, a crescent of eclipse, 10
Dreams over lake and lawn, and isles and capes—
Suffused them, sitting, lying, languid shapes,
By heaps of gourds, and skins of wine, and piles of
    grapes.

II

Then methought I heard a mellow sound,
Gathering up from all the lower ground; 15
Narrowing in to where they sat assembled
Low voluptuous music winding trembled,
Wov'n in circles: they that heard it sigh'd,
Panted hand-in-hand with faces pale,
Swung themselves, and in low tones replied; 20
Till the fountain spouted, showering wide
Sleet of diamond-drift and pearly hail;
Then the music touch'd the gates and died;
Rose again from where it seem'd to fail,
Storm'd in orbs of song, a growing gale; 25
Till thronging in and in, to where they waited,
As 'twere a hundred-throated nightingale,
The strong tempestuous treble throbb'd and
    palpitated;

Ran into its giddiest whirl of sound,
   Caught the sparkles, and in circles, 30
   Purple gauzes, golden hazes, liquid mazes,
   Flung the torrent rainbow round:
   Then they started from their places,
   Moved with violence, changed in hue,
   Caught each other with wild grimaces, 35
   Half-invisible to the view,
   Wheeling with precipitate paces
   To the melody, till they flew,
   Hair, and eyes, and limbs, and faces,
   Twisted hard in fierce embraces, 40
   Like to Furies, like to Graces,
   Dash'd together in blinding dew:
   Till, kill'd with some luxurious agony,
   The nerve-dissolving melody
   Flutter'd headlong from the sky. 45

III

   And then I look'd up toward a mountain-tract,
   That girt the region with high cliff and lawn:
   I saw that every morning, far withdrawn
   Beyond the darkness and the cataract,
   God made Himself an awful rose of dawn, 50
   Unheeded: and detaching, fold by fold,
   From those still heights, and, slowly drawing near,
   A vapour heavy, hueless, formless, cold,
   Came floating on for many a month and year,
   Unheeded: and I thought I would have spoken, 55
   And warn'd that madman ere it grew too late:
   But, as in dreams, I could not. Mine was broken,
   When that cold vapour touch'd the palace gate,
   And link'd again. I saw within my head
   A gray and gap-tooth'd man as lean as death, 60
   Who slowly rode across a wither'd heath,
   And lighted at a ruin'd inn, and said:

IV

'Wrinkled ostler, grim and thin!
  Here is custom come your way;
Take my brute, and lead him in,
  Stuff his ribs with mouldy hay.

'Bitter barmaid, waning fast!
  See that sheets are on my bed;
What! the flower of life is past:
  It is long before you wed.

'Slip-shod waiter, lank and sour,
  At the Dragon on the heath!
Let us have a quiet hour,
  Let us hob-and-nob with Death.

'I am old, but let me drink;
  Bring me spices, bring me wine;
I remember, when I think,
  That my youth was half divine.

'Wine is good for shrivell'd lips,
  When a blanket wraps the day,
When the rotten woodland drips,
  And the leaf is stamp'd in clay.

'Sit thee down, and have no shame,
  Cheek by jowl, and knee by knee:
What care I for any name?
  What for order or degree?

'Let me screw thee up a peg:
  Let me loose thy tongue with wine:
Callest thou that thing a leg?
  Which is thinnest? thine or mine?

'Thou shalt not be saved by works:
  Thou hast been a sinner too:
Ruin'd trunks on wither'd forks,
  Empty scarecrows, I and you!

'Fill the cup, and fill the can: 95
  Have a rouse before the morn:
Every moment dies a man,
  Every moment one is born.

'We are men of ruin'd blood;
  Therefore comes it we are wise. 100
Fish are we that love the mud,
  Rising to no fancy-flies.

'Name and fame! to fly sublime
  Thro' the courts, the camps, the schools,
Is to be the ball of Time, 105
  Bandied by the hands of fools.

'Friendship!—to be two in one—
  Let the canting liar pack!
Well I know, when I am gone,
  How she mouths behind my back. 110

'Virtue!—to be good and just—
  Every heart, when sifted well,
Is a clot of warmer dust,
  Mix'd with cunning sparks of hell.

'O! we two as well can look 115
  Whited thought and cleanly life
As the priest, above his book
  Leering at his neighbour's wife.

'Fill the cup, and fill the can:
   Have a rouse before the morn:
Every moment dies a man,
   Every moment one is born.

'Drink, and let the parties rave:
   They are fill'd with idle spleen;
Rising, falling, like a wave,
   For they know not what they mean.

'He that roars for liberty
   Faster binds a tyrant's power;
And the tyrant's cruel glee
   Forces on the freer hour.

'Fill the can, and fill the cup:
   All the windy ways of men
Are but dust that rises up,
   And is lightly laid again.

'Greet her with applausive breath,
   Freedom, gaily doth she tread;
In her right a civic wreath,
   In her left a human head.

'No, I love not what is new;
   She is of an ancient house:
And I think we know the hue
   Of that cap upon her brows.

'Let her go! her thirst she slakes
   Where the bloody conduit runs,
Then her sweetest meal she makes
   On the first-born of her sons.

'Drink to lofty hopes that cool—
  Visions of a perfect State:
Drink we, last, the public fool,
  Frantic love and frantic hate.   150

'Chant me now some wicked stave,
  Till thy drooping courage rise,
And the glow-worm of the grave
  Glimmer in thy rheumy eyes.

'Fear not thou to loose thy tongue;   155
  Set thy hoary fancies free;
What is loathsome to the young
  Savours well to thee and me.

'Change, reverting to the years,
  When thy nerves could understand   160
What there is in loving tears,
  And the warmth of hand in hand.

'Tell me tales of thy first love—
  April hopes, the fools of chance;
Till the graves begin to move,   165
  And the dead begin to dance.

'Fill the can, and fill the cup:
  All the windy ways of men
Are but dust that rises up,
  And is lightly laid again.   170

'Trooping from their mouldy dens
  The chap-fallen circle spreads:
Welcome, fellow-citizens,
  Hollow hearts and empty heads!

'You are bones, and what of that?   175
  Every face, however full,

Padded round with flesh and fat,
  Is but modell'd on a skull.

'Death is king, and Vivat Rex!
  Tread a measure on the stones, 180
Madam—if I know your sex,
  From the fashion of your bones.

'No, I cannot praise the fire
  In your eye—nor yet your lip:
All the more do I admire 185
  Joints of cunning workmanship.

'Lo! God's likeness—the ground-plan—
  Neither modell'd, glazed, nor framed:
Buss me, thou rough sketch of man,
  Far too naked to be shamed! 190

'Drink to Fortune, drink to Chance,
  While we keep a little breath!
Drink to heavy Ignorance!
  Hob-and-nob with brother Death!

'Thou art mazed, the night is long, 195
  And the longer night is near:
What! I am not all as wrong
  As a bitter jest is dear.

'Youthful hopes, by scores, to all,
  When the locks are crisp and curl'd, 200
Unto me my maudlin gall
  And my mockeries of the world.

'Fill the cup, and fill the can:
  Mingle madness, mingle scorn!
Dregs of life, and lees of man: 205
  Yet we will not die forlorn.'

V

The voice grew faint: there came a further change:
Once more uprose the mystic mountain-range:
Below were men and horses pierced with worms,
And slowly quickening into lower forms; 210
By shards and scurf of salt, and scum of dross,
Old plash of rains, and refuse patch'd with moss.
Then some one spake: 'Behold! it was a crime
Of sense avenged by sense that wore with time.'
Another said: 'The crime of sense became 215
The crime of malice, and is equal blame.'
And one: 'He had not wholly quench'd his power;
A little grain of conscience made him sour.'
At last I heard a voice upon the slope
Cry to the summit, 'Is there any hope?' 220
To which an answer peal'd from that high land,
But in a tongue no man could understand;
And on the glimmering limit far withdrawn
God made Himself an awful rose of dawn.

THE SKIPPING-ROPE

SURE never yet was Antelope
  Could skip so lightly by.
Stand off, or else my skipping-rope
  Will hit you in the eye.
How lightly whirls the skipping-rope! 5
  How fairy-like you fly!
Go, get you gone, you muse and mope—
  I hate that silly sigh.
Nay, dearest, teach me how to hope,
  Or tell me how to die. 10
There, take it, take my skipping-rope,
  And hang yourself thereby.

'MOVE EASTWARD, HAPPY EARTH, AND LEAVE'

Move eastward, happy earth, and leave
    Yon orange sunset waning slow:
From fringes of the faded eve,
    O, happy planet, eastward go;
Till over thy dark shoulder glow   5
    Thy silver sister-world, and rise
    To glass herself in dewy eyes
That watch me from the glen below.

Ah, bear me with thee, smoothly borne,
    Dip forward under starry light,   10
And move me to my marriage-morn,
    And round again to happy night.

'BREAK, BREAK, BREAK'

Break, break, break,
    On thy cold gray stones, O Sea!
And I would that my tongue could utter
    The thoughts that arise in me.

O well for the fisherman's boy,   5
    That he shouts with his sister at play!
O well for the sailor lad,
    That he sings in his boat on the bay!

And the stately ships go on
    To their haven under the hill;   10
But O for the touch of a vanish'd hand,
    And the sound of a voice that is still!

Break, break, break,
  At the foot of thy crags, O Sea!
But the tender grace of a day that is dead   15
  Will never come back to me.

THE POET'S SONG

THE rain had fallen, the Poet arose,
  He pass'd by the town and out of the street,
A light wind blew from the gates of the sun,
  And waves of shadow went over the wheat,
And he sat him down in a lonely place,   5
  And chanted a melody loud and sweet,
That made the wild-swan pause in her cloud,
  And the lark drop down at his feet.

The swallow stopt as he hunted the fly,
  The snake slipt under a spray,   10
The wild hawk stood with the down on his beak,
  And stared, with his foot on the prey,
And the nightingale thought, 'I have sung many songs,
  But never a one so gay,
For he sings of what the world will be   15
  When the years have died away.'

Notes

CLARIBEL

19 Published *1830*; from *1870*, among 'Juvenilia'. Tennyson said of these love-portraits: 'All these ladies were evolved, like the camel, from my own consciousness.'

LILIAN

20 Published *1830*; from *1870*, among 'Juvenilia'.
16-7. In his review of *1842*, Leigh Hunt gave these lines as 'an instance of that injudicious crowding of images which sometimes results from Mr. Tennyson's desire to impress upon us the abundance of his thoughts.'
23. From *The Song of Solomon* 4:3, 'Thy lips are like a thread of scarlet.'

ISABEL

21 Published *1830*; from *1870*, among 'Juvenilia'. It describes Tennyson's mother, and—in lines 30-7—her relationship to his father.
1-4. Cp. Shelley, *Dedication to The Revolt of Islam* 98-9 (1818):

> And through thine eyes, even in thy soul I see
> A lamp of vestal fire burning internally.

5. The chaste Belphoebe in Spenser's *Faerie Queene*, II, iii, xxx, has 'lockes.... wide dispred'.
12. *lowlihead:* Tennyson apparently revived this word, not used since Lydgate in 1426.
17. In his review of *1842*, Leigh Hunt compared Thomas Heywood's famous phrase in *A Woman Killed with Kindness* (1607): 'The expression "*blanched* tablets of the heart," will not do at all after its beautiful original in the old poet, "the *red-leaved* tablets [read 'tables'] of the heart".'

NOTES

MARIANA

23 Published *1830*; from *1870*, among 'Juvenilia'. Tennyson's epigraph shows that the poem was suggested by Shakespeare's *Measure for Measure*; 'She should this Angelo have married: was affianced to her by oath, and the nuptial appointed . . . Left her in her tears, and dried not one of them with his comfort . . . What a merit were it in death to take this poor maid from the world! . . . There, at the moated grange, resides this dejected Mariana' (III, i, 212 ff.). The poem was influenced by Keats's *Isabella* 233 ff. (1820), where she waits in vain:

> She weeps alone for pleasures not to be;
> Sorely she wept until the night came on. . . .
> And so she pined, and so she died forlorn.

Keats's rhyme *aloof/roof* may have suggested lines 73-5. Tennyson seems to have invented the stanza-form; the best of his early poems are those which, like *Mariana*, stay most strictly with a stanza-form. Here the regularity suggests the unending monotony of Mariana's waiting, 'without hope of change'. Cp. *Mariana in the South* (p. 63), together with Arthur Hallam's comparison of the two poems (p. 292).

4. In *1862* Tennyson changed 'peach' to 'pear'. He later commented: ' "peach" spoils the desolation of the picture. It is not a characteristic of the scenery I had in mind.'

15. Cp. the deserted Dido, in *Aeneid*, IV, 451: *taedet caeli convexa tueri* ('she is weary of gazing on the arch of heaven').

18. *trance:* to entrance, throw into a trance. Tennyson's is the earliest figurative use given in the *Oxford English Dictionary*.

20. Cp. *Fatima* 13: 'I look'd athwart the burning drouth,' where the suffering heroine awaits her lover.

25. Another reminiscence of *Measure for Measure*, IV, i, 35: 'Upon the heavy middle of the night.' Cp. also Keats's love-poem, *The Eve of St. Agnes* 49 (1820): 'Upon the honey'd middle of the night.'

24 31. *gray-eyed morn:* from *Romeo and Juliet*, II, iii, 1.

NOTES

24 40. *marish-mosses:* Tennyson commented, 'the little marsh-moss lumps that float on the surface of water.'

54. *cell:* the cave of Aeolus, guardian of the winds. He is mentioned in Milton's *Lycidas* 97; see the note to line 80 below.

63. T. S. Eliot remarked: 'The line would be ruined if you substituted *sang* for *sung*.'

80. In *1830*: 'Downsloped was westering in his bower.' Tennyson probably thought that this was too close to *Lycidas* 31: 'had sloped his westering wheel.'

TO——

26 Published *1830*; from *1870*, among 'Juvenilia'. Tennyson said that the opening was addressed to his Cambridge friend J. W. Blakesley, 'but the poem wandered off to describe an imaginary man.'

6. Combining Keats's *Endymion*, II, 563 (1818): 'fringed lids'; with (as Tennyson acknowledged) *Lycidas* 26: 'Under the opening eyelids of the morn'. (Milton's poem, too, was about a Cambridge friend.)

10. *Sophist:* originally (in Greek) a wise or learned man; subsequently, a man who uses false arguments.

11-2. Cp. *Endymion*, I, 759-62:
'Why pierce high-fronted honour to the quick
For nothing but a dream?' Hereat the youth
Look'd up: a conflicting of shame and ruth
Was in his plaited brow.

20-3. Thy intellect shall feed Truth [not *vice versa*] until she, Truth, wearies the limbs of Falsehood.

24-9. *Genesis* 32: 22-31, Jacob 'passed over the ford Jabbok . . . And Jacob was left alone: and there wrestled a man with him, until the breaking of the day. And when he saw, that he prevailed not against him, he touched the hollow of his thigh: and the hollow of Jacob's thigh was out of joint, as he wrestled with him . . . And he said, "Thy name shall be called no more Jacob, but Israel: for as a prince hast thou power with God, and with men, and hast prevailed" . . . And Jacob called the name of the place Penuel: for I have

NOTES

26 seen God face to face, and my life is preserved. And as he passed over Penuel, the sun rose upon him, and he halted upon his thigh.' Tennyson commented: 'Jabbock not so sweet as Yabbock ... The Hebrew J is Y.' For the critic, the problem is whether there is a relevant parallel between the conflict of Truth and Falsehood (lines 21-3) and that of Jacob and the angel.

MADELINE

27 Published *1830*; from *1870*, among 'Juvenilia'. The name was perhaps suggested by the heroine of Keats's *Eve of St. Agnes*; *Madeline* has many Keatsian reminiscences.

1. Cp. Keats's *Ode on Indolence* 47: 'steep'd in honied indolence' (written 1819, but not published till 1848).

2. The contrast is with the 'summer calm' of *Isabel* (p. 21). *tranced summer:* from Keats's *Hyperion*, I, 72 (1820).

7. Keats has 'airy form', *Endymion*, II, 301.

16-7. Cp. *Endymion*, III, 872: 'thunder-gloomings'. Keats's Madeline has 'maiden eyes divine', rhyming with her name, in *Eve of St. Agnes* 57.

28 44. *taper fingers:* from Keats's *I stood tip-toe* 59 (1817). *amorously:* until corrected in the Errata, this stood in *1830*: 'three-times-three'. Tennyson perhaps meant 'nine times', but the phrase suggested that Madeline had nine fingers.

45. Cp. *Hyperion*, I, 182: 'Flush'd angerly.'

SONG—THE OWL

28 Published *1830*; from *1870*, among 'Juvenilia'. Based on the song, 'When icicles hang by the wall', in *Love's Labour's Lost*, V, ii:

Then nightly sings the staring owl...
Tu-whit to-who.

5. The manuscript version of the poem did not repeat line 4 or line 11; doing so enforces the sense of 'goes round' and 'twice or thrice'. The similar addition of line 5 to the *Second Song* enforces the 'echo'.

NOTES

28 6. Tennyson quoted *King Lear*, III, iv, 56: 'Bless thy five wits! Tom's a-cold'; and he glossed *wits* as 'senses'.

SECOND SONG. TO THE SAME

29 Published *1830*; from *1870*, among 'Juvenilia'.

3-4. Miltonic. Cp. *Comus* 249-52: 'float upon the wings / Of silence ... smoothing the Raven doune / Of darknes till it smil'd'; and *At a Vacation Exercise* 20: 'takes ... with delight'.

5. See the previous poem, line 5 note.

RECOLLECTIONS OF THE ARABIAN NIGHTS

30 Published *1830*; from *1870*, among 'Juvenilia'. Tennyson said that it was based on two stories from the *Arabian Nights*: 'The History of Aboulhassen', and 'Noureddin and the Fair Persian'.

10. *the golden prime:* from *Richard III*, I, ii, 247. Also (noting line 1) Shelley's *Epipsychidion* 192 (1821): 'In the clear golden prime of my youth's dawn.'

13-4. 'The deeps were driven before the prow' (Tennyson).

32 58. *engrain'd:* dyed in grain. Cp. Spenser, *Shepherd's Calendar: February* 131 (1579): 'With Leaves engrained in lusty greene.'

64. *tiar:* poetic form for 'tiara', as in Milton, Pope and Keats.

68. *coverture:* Tennyson cited the word from *Much Ado about Nothing*, III, i, 30.

70. *bulbul:* 'the Persian name for Nightingale' (Tennyson).

76. *flattering:* making beautiful, as in Shakespeare's Sonnet 33, where the proximity of 'golden' to 'flatter' suggests that Tennyson remembered this sonnet.

84. *counterchanged:* chequered (a heraldic term).

33 90. *Distinct:* adorned (a Latinism, chiefly poetic, found in Spenser and Milton). *inlaid:* cp. *Cymbeline*, V, v, 352: 'To inlay heaven with stars'. For 'inlaid,' *1830* read 'unrayed'—a word to which Tennyson's friend Arthur

279

NOTES

33 Hallam objected in his review of *1830*, as not conveying 'a very precise notion'.

103. *Henry V*, Prologue to Act IV, has 'stilly sounds'.

34 127. Tennyson commented: 'Crowned with the Mohammedan crescent moon. The crescent is Ottoman, not Arabian, an anachronism pardonable in a boy's vision.'

148. *diaper'd:* diversified like fretwork (a heraldic and Spenserian word).

ODE TO MEMORY

35 Published *1830*; from *1870*, among 'Juvenilia'. *1830* had the note: 'Written very early in life.' Tennyson said that it was 'a very early poem; all except [lines 119-21], which were addressed to Arthur Hallam and added.' Hallam Tennyson reports that 'my father considered this one of the best of his early and peculiarly concentrated Nature-poems.' The versification at times recalls *Lycidas* in its use of 5-stress and 3-stress iambic lines, but more particularly Wordsworth's *Immortality Ode* (1807).

25. Cp. *Lycidas* 2: 'with Ivy never-sear'. *sere:* dried up.

36 41. *listening:* listening to (not yet an archaic form, and used by Wordsworth in 1793). Lines 40-2 were incorporated from an earlier poem by Tennyson, *Timbuctoo* (1829):

I have rais'd thee nigher to the spheres of Heaven,
Man's first, last home: and thou with ravish'd sense
Listenest the lordly music flowing from
The illimitable years.

48-54. The landscape of Tennyson's tour of the Pyrenees in 1830. *flaunting:* Milton's 'flaunting Honysuckle', *Comus* 545.

56-9. 'The rectory at Somersby' (Tennyson), like lines 105-10.

37 66. Cp. *Comus* 344: 'The folded flocks, penned in their wattled cotes.'

38 96. *Pike:* 'Cumberland word for Peak' (Tennyson).

100-4. Tennyson said that this describes Mablethorpe on the Lincolnshire coast, where the Tennysons had a cottage.

NOTES

38 118. *myriad-minded:* an epithet which Coleridge had devised for Shakespeare, in *Biographia Literaria* (1817).

SONG [A SPIRIT]

39 Published *1830*; from *1870*, among 'Juvenilia'. One of the finest of Tennyson's minglings of natural setting and mood, the mood itself being very equivocal; there is not only grief but also a luxuriant pleasure at the 'moist rich smell' of the last days of autumn.

16. In the manuscript, 'very' and 'whole' were transposed.

19. *box:* a dark evergreen shrub.

ADELINE

40 Published *1830*; from *1870*, among 'Juvenilia'. A companion-poem to *Margaret* (p. 128). The name may be from Byron's *Don Juan*, Canto XIII (1823), where Adeline is 'not indifferent', but 'a hidden nectar under a cold presence'.

16. *Naiad:* a nymph or deity of river or spring.

26. *salient springs:* i.e. leaping. Poetic diction used by Tennyson in *Supposed Confessions* 56. Wordsworth has 'salient spring', *The Borderers* 1788 (written 1797, but not published till 1842).

41 43. *odorous sighs* were emitted by the flowers in Shelley's *Triumph of Life* 14 (1824).

47. Cp. William Collins, *Ode to Pity* 12 (1747): 'Eyes of dewy Light.'

53. *Sabæan:* Arabian. Cp. *Paradise Lost*, IV, 162: 'Sabean Odours from the spicy shore.'

62. Tennyson commented: 'The red spots on the cowslip bell, as if . . . letters of a fairy alphabet.' He compared *Cymbeline*, II, ii, 39; there too the context is erotic:

> On her left breast
> A mole cinque-spotted like the crimson drops
> I' th' bottom of a cowslip.

NOTES

A CHARACTER

42 Published *1830*; from *1870*, among 'Juvenilia'. It is a 'character' in the manner of the Greek writer Theophrastus, whose *Characters* epigrammatically combine a moral temperament and a personal sketch. Tennyson's poem is an attack on a man who was at Cambridge with him, Thomas Sunderland, 'a very plausible, parliament-like, and self-satisfied speaker at the Union' (said Edward FitzGerald). It is one of Tennyson's few poems of personal satire. Leigh Hunt quoted and praised it in his review of *1842*: 'We look upon the above, after its kind, as a faultless composition; and its kind is no mean one. Considered as a poetical satire, it brings an atmosphere of imagination round the coldest matter of fact; and the delicate *blank* effect of the disposition of the rhymes completes the seemingly passionless exposure of its passionless object.'

5-6. Yet in fact all the physical creation could not enter into his soul but remained mere seeing.

11. *sleek'd:* smoothed, as in *Comus* 882: 'sleeking her soft alluring locks'.

15. *Pallas and Juno:* the goddesses of wisdom and of empire.

17. The moralizing fool in *As You Like It*, II, vii, 21, had a 'lack-lustre eye'.

18. Itself deliberately using a traditional diction of eloquence. Cp. James Thomson, *Autumn* 16-7 (1730): 'Devolving through the maze of eloquence / A roll of periods.' From Horace's *verba devolvit* (*Odes*, IV, ii, 11).

21. *on silk:* mincingly.

27. Cp. (noting also line 10) *Troilus and Cressida*, II, iii, 153-4: 'He that is proud eats up himself: pride is his own glass.'

29. Coldly unimaginative, and quite different from his airy beliefs.

THE POET

43 Published *1830;* from *1870*, among 'Juvenilia'. It was influenced by the lofty opinions of poetry current at Cambridge when Tennyson was an undergraduate—

NOTES

43 especially those of the religious thinker F. D. Maurice. Cp. *The Poet's Mind* (p. 45). The stanza-form resembles *The Palace of Art* and *A Dream of Fair Women*.

1. *golden clime:* Keats, *Endymion*, III, 455.

3. Tennyson paraphrased: 'The poet hates hate; and scorns scorn' (rather than being dowered with the quintessence of these). F. D. Maurice had said in 1828 of the poet: 'He cannot be a scorner.' Victorian poetry held a low view of satire.

11-2. A poem *To Poesy*, written jointly by Tennyson and Arthur Hallam, says:

> Oh might I be an arrow in thy hand,
> And not of viewless flight, but trailing flame.

viewless: invisible; cp. Keats, *Ode to a Nightingale* 33 (1820): 'the viewless wings of Poesy'.

13. Blow-pipes.

15. *Calpe:* Gibraltar, 'the western limit of the old world, as Caucasus was the eastern' (Tennyson).

19. 'The dandelion' (Tennyson).

44 27. *breathing spring:* traditional poetic diction, as in Pope and Collins.

41-6. *Revelation* 19:12-3, 'His eyes were as a flame of fire, and on his head were many crowns; and he had a name written, that no man knew, but he himself. And he was clothed with a vesture dipped in blood ... And out of his mouth goeth a sharp sword [cp. lines 53-4] ... And he hath on his vesture and on his thigh a name written, King of Kings.' But Tennyson's substitution of 'eyes' for 'thigh' confuses the meaning. T. O. Mabbott ingeniously suggests that Tennyson refers to the image of the word (Wisdom) on the garments of Freedom as it is reflected in the retina of the eye. In *1830*, lines 45 and 47 read:

> And in the bordure of her robe was writ ...
> Hoar anarchies, as with a thunderfit.

THE POET'S MIND

45 Published *1830;* from *1870,* among 'Juvenilia'. The main influence, as G. H. Ford pointed out, is the end of Keats's *Lamia* (1820):

45
>   Do not all charms fly
>   At the mere touch of cold philosophy? . . .
>   The stately music no more breathes;
>   The myrtle sicken'd in a thousand wreaths.

Lamia died after 'the sophist's eye' had been 'browbeating her fair form'.

7. Following this line, *1830* had:
>   Clear as summer mountainstreams,
>   Bright as the inwoven beams,
>   Which beneath their crisping sapphire
>   In the midday, floating o'er
>   The golden sands, make evermore
>   To a blossomstarréd shore.
>   Hence away, unhallowed laughter!

8-9. Wordsworth's *A Poet's Epitaph* (1800) opposes poetry to the philosopher, 'all eyes', and to the lawyer: 'draw not nigh'. Gray's *Ode for Music* 10-2 (1769) speaks of 'the Muse's walk': 'Hence, away, 'tis holy Ground.' *Exodus* 3:5, 'Draw not nigh hither: put off thy shoes from off thy feet, for the place whereon thou standest, is holy ground.'

12. As an exorcism.

THE DYING SWAN

46 Published *1830*; from *1870*, among 'Juvenilia'. The widespread tradition of the swan's death-song had been discussed in William Hone's *Every-Day Book* (1825; 1827 ed., ii, 964-8), which Tennyson acknowledged as a source for *St. Simeon Stylites*.

9. *weary wind:* poetic diction, as in *Ode to Memory* 113 (p. 38), and three times in Shelley.

17. Cp. Wordsworth, *Westminster Bridge* 12 (1807): 'The river glideth at his own sweet will.'

47 21. *wild swan:* since the tradition did not include the domestic swan, a point made by Hone.

26. *coronach:* 'Gaelic funeral-song' (Tennyson).

30. *free and bold:* 'with the sentiment of entire liberty, it has also the tones' (Hone).

31-4. Based on *Iliad*, IV, 452-5.

NOTES

47 32. *shawms:* reeded musical instruments.

33. *To Poesy*, by Tennyson and Arthur Hallam, spoke of 'tumult of acclaim'.

38. *soughing:* Tennyson commented, 'Anglo-Saxon *sweg*, a sound. Modified into an onomatopœic word for the soft sound or the deep sighing of the wind.'

A DIRGE

47 Published *1830*; from *1870*, among 'Juvenilia'. It is based on the dirge in *Cymbeline*, IV, ii, 258, 'Fear no more the heat o' th' sun.' It was probably influenced by William Collins's imitation of that dirge, *Song from Shakespear's Cymbeline* (1744).

1. Cp. the dirge in *Cymbeline*: 'Thou thy worldly task hast done.'

48 23. *eglatere:* eglantine. Tennyson quoted the word from the 15th-century poem, *The Flower and the Leaf*.

29. *pleached:* plaited, as in Shakespeare and Keats.

31. *long purples:* 'the purple vetch' (Tennyson). In *1830* the two words were in quotation-marks, suggesting the reference in *Hamlet*, IV, vii, 168, where the context is again of death. Tennyson removed the quotation-marks, and later explicitly disowned a debt to *Hamlet* here, probably because there the context includes an obscene reference.

LOVE AND DEATH

49 Published *1830*; from *1870*, among 'Juvenilia'.

1. From Virgil, *Georgics*, I, 427: *luna revertentis cum primum colligit ignis*. *mighty moon:* as in Wordsworth and Shelley.

3. Cp. Keats, *Ode to a Nightingale* 29-30: 'Where Beauty cannot keep her lustrous eyes / Or new Love....' The 'moon' and 'plots' also suggest the *Ode*.

4. *cassia:* 'a kind of laurel' (Tennyson).

8. *vans:* wings. Tennyson compared *Paradise Lost*, II, 927-8: 'his Sail-broad Vans / He spreads for flight.' Cp. also 'sheeny vans' with *Paradise Regained*, IV, 583: 'plumy Vans'.

49 13. *eminent:* 'standing out like a tree' (Tennyson). Milton's 'Tree of Life' was 'High eminent', *Paradise Lost*, IV, 219.

THE BALLAD OF ORIANA

50 Published *1830*; from *1870*, among 'Juvenilia'. In his copy of *1842* (now at Trinity College, Cambridge), Edward FitzGerald noted that the poem was 'in some measure inspired' by the ballad of Helen of Kirkconnell. Tennyson knew the ballad by heart (*Memoir*, i, 48), in the version given in Scott's *Minstrelsy*. The name Oriana is from the chivalric romance *Amadis de Gaula*, and Scott mentions Oriana in *Marmion* (1808)—of which a copy was at Tennyson's home at Somersby.

12. Cp. the ballad of Clerk Saunders, which Tennyson also knew by heart: 'O, cocks are crowing a merry midnight.'

14-7. Adapted from an earlier poem by Tennyson, *The Vale of Bones* 57-9 (1827):

> When on to battle proudly going,
> Your plumage to the wild winds blowing,
> Your tartans far behind ye flowing.

CIRCUMSTANCE

53 Published *1830*; from *1870*, among 'Juvenilia'. 'Circumstance' was an important word to Tennyson, in that it suggested an earlier usage as 'the totality of surrounding things', hence 'the heavens'. See his note to 'The hollow orb of moving Circumstance', *The Palace of Art* 255 (p. 100).

THE MERMAN

53 Published *1830*; from *1870*, among 'Juvenilia'. See the note to the next poem, *The Mermaid*.

54 32. *Turkis:* a Miltonic form for 'turquoise' (*Comus* 894), to avoid the 'ugly nasal sound' (Tennyson). *almondine:* 'a small violet garnet' (Tennyson).

40. The refrain was suggested by Ariel's in *The Tempest*, V, i, 92-3:

> Merrily, merrily, shall I live now,
> Under the blossom that hangs on the bough.

NOTES

THE MERMAID

55 Published *1830*; from *1870*, among 'Juvenilia'. Tennyson had many sources for this and *The Merman*, among them Walter Scott's *Minstrelsy of the Scottish Border* (1802-3), which included John Leyden's *The Mermaid*. In his notes Tennyson quoted from Scott:

No more misshapen from the waist,
But like a maid of mortal frame.

And he said: 'I never thought of Mermen and Mermaidens with tails.' W. D. Paden has pointed out that mermen and mermaids were types of the great deities in G. S. Faber's religious mythologizing (which influenced many of Tennyson's early poems)—and so less trivial than they now seem.

16. Combining Shelley's 'crowns of sea-buds', *Rosalind* 1081 (1819), with his 'starry sea-flower crowns', *Prometheus Unbound*, III, ii, 47 (1820), on the Nereids under the sea.

29-30. Referring to the belief that true human love extinguishes the immortality of a merman.

56 48. *dry:* probably meaning 'crustaceous'; contrast 'soft' in line 53.

54. 'An underworld of which the sea is the heaven' (Tennyson).

TO J.M.K.

57 Published *1830*; from *1870*, as 'Juvenilia: Early Sonnets, II'. It was written to Tennyson's college-friend, J. M. Kemble, who later 'gave up his thought of taking Orders, and devoted himself to Anglo-Saxon history and literature' (Hallam Tennyson). It is the only sonnet of *1830* which Tennyson reprinted.

2. Martin Luther (1483-1546), the great German religious reformer.

3. Cp. *Paradise Regained*, II, 402-3 (after the tempting of Christ):

Both Table and Provision vanish'd quite
With sound of Harpies wings, and Talons heard.

9. *proof:* including the earlier sense of 'armour'.

NOTES

57 12-4. *Zechariah* 9:14, 'And the Lord shall be seen over them, and his arrow shall go forth as the lightning.'

THE LADY OF SHALOTT

57 Published *1832*; much revised in *1842*. All the textual changes are given below. Tennyson said that it was 'taken from an Italian novelette, *Donna di Scalotta*'. But this source (which is quoted at *Materials*, iv, 461) is very different; it has no Arthur, Queen, mirror, weaving, curse, song, river, or island. Apart from the Lady's death, the main links are that Camelot is the end of the funeral voyage, and is—unusually—on the sea-shore, and that there is an astonished crowd about the body. The *1832* text is slightly closer in some details, e.g. her death-letter. F. J. Furnivall quotes Tennyson in January 1868: 'I met the story first in some Italian *novelle*: but the web, mirror, island, etc., were my own. Indeed, I doubt whether I should ever have put it in that shape if I had been then aware of the Maid of Astolat in *Mort Arthur*' (*Rossetti Papers 1862-70*, ed. W. M. Rossetti, 1903, p. 341). Tennyson also said: 'The Lady of Shalott is evidently the Elaine of the *Morte d'Arthur* [by Malory], but I do not think that I had ever heard of the latter when I wrote the former. Shalott was a softer sound than "Scalott".' He later wrote the story of Elaine in the *Idylls of the King: Lancelot and Elaine* (1859). On the meaning of the poem, he remarked: 'The new-born love for something, for some one in the wide world from which she has been so long secluded, takes her out of the region of shadows into that of realities.' Hallam Tennyson added: 'The key to this tale of magic symbolism is of deep human significance and is to be found in the lines [69-72].' Lionel Stevenson has suggested the influence of Shelley's *Witch of Atlas* (1824), for an onlooker who weaves, and who has a magic boat:

'Tis said in after times her spirit free
  Knew what love was, and felt itself alone.

NOTES

57 6-9. In *1832*:
>The yellowleavèd waterlily,
>The greensheathèd daffodilly,
>Tremble in the water chilly,
>   Round about Shalott.

58 10. *quiver:* in *1832*, 'shiver'.

11-2. In *1832*:
>The sunbeam-showers break and quiver
>In the stream that runneth ever

19-27. These lines were transposed with lines 28-36 in *1832*.

19-21. In *1832*:
>The little isle is all inrailed
>With a rose-fence, and overtrailed
>With roses: by the marge unhailed

24-6. In *1832*:
>A pearlgarland winds her head:
>She leaneth on a velvet bed,
>Full royally apparellèd,

27. *Shalott?:* in *1832*, 'Shalott.'.

28-34. In *1832*:
>Underneath the bearded barley,
>The reaper, reaping late and early,
>Hears her ever chanting cheerly,
>Like an angel, singing clearly,
>   O'er the stream of Camelot.
>Piling the sheaves in furrows airy,
>Beneath the moon, the reaper weary

30. *cheerly:* Tennyson compared *Richard II*, I, iii, 66: 'But lusty, young, and cheerly drawing breath.'

34. Thomas Warton has 'airy uplands' in his *Sonnet II*, 'When late the trees' (1777).

37-40. In *1832*:
>No time hath she to sport and play:
>A charmèd web she weaves alway.
>A curse is on her, if she stay
>Her weaving, either night or day,

59 43. *And so:* in *1832*, 'Therefore'.

44. *And little:* in *1832*, 'Therefore no'.

NOTES

59 46-51. In *1832*:
>   She lives with little joy or fear.
>   Over the water, running near,
>   The sheepbell tinkles in her ear.
>   Before her hangs a mirror clear,
>   Reflecting tower'd Camelot.
>   And, as the mazy web she whirls,

46. The mirror is not there simply for the fairy-tale; it was set behind the tapestry so that the worker could see the effect on the right side. This was slightly clearer in the sequence of lines in *1832*. Tennyson was much influenced by Spenser's *Faerie Queene*, III, ii, on Britomart and Artegall: 'The wondrous myrrhour, by which she in love with him did fall.' Spenser mentions the Towre,
>   Wherein th' Ægyptian *Phao* long did lurke
>   From all mens vew, that none might her discoure,
>   Yet she might all men vew out of her bowre.

Britomart looks in the mirror:
>   Eftsoones there was presented to her eye
>   A comely knight, all arm'd in complet wize.

She is then languishing: 'Till death make one end of my dayes and miserie.'

52. *And there:* in *1832*, 'She sees'.

68. *went to:* in *1832*, 'came from'.

60 78. *red-cross knight:* again a Spenserian influence.

82 ff. For the knight's appearance, Tennyson takes up details from *Faerie Queene*, I, vii, xxix ff.

86. *to:* in *1832*, 'from'. Likewise in lines 95, 104.

99. *still:* in *1832*, 'green'.

61 107. In *1832*: ' "Tirra lirra, tirra lirra,".' From *Winter's Tale*, IV, iii, 9.

111. *water-lily:* in *1832*, 'waterflower'.

123. In *1832*: 'Outside the isle a shallow boat'.

124. *left:* in *1832*, 'lay'.

125. *And . . . prow:* in *1832*, 'Below the carven stern.' Following this stanza, *1832* had (cp. line 136):
>   A cloudwhite crown of pearl she dight.
>   All raimented in snowy white
>   That loosely flew, (her zone in sight,

NOTES

61   Clasped with one blinding diamond bright,)
          Her wide eyes fixed on Camelot,
          Though the squally eastwind keenly
          Blew, with folded arms serenely
          By the water stood the queenly
            Lady of Shalott.

127. In *1832*: 'With a steady, stony glance—'.
129. *Seeing:* in *1832*, 'Beholding'.
130. *With:* in *1832*, 'Mute, with'.
131. *Did she look:* in *1832*, 'She looked down'.

62 132. *And at:* in *1832*, 'It was'.
136-41. In *1832*:

      As when to sailors while they roam,
      By creeks and outfalls far from home,
      Rising and dropping with the foam,
      From dying swans wild warblings come,
         Blown shoreward; so to Camelot
      Still as . . .

143. *singing . . . song:* in *1832*, 'chanting her deathsong'. With this stanza, especially in *1832*, cp. *The Dying Swan* (p. 47), and *Morte d'Arthur* 266-9 (p. 153).
145. *Heard a:* in *1832*, 'A longdrawn'.
146. *Chanted:* in *1832*, 'She chanted'.
147, 148. These lines were transposed in *1832* ('Till her eyes . . .').
148. In *1832*: 'And her smooth face sharpened slowly,'. Tennyson reported that 'George Eliot liked my first [version] the best.'
156. *gleaming shape:* in *1832*, 'pale, pale corpse'.
157. *Dead-pale:* Tennyson's final reading, adopted in *1855*; in *1832*, 'Deadcold'; *1842-53*, 'A corse'.
158. In *1832*: 'Dead into towered Camelot.'
159, 160. These lines were transposed in *1832*.
159. In *1832*: 'To the plankèd wharfage came:'.
161. *And . . . prow:* in *1832*, 'Below the stern'. A reviewer, J. W. Croker, had ridiculed the fact that the name of the boat was below its stern.

63 163-71. In *1832*:

      They crossed themselves, their stars they blest,
      Knight, minstrel, abbot, squire and guest.

NOTES

63   There lay a parchment on her breast,
        That puzzled more than all the rest,
          The wellfed wits at Camelot.
    '*The web was woven curiously
    The charm is broken utterly,
    Draw near and fear not—this is I,
      The Lady of Shalott.*'

John Stuart Mill objected to the *1832* stanza (*London Review*, July 1835).

MARIANA IN THE SOUTH

63 Published *1832*; from *1870*, among 'Juvenilia'. It was much re-written for *1842*; all the textual changes are given below. Tennyson set to work revising it soon after *1832*. It was written 1830-1: 'the idea of this came into my head between Narbonne and Perpignan' (Tennyson), during his tour of the Pyrenees with Arthur Hallam, summer 1830.

Hallam wrote to W. B. Donne in 1831 (*Memoir*, i, 500-1):
It is intended, you will perceive, as a kind of pendant to his former poem of *Mariana* [p. 23], the idea of both being the expression of desolate loneliness, but with this distinctive variety in the second, that it paints the forlorn feeling as it would exist under the influence of different impressions of sense. When we were journeying together this summer through the South of France we came upon a range of country just corresponding to his preconceived thought of a barrenness, so as in the South, and the portraiture of the scenery in this poem is most faithful. You will, I think, agree with me that the essential and distinguishing character of the conception requires in the *Southern Mariana* a greater lingering on the outward circumstances, and a less palpable transition of the poet into Mariana's feelings, than was the case in the former poem.

The reviewer of *1832* in the *True Sun* spoke of Tennyson's heroine as 'exceedingly lovely in her desertion, with the scenery around in keeping with her heart' (E.

NOTES

63 F. Shannon, *Tennyson and the Reviewers*, 1952, p. 18).
It was influenced by Sappho's *Fragment* 111, of which
the Loeb translation is:

> The Moon is gone
> And the Pleiads set,
>   Midnight is nigh;
> Time passes on,
> And passes; yet
>   Alone I lie.

Arthur Hallam referred to 'the fragments of Sappho, in
which I see much congeniality to Alfred's peculiar
power', when enclosing the poem. Of Tennyson's
revisions: in *1832* the first stanza violated the scheme
by having twelve lines plus refrain; the last stanza
likewise, and with a false rhyme. A manuscript at
Trinity College shows that at an earlier stage the poem
consisted of stanzas of 16 lines plus refrain, i.e. joining
two of the final stanzas. In *The Formation of Tennyson's
Style* (1921, pp. 59-60), J. F. A. Pyre shows that the
1842 changes make for regularity of rhythm, which is
apt to the persistent monotony.

1-12. In *1832*:

> Behind the barren hill upsprung
>   With pointed rocks against the light,
> The crag sharpshadowed overhung
>   Each glaring creek and inlet bright.
> Far, far, one lightblue ridge was seen,
>   Looming like baseless fairyland;
>   Eastward a slip of burning sand,
> Dark-rimmed with sea, and bare of green.
> Down in the dry salt-marshes stood
>   That house darklatticed. Not a breath
>   Swayed the sick vineyard underneath,
> Or moved the dusty southernwood.
> 'Madonna,' with melodious moan
> Sang Mariana, night and morn,
> 'Madonna! lo! I am all alone,
>   Love-forgotten and love-forlorn.'

14. In *1832*: 'From her warm brow and bosom down'.

NOTES

63 15. *taper fingers:* from Keats, *I stood tip-toe* 59, as in Tennyson's *Madeline* 44 (p. 28).

17. *To . . . right:* in *1832*, 'On either side'.

64 21-4. *1832* has the refrain as in its first stanza.

25. *Till . . . crimson:* in *1832*, 'When the dawncrimson'.

28. *Before . . . murmur'd:* in *1832*, 'Unto . . . prayèd'.

29-36. In *1832*:

> She moved her lips, she prayed alone,
>   She praying disarrayed and warm
>   From slumber, deep her wavy form
> In the darklustrous mirror shone.
>   'Madonna,' in a low clear tone
> Said Mariana, night and morn,
> Low she mourned, 'I am all alone,
> Love-forgotten, and love-forlorn.'

31. *liquid mirror:* as in Shelley, *Alastor* 462 (1816), where it has the more common application to water.

37-48. In *1832*:

> At noon she slumbered. All along
>   The silvery field, the large leaves talked
> With one another, as among
>   The spikèd maize in dreams she walked.
> The lizard leapt: the sunlight played:
>   She heard the callow nestling lisp,
>   And brimful meadow-runnels crisp,
> In the full-leavèd platan-shade.
>   In sleep she breathed in a lower tone,
> Murmuring as at night and morn,
> 'Madonna! lo! I am all alone,
> Love-forgotten and love-forlorn.'

Cp. *Claribel* 17-9:

>   The callow throstle lispeth . . .
>   The babbling runnel crispeth.

49-50. *dream: / She felt he:* in *1832*, 'dream / Most false: *he*'.

53. *one:* Tennyson's final reading, adopted in *1850*; *1832-48*, 'the'. *willow:* Tennyson's final reading, adopted in *1853*; *1832-51*, 'olive'.

65 55-6. In *1832*:
>From the bald rock the blinding light
>Beat ever on the sunwhite wall.

59-60. In *1832*:
>'Madonna, leave me not all alone,
>To die forgotten and live forlorn.'

61-84. These were not in *1832*, but added in *1842*. Possibly they were precipitated by the death of Arthur Hallam. Cp. the 'letters' ('love', 'worth') with the mention of Hallam's letters in *In Memoriam* XCV. The 'image' which speaks makes use of the *In Memoriam* stanza-form in lines 65-8.

85-6. In *1832*:
>One dry cicala's summer song
>   At night filled all the gallery,

66 89-91. Cp. the opening of James Beattie's *Retirement* (1758):
>When in the crimson cloud of even
>   The lingering light decays,
>And Hesper on the front of heaven
>   Her glittering gem displays;
>Deep in the silent vale . . .

There was a copy of Beattie's *Minstrel* at Tennyson's home at Somersby.

89-96. In *1832*:
>Ever the low wave seemed to roll
>   Up to the coast: far on, alone
>   In the East, large Hesper overshone
>The mourning gulf, and on her soul
>Poured divine solace, or the rise
>   Of moonlight from the margin gleamed,
>   Volcano-like, afar, and streamed
>On her white arm, and heavenward eyes.
>   Not all alone she made her moan,
>   Yet ever sang she, night and morn,
>   'Madonna, lo! I am all alone,
>   Love-forgotten and love-forlorn.'

The revision abolishes the 'divine solace', 'not all alone'.

90. Cp. Keats, *Hyperion*, II, 5-6: 'light / Could glimmer

66 on their tears.' And James Thomson, *Autumn* 200-1, where Lavinia's eyes 'like the dewy star / Of evening, shone in tears.'

ELEÄNORE

66 Published *1832*; from *1870*, among 'Juvenilia'.

12. *floating shades:* as in Shelley, *Alastor* 124.

67 44. Cp. Shakespeare, Sonnet 86: 'the proud full sail of his great verse.'

68 53. Cp. the 'lineaments divine' of Milton's bird-like angel, *Paradise Lost*, V, 278.

64. Cp. Keats, *Ode on a Grecian Urn* 11-2 (1820): 'Heard melodies are sweet, but those unheard / Are sweeter.'

69 108-9. In *1832*:

> As waves that from the outer deep
> > Roll into a quiet cove,
> > There fall away, and lying still,
> > Having glorious dreams in sleep,

A reviewer objected to the last line.

117. *languid Love:* as twice in Shelley. J. C. Collins suggested the influence of Horace's *Odes*, III, xxvii, 67-8: Cupid is with *remisso arcu* instead of *intento arcu*. Alongside this suggestion, Tennyson jotted: 'possibly'.

70 122-3. Cp. Byron, *Maid of Athens* 7-8 (1812):

> By those tresses unconfined,
> Wooed by each Aegean wind.

odorous wind: as four times in Shelley.

122-44. Tennyson compared Sappho, *Fragment 2*. In the Loeb translation:

> It is to be a God, methinks, to sit before you and listen close by to the sweet accents and winning laughter which have made the heart in my breast beat fast, I warrant you. When I look on you, Brocheo, my speech comes short or fails me quite, I am tongue-tied; in a moment a delicate fire has overrun my flesh, my eyes grow dim and my ears sing, the sweat runs down me and a trembling takes me altogether, till I am as green and pale as the grass, and

NOTES

70   death itself seems not very far away;—but now that
I am poor, I must fain be content.

This was also a source for *Fatima* (p. 79).

THE MILLER'S DAUGHTER

71 Published *1832*; much revised in *1842*. Only a selection
of the revisions is given below. It was influenced by
Mary Russell Mitford's idyll, *The Queen of the Meadow*
(1827, reprinted in *Our Village*, 1828), a story which
also suggested details in a later Tennyson poem, *The
Brook* (1855). Tennyson may have remembered Robert
Bloomfield's *The Miller's Maid*, about an adopted
daughter, in *Rural Tales* (1801), of which a copy was at
Somersby. Tennyson had thought of a series of
'Daughter' poems; he published *The Gardener's
Daughter* (p. 154), left unpublished a short poem, *The
Doctor's Daughter*, and planned to write an *Innkeeper's
Daughter* in 1832. The graceful fluency of *The Miller's
Daughter*, what Edward FitzGerald picked out as 'the
easy character of "talk over the walnuts and the wine" ',
links it with Tennyson's 'English Idyls'. FitzGerald
thought that 'in some respects' Tennyson's changes
were 'not for the better'.

1. In *1832* this was preceded by the stanza:

> I met in all the close green ways,
>   While walking with my line and rod,
> The wealthy miller's mealy face,
>   Like the moon in an ivytod.
> He looked so jolly and so good—
>   While fishing in the milldam-water,
> I laughed to see him as he stood,
>   And dreamt not of the miller's daughter.

The reviewer 'Christopher North' (John Wilson)
objected.

13. *lightnings of a soul:* from Shelley, *Epipsychidion* 89.

72 25-32. These lines were not in *1832*, but added in *1842*.

33-7. In *1832*:

> My father's mansion, mounted high,
>   Looked down upon the village-spire.
> I was a long and listless boy.

297

NOTES

72   And son and heir unto the squire.
     In these dear walls, where . . .

48. After this line, *1832* had:
>Sometimes I whistled in the wind,
> Sometimes I angled, thought and deed
>Torpid, as swallows left behind
> That winter 'neath the floating weed:
>At will to wander everyway
> From brook to brook my sole delight,
>As lithe eels over meadows gray
> Oft shift their glimmering pool by night.

1832 followed these lines with its text of lines 97-104.

49-56. In *1832*:
>I loved from off the bridge to hear
> The rushing sound the water made,
>And see the fish that everywhere
> In the backcurrent glanced and played;
>Low down the tall flagflower that sprung
> Beside the noisy steppingstones,
>And the massed chestnutboughs that hung
> Thickstudded over with white cones.

73 60-3. In *1832*:
>Beneath those gummy chestnutbuds
> That glistened in the April blue.
>Upon the slope so smooth and cool,
> I lay and never thought of *you*,

65-72. These lines were not in *1832*, but added in *1842*.

73-80. In *1832*:
>A water-rat from off the bank
> Plunged in the stream. With idle care,
>Downlooking thro' the sedges rank,
> I saw your troubled image there.
>Upon the dark and dimpled beck
> It wandered like a floating light,
>A full fair form, a warm white neck,
> And two white arms—how rosy white!

In his very hostile review, J. W. Croker pretended to understand this as meaning that the 'rat' is an 'image' of the girl.

NOTES

74 89-96. In *1832*:
> That slope beneath the chestnut tall
>   Is wooed with choicest breaths of air:
> Methinks that I could tell you all
>   The cowslips and the kingcups there.
> Each coltsfoot down the grassy bent,
>   Whose round leaves hold the gathered shower,
> Each quaintly-folded cuckoopint,
>   And silver-paly cuckooflower.

91-2. Cp. Shelley, *To Jane—The Recollection* 51-4 (written 1822):
> One fair form that filled with love
>   The lifeless atmosphere

continuing in the manner of Tennyson's poem:
> We paused beside the pools that lie
>   Under the forest bough.

105-8. In *1832*:
> In rambling on the eastern wold,
>   When thro' the showery April nights
> Their hueless crescent glimmered cold,
>   From all the other village-lights

113-20. In *1832*:
> The white chalkquarry from the hill
>   Upon the broken ripple gleamed,
> I murmured lowly, sitting still
>   While round my feet the eddy streamed:
> 'Oh! that I were the wreath she wreathes,
>   The mirror where her sight she feeds,
> The song she sings, the air she breathes,
>   The letters of the book she reads.'

75 137-60. In *1832*:
> Remember you the clear moonlight,
>   That whitened all the eastern ridge,
> When o'er the water, dancing white,
>   I stepped upon the old millbridge.
> I heard you whisper from above
>   A lutetoned whisper, 'I am here;'
> I murmured, 'Speak again, my love,
>   The stream is loud: I cannot hear.'

NOTES

76
      I heard, as I have seemed to hear,
        When all the under-air was still,
      The low voice of the glad new year
        Call to the freshly-flowered hill.
      I heard, as I have often heard
        The nightingale in leavy woods
      Call to its mate, when nothing stirred
        To left or right but falling floods.

169-86. Tennyson re-wrote the song for *1842*. The lover's wishes in these songs are traditional; cp. in particular Anacreon, *Ode XXII*.

77 189-98. In *1832*:
      For o'er each letter broods and dwells,
        (Like light from running waters thrown
      On flowery swaths) the blissful flame
        Of his sweet eyes, that, day and night,
      With pulses thrilling thro' his frame
        Do inly tremble, starrybright.

      How I waste language—yet in truth
        You must blame love, whose early rage
      Made me a rhymster in my youth,
        And over-garrulous in age.

203-14. *1832* had a different song, on the same theme of 'forget me not'.

78 223-38. These lines were not in *1832*, but added in *1842*.

FATIMA

79 Published *1832*, with no title but with an epigraph from Sappho's *Fragment 2*. This Fragment is Tennyson's main source (quoted on p. 296), as for the end of *Eleänore*. But, as W. D. Paden observed, it merges with the story of Jemily in Savary's *Letters on Egypt* (of which the 1799 translation was at Somersby). She waits for her lover who dare not come because of her husband: 'extending herself on the ground, [she] rolled among and crushed the tender flowers' (cp. lines 11-2). For the scheme of rhyme and metre, cp. *The Lady of Shalott* (p. 57), which simply adds rhyming refrains.

8-14. These lines were not in *1832*, but added in *1842*.

NOTES

79 13. Cp. *Mariana* 20 (a similar situation): 'And glanced athwart the glooming flats' (p. 23).

19-21. A traditional notion, as in *Locksley Hall* 38 (p. 198). Cp. Marlowe's *Dr Faustus* 1331 (1604): 'Her lips sucke forth my soule'; and Donne's *The Expiration* (1609):

> So, so, breake off this last lamenting kisse,
> Which sucks two soules, and vapors both away.

ŒNONE

80 Published *1832*; much revised for *1842*. Only a selection of the revisions is given below. The changes are interestingly discussed by P. F. Baum in *Tennyson Sixty Years After* (1948), pp. 75-82. Tennyson began revising it soon after *1832*. He wrote it 1830-2; the scenery was suggested by the Pyrenees, where part of it was written, summer 1830. Tennyson commented: Œnone was 'married to Paris, and afterwards deserted by him for Helen. The sequel of the tale is poorly given in Quintus Calaber' (which Tennyson was to adapt for *The Death of Œnone*, 1892). The sources and classical allusions—in particular Ovid's *Heroides* and Theocritus—have been comprehensively discussed by Paul Turner (*Journal of English and Germanic Philology*, 1962, lxi, 57-72), who subsumes previous commentators and on whom the following notes draw extensively. Douglas Bush describes the poem as an epyllion, or minor epic, in the manner of Theocritus.

1-14. In *1832*:

> There is a dale in Ida, lovelier
> Than any in old Ionia, beautiful
> With emerald slopes of sunny sward, that lean
> Above the loud glenriver, which hath worn
> A path thro' steepdown granite walls below
> Mantled with flowering tendriltwine. In front
> The cedarshadowy valleys open wide.
> Far-seen, high over all the Godbuilt wall
> And many a snowycolumned range divine,
> Mounted with awful sculptures—men and Gods,
> The work of Gods—bright on the darkblue sky

NOTES

80
>The windy citadel of Ilion
>Shone, like the crown of Troas. Hither came

1. *Ida:* the mountain on the south of the Troas (Troy). Tennyson's opening paragraphs follow the pastoral love-lament: hopeless lover, loved one, setting.

10. *Gargarus:* 'the highest part of Mount Ida' (Tennyson). He compared Virgil's *Georgics*, I, 103: *Ipsa suas mirantur Gargara messes.*

81 15-6. *forlorn of:* Spenserian and Miltonic. Paul Turner suggests that lines 17-8 associate Œnone ominously with Cassandra (*diffusis comis* in Ovid), and with Dido (*aut videt aut vidisse putat* in *Aeneid*, VI, 454).

22. Tennyson remarked that 'this sort of refrain is found in Theocritus.' *ere I die:* a traditional feature of the pastoral love-poem.

24. This line was not in *1832*, but added in *1842*.

25-9. Based on Virgil's *Eclogues*, II. 8-13, where *cicadis* suggested the cicala of *1832*. The antithesis, *rests / awake*, is from Theocritus II, 38-9; and the lizard, from VII, 21-3.

27. Tennyson's final reading, adopted in *1883*. In *1832*:
>Sleeps like a shadow, and the scarletwinged
>Cicala in the noonday leapeth not
>Along the water-rounded granite-rock.

1842-82: 'Rests like a shadow, and the cicala sleeps.' Tennyson remarked: 'In these lines describing a perfect stillness, I did not like the jump, "Rests like a shadow—and the cicala sleeps". Moreover, in the heat of noon the cicala is generally at its loudest, though I have read that, in extreme heat, it is silent. Someone (I forget who) found them silent at noon on the slopes of Etna.'

30. Tennyson denied the influence of *2 Henry VI*, II, iii, 17: 'Mine eyes are full of tears, my heart of grief.'

38-41. Suggested by Ovid's Œnone, who boasts that Apollo was her first lover—Apollo, *Troiae munitor*. For the building of Troy to music, cp. Tennyson's later poem, *Tithonus* (1860, though originally drafted in 1833):
>Like that strange song I heard Apollo sing,
>While Ilion like a mist rose into towers.

NOTES

81 46. This line was not in *1832*, but added in *1842*. *the dawning hills: Paradise Lost*, VI, 528.

82 50. Together with the apple of line 65, the traditional rustic gifts of the pastoral.

51. *Simois:* one of the two rivers of the plain of Troy.
53-6. In *1832*:

> I sate alone: the goldensandalled morn
> Rosehued the scornful hills: I sate alone
> With downdropt eyes: whitebreasted ...

60. *foam-bow:* 'the rainbow in the cataract' (Tennyson).
65. A pastoral gift, as in Theocritus, but here the apple of Discord.

65-7. In *1832*:

> Close-held a golden apple, lightningbright
> With changeful flashes, dropt with dew of Heaven
> Ambrosially smelling. From his lip,
> Curved crimson, the fullflowing ...

69, 74. Eyebrows that met were thought beautiful in classical times, as in Theocritus.

71-87. In *1832*:

> 'For the most fair,' in aftertime may breed
> Deep evilwilledness of heaven and sere
> Heartburning toward hallowed Ilion;
> And all the colour of my afterlife
> Will be the shadow of today. Today
> Herè and Pallas and the floating grace
> Of laughterloving Aphrodite meet
> In manyfolded Ida to receive
> This meed of beauty, she to whom my hand
> Award the palm. Within the green hillside,
> Under yon whispering tuft of oldest pine,
> Is an ingoing grotto, strown with spar
> And ivymatted at the mouth, wherein
> Thou unbeholden may'st behold, unheard

72. *Oread:* mountain-nymph.
76. Ominously recalling Bion's *Lament for Adonis* 11-2:

303

NOTES

82 'The rose departs from his lip, and the kiss that [Aphrodite] shall never have so again, that kiss dies upon it and is gone' (Loeb translation).

83 81. *Iris:* the messenger of the gods, especially of Juno.

91. Cp. James Thomson, *Summer* 1304-5 (1727): 'Paris on the piny top / Of Ida.'

93 ff. The setting is from *Iliad*, XIV, 346-51, where the cloud dropping dew (lines 103-4) envelops Herè (Hera) and not her peacock. Cp. *Paradise Lost*, IV, 700-02, the bower of Adam and Eve.

> underfoot the Violet,
> Crocus, and Hyacinth with rich inlay
> Broiderd the ground.

94-7. In *1832*:

> Lustrous with lilyflower, violeteyed
> Both white and blue, with lotetree-fruit thickset,
> Shadowed with singing pine; and all the while,
> Above, the overwandering ivy and vine

like fire: Tennyson spoke of the 'flame-like petal ... not only the colour'.

101-8. In *1832*:

> On the treetops a golden glorious cloud
> Leaned, slowly dropping down ambrosial dew.
> How beautiful they were, too beautiful
> To look upon! but Paris was to me
> More lovelier than all the world beside.
>   O mother Ida, hearken ere I die.
> First spake the imperial Olympian
> With archèd eyebrow smiling sovranly,
> Fulleyèd Herè. She to Paris made

102. *peacock:* 'sacred to Herè' (Tennyson).

84 113. In *1832*: 'Or upland glebe wealthy in oil and wine—.' This brings out more clearly the debt in lines 112-3 to *Paradise Regained*, III, 257-60:

> Fair champaign, with less rivers interveined,
> Then meeting joined their tribute to the sea.
> Fertile of corn the glebe, of oil, and wine;
> With herds the pastures throng'd ...

The reminiscence is due to the similar situation, of tempting offers being made.

NOTES

84 127-31. Based, as Tennyson says, on Lucretius's account of the Epicurean gods, III, 18-24.

137. *O'erthwarted:* Tennyson said the word was founded on the Chaucerian 'overthwart': across.

85 148. Traditionally Pallas had offered Paris success in war, until (as Douglas Bush observed) the 5th-century writer Fulgentius modified the offer to that of wisdom.

150-64. In *1832*:

> Not as men value gold because it tricks
> And blazons outward Life with ornament,
> But rather as the miser, for itself.
> Good for selfgood doth half destroy selfgood.
> The means and end, like two coiled snakes, infect
> Each other, bound in one with hateful love.
> So both into the fountain and the stream
> A drop of poison falls. Come hearken to me,
> And look upon me and consider me,
> So shalt thou find me fairest, so endurance,
> Like to an athlete's arm, shall still become
> Sinewed with motion, till thine active will
> (As the dark body of the Sun robed round
> With his own ever-emanating lights)
> Be flooded o'er with her own effluences,
> And thereby grow to freedom.

151. *Sequel of guerdon:* 'addition of reward' (Tennyson).

162. Cp. *2 Henry IV*, IV, i, 172: 'Insinewed to this action.'

166-7. The antithesis, *heard / hear*, is from Aeschylus, *Prometheus Vinctus* 448. Turner observes that it 'carries the implication that Paris is in the same state of primitive animalism as the human race before Prometheus began to civilize it.'

170-1. 'Idalium and Paphos in Cyprus are sacred to Aphrodite' (Tennyson); she was born from the sea-foam.

174-6. In *1832:*

> Fragrant and thick, and on her head upbound
> In a purple band: below her lucid neck
> Shone ivorylike, and from the ground her foot
> Gleamed rosywhite ...

NOTES

86 184. This line was not in *1832*, but added in *1842*.

195-7. Cp. Keats, *Lamia*, I, 49-50 (1820): 'freckled like a pard, / Eyed like a peacock.' Turner remarks that this context brings 'with it associations of illusory and evanescent love.'

204-5. Suggested by *Heroides*, V, 41-2, but there, as Turner says, 'Œnone's only objection to the felling of the pines is that it provides transport for Paris and Helen.'

87 216-25. These lines were not in *1832*, but added in *1842*.

220. Eris, 'the goddess of strife' (Tennyson).

233. A classical commonplace.

88 253-6. The association of Œnone and Dido (cp. line 18) was, as Turner says, 'inevitable, considering the similarity of their histories (both being deserted by Trojan lovers, and both committing suicide on funeral pyres).' The image here is from Dido's dream, *Aeneid*, IV, 465-8.

259. Turner points out that 'Ovid's Œnone refers to Cassandra's prophecy that Helen will be the ruin of Troy, but she is also perfectly aware ... that the rape of Helen is going to cause a major war.' Tennyson gives Œnone 'some of Cassandra's vague prophetic power ... depriving her of any accurate knowledge.'

260-4. Turner links *fire* as a traditional metaphor for love, with it as magic to bring back the faithless lover (Theocritus); with Hecuba's dream before the birth of Paris; and with the fires of Dido, including her funeral pyre. In *The Death Of Œnone*, Tennyson tells how she flings herself on to the funeral-pyre of Paris.

THE SISTERS

88 Published *1832*. It was influenced by Scott's *Minstrelsy of the Scottish Border* (from which Tennyson knew ballads by heart)—e.g. *The Cruel Sister*.

19-20. Cp. Byron, *The Bride of Abydos* 301-2 (1813):
> Come, lay thy head upon my breast,
> And I will kiss thee into rest.

NOTES

TO—WITH THE FOLLOWING POEM

90 Published *1832*. It is addressed to Tennyson's college friend R. C. Trench, a remark by whom prompted *The Palace of Art* (p. 91). It proclaims the view of poetry (morally opposed to aestheticism) which was strongly held by the Cambridge 'Apostles'.

15-6 Cp. *Hamlet*, V, i, 234-6:
> I tell thee, churlish priest,
> A minst'ring angel shall my sister be,
> When thou liest howling.

Hence 'he that shuts Love out' suggests the priest's 'She should in ground unsanctified have lodged.' *Matthew* 8:12, 'But the children of the kingdom shall be cast out into outer darkness: there shall be weeping and gnashing of teeth.'

18-9. Cp. *Genesis* 2:7. But Tennyson also uses Sir William Jones's translation of the *Khelassut ul Akhbar* of Khondemeer. At the creation of Adam, Gabriel and the other angels were 'compassionating the earth's distress' when the earth feared it might be involved in any 'offence' caused by man; 'In the space of forty days, the clay was kneaded into form by the hands of the angels.' Jones's *Works* (1799) were at Somersby. It is Tennyson who links the angels' tears with the actual making of man.

THE PALACE OF ART

91 Published *1832*; much-revised in *1842*. Only a selection of the revisions is given below. R. C. Trench 'said, when we were at Trinity (Cambridge) together, "Tennyson, we cannot live in Art". This poem is the embodiment of my own belief that the Godlike life is with man and for man.' Tennyson had many sources or analogues. *Ecclesiastes* 2:1-17:

> I said in mine heart, Go to now, I will prove thee with mirth, therefore enjoy pleasure .. I made me great works; I builded me houses. I gathered me also silver and gold, and the peculiar treasure of kings ... And whatsoever mine eyes desired I kept not from

91 them, I withheld not my heart from any joy ... Then I looked on all the works that my hands had wrought, and on the labour that I had laboured to do: and, behold, all was vanity and vexation of spirit, and there was no profit under the sun ... Therefore I hated life.

Luke 12:19-20, 'And I will say to my soul, Soul, thou hast much goods laid up for many years; take thine ease, eat, drink, and be merry. But God said unto him, Thou fool, this night thy soul shall be required of thee.' H. N. Fairchild suggested the influence of Shelley's *Queen Mab*, II, 56-64 (1813): the Fairy

> ... pointed to the gorgeous dome,
> 'This is a wondrous sight
> And mocks all human grandeur;
> But, were it virtue's only meed, to dwell
> In a celestial palace, all resigned
> To pleasurable impulses, immured
> Within the prison of itself, the will
> Of changeless Nature would be unfulfilled.
> Learn to make others happy.'

The stanza-form was independently developed; Tennyson approached it in *The Poet* (p. 43), and cp. *A Dream of Fair Women* (p. 118), but it is that of Henry Vaughan's *They are all gone into the world of light* (1655).

15-6. Hallam Tennyson commented: 'The shadow of Saturn thrown on the luminous ring, though the planet revolves in ten and a half hours, appears to be motionless.' After line 16, *1832* had:

> 'And richly feast within thy palacehall,
> Like to the dainty bird that sups,
> Lodged in the lustrous crown-imperial,
> Draining the honeycups.'

92 27. *sonorous:* sonórous.

30. *broad verge:* 'a broad horizon' (Tennyson).

37-47. In *1832*:

> Huge incense-urns along the balustrade,
> Hollowed of solid amethyst,
> Each with a different odour fuming, made
> The air a silver mist.

NOTES

92 Far-off 'twas wonderful to look upon
    Those sumptuous towers between the gleam
Of that great foambow trembling in the sun,
    And the argent incense-steam;

And round the terraces and round the walls,
    While day sank lower or rose higher,
To see those rails with all their knobs and balls,

93 61 ff. Resembling the scenes depicted in James Thomson's *Castle of Indolence*, I, xxxvi ff. (1748), where 'the rooms with costly tapestry were hung'.

65-8. In *1832*:
    Some were all dark and red, a glimmering land
        Lit with a low round moon,
    Among brown rocks a man upon the sand
        Went weeping all alone.

69-80. In *1832*:
Some showed far-off thick woods mounted with towers,
    Nearer, a flood of mild sunshine
Poured on long walks and lawns and beds and bowers
    Trellised with bunchy vine.

80. 'The underside of the olive leaf is white' (Tennyson).

94 83. Cp. Keats, *To Autumn* 25 (1820): 'barred clouds'.

86-7. From Virgil's *somno mollior herba* (*Eclogues*, VII, 45).

93. *1832* had a note:
When I first conceived the plan of the Palace of Art, I intended to have introduced both sculptures and paintings into it; but it is the most difficult of all things to *devise* a statue in verse. Judge whether I have succeeded in the statues of Elijah and Olympias.

One was the Tishbite whom the raven fed,
    As when he stood on Carmel-steeps,
With one arm stretched out bare, and mocked and said,
    'Come cry aloud—he sleeps.'

Tall, eager, lean and strong, his cloak windborne
    Behind, his forehead heavenly-bright
From the clear marble pouring glorious scorn,
    Lit as with inner light.

NOTES

94 One was Olympias: the floating snake
   Rolled round her ancles, round her waist
Knotted, and folded once about her neck,
    Her perfect lips to taste

Round by the shoulder moved: she seeming blythe
   Declined her head: on every side
The dragon's curves melted and mingled with
    The woman's youthful pride

Of rounded limbs.

1842 dropped this. See lines 186-92 note. Elijah, from *1 Kings* 18:27. 'Olympias was the mother of Alexander the Great, and devoted to the Orphic rites' (Tennyson).
95. Tennyson commented: 'The Parisian jewellers apply graduated degrees of heat to the sardonyx, by which the original colour is changed to various colours. They imitate thus, among other things, bunches of grapes with green tendrils.'
96. After this line, *1832* had:
    Or Venus in a snowy shell alone,
       Deepshadowed in the glassy brine,
    Moonlike glowed double on the blue, and shone
       A naked shape divine.
97-100. St Cecilia, patroness of church music.
101-4. The Mahometan paradise.
105-8. In *1832*:
    Or that deepwounded child of Pendragon
       Mid misty woods on sloping greens
    Dozed in the valley of Avilion,
       Tended by crownèd queens.

Cp. this account of the death of King Arthur (son of Uther Pendragon) with *Morte d'Arthur* (p. 145).
95 109-16. In *1832*:
    Or blue-eyed Kriemhilt from a craggy hold,
       Athwart the lightgreen rows of vine,
    Poured blazing hoards of Nibelungen gold,
       Down to the gulfy Rhine.

The princess Kriemhild, in the heroic epic, *Nibelungenlied*.

NOTES

95 111. The nymph is 'Egeria, who gave the laws to Numa Pompilius' (Tennyson).

113. *engrail'd:* 'heraldic term for serrated' (Hallam Tennyson). *peaky:* Tennyson's is the earliest usage in the *Oxford English Dictionary*.

115. *Cama:* 'The Hindu God of young love, son of Brahma' (Tennyson).

117-20. Jupiter seduced Europa by taking the shape of a bull, and then carrying her into the sea. *1832* followed this stanza with:

> He thro' the streaming crystal swam, and rolled
>   Ambrosial breaths that seemed to float
> In lightwreathed curls. She from the ripple cold
>   Updrew her sandalled foot.

121-4. The youth Ganymede was carried away to be the cupbearer of the gods.

126. *Caucasian:* Indo-European, Western (an early 19th-century sense).

128. After this line, *1832* had the following, referring to the theory that the embryo passes through the evolutionary stages that culminate in man:

> So that my soul beholding in her pride
>   All these, from room to room did pass;
> And all things that she saw, she multiplied,
>   A manyfacèd glass;
>
> And, being both the sower and the seed,
>   Remaining in herself became
> All that she saw, Madonna, Ganymede,
>   Or the Asiatic dame—
>
> Still changing, as a lighthouse in the night
>   Changeth athwart the gleaming main,
> From red to yellow, yellow to pale white,
>   Then back to red again.
>
> 'From change to change four times within the womb
>   The brain is moulded,' she began,
> 'So through all phases of all thought I come
>   Into the perfect man.

NOTES

95   'All nature widens upward: evermore
      The simpler essence lower lies.
  More complex is more perfect, owning more
      Discourse, more widely wise.

  'I take possession of men's minds and deeds.
      I live in all things great and small.
  I dwell apart, holding no forms of creeds,
      But contemplating all.'

In revision, some of these lines became lines 209-12.

96 137. Homer.

137-64. In *1832*:

  And underneath freshcarved in cedarwood,
      Somewhat alike in form and face,
  The Genii of every climate stood,
      All brothers of one race:

  Angels who sway the seasons by their art,
      And mould all shapes in earth and sea;
  And with great effort build the human heart
      From earliest infancy.

  And in the sunpierced Oriel's coloured flame
      Immortal Michael Angelo
  Looked down, bold Luther, largebrowed Verulam,
      The king of those who know.

  Cervantes, the bright face of Calderon,
      Robed David touching holy strings,
  The Halicarnasseän, and alone,
      Alfred the flower of kings,

  Isaïah with fierce Ezekiel,
      Swarth Moses by the Coptic sea,
  Plato, Petrarca, Livy, and Raphaël,
      And eastern Confutzee:

164. *1832* note: '*Il maëstro di color chi sanno*—Dante, *Inferno* III'. (In fact, IV, 131: *vidi 'l maestro di color che sanno*.) Tennyson remarked that this praise of Francis Bacon (Lord Verulam) was Dante's praise of Aristotle.

NOTES

97 171. *Memnon:* the statue that made music when touched by the sun.
181-3. In *1832*:
As some rich tropic mountain, that infolds
   All change, from flats of scattered palms
Sloping thro' five great zones of climate, holds
     His head in snows and calms—

Full of her own delight and nothing else,
   My vainglorious, gorgeous soul
Sat throned between the shining oriels,
     In pomp beyond control;

With piles of flavorous fruits in basket-twine
   Of gold, upheapèd, crushing down
Muskscented blooms—all taste—grape, gourd or pine—
     In bunch, or singlegrown—

Our growths, and such as brooding Indian heats
   Make out of crimson blossoms deep,
Ambrosial pulps and juices, sweets from sweets
     Sunchanged, when seawinds sleep.

With graceful chalices of curious wine,
   Wonders of art—and costly jars,
And bossèd salvers. Ere young night divine
186. *anadems:* 'crowns' (Tennyson). Hallam Tennyson compared Shelley, *Adonais* 94 (1821): 'the wreath upon him, like an anadem'.
186-92. In *1832:*
     She lit white streams of dazzling gas,
       And soft and fragrant flames of precious oils
          In moons of purple glass

     Ranged on the fretted woodwork to the ground.
       Thus her intense untold delight,
     In deep or vivid colour, smell and sound,
         Was flattered day and night.
1832 continued with a note (omitted in *1842*):
'If the Poem were not already too long, I should have

NOTES

97 inserted in the text the following stanzas, expressive of the joy wherewith the soul contemplated the results of astronomical experiment. In the centre of the four quadrangles rose an immense tower.

> Hither, when all the deep unsounded skies
>   Shuddered with silent stars, she clomb,
> And as with optic glasses her keen eyes
>   Pierced thro' the mystic dome,
>
> Regions of lucid matter taking forms,
>   Brushes of fire, hazy gleams,
> Clusters and beds of worlds, and bee-like swarms
>   Of suns, and starry streams.
>
> She saw the snowy poles of moonless Mars,
>   That marvellous round of milky light
> Below Orion, and those double stars
>   Whereof the one more bright
>
> Is circled by the other, etc.'

The allusion is to the theory of the nebulous matter diffused through the universe; 'lucid', 'matter', and 'forms' are all scientific terms. Of these incorporations (here and at line 93) in *1832*, the reviewer J. W. Croker was most contemptuous, and he spoke of Tennyson's 'ingenious device . . . for reconciling the rigour of criticism with the indulgence of parental partiality.'

188. 'Gems hollowed out for lamps' (Hallam Tennyson).

98 193-204. These lines were not in *1832*; they did not reach their final form till *1851*.

205-8. These lines were not in *1832*, but added in *1842*.

209-12. These lines were not in *1832*; a version of them was added in *1842*, but they did not reach their final form till *1850*.

219-20. *Acts* 12:21-3, 'And upon a set day Herod, arrayed in royal apparel, sat upon his throne, and made an oration unto them. And the people gave a shout, saying, It is the voice of a god, and not of a man. And immediately the angel of the Lord smote him, because

NOTES

98 he gave not God the glory: and he was eaten of worms' and gave up the ghost.'

99 223. Tennyson pointed out that this was from Arthur Hallam's *Theodicaea Novissima* (1831): 'God's election, with whom alone rest the abysmal secrets of personality.' Cp. *Psalm* 139: 1-4, 'O Lord, thou hast searched me and known me . . .'

227. As at the feast of Belshazzar (*Daniel* 5), who 'hast praised the gods of silver, and gold, of brass, iron, wood, and stone, which see not, nor hear, nor know: and the God in whose hand thy breath is, and whose are all thy ways, hast thou not glorified . . . This is the interpretation of the thing: MENE; God hath numbered thy kingdom, and finished it. TEKEL; Thou art weighed in the balances, and art found wanting. PERES; Thy kingdom is divided.'

232. After this line, *1832* had:
'Who hath drawn dry the fountains of delight,
   That from my deep heart everywhere
Moved in my blood and dwelt, as power and might
   Abode in Sampson's hair?

239. Cp. another guilty soul, that of Faustus, in Marlowe's *Dr Faustus* 1386-8: 'I would weep, but the devil draws in my tears. Gush forth blood, instead of tears.' Also Shelley, *Prologue to Hellas* 88 (1822): 'Whose pores wept tears of blood.'

241. Beckford's *Vathek* (1786), which has a palace, mentions spirits with hearts like Soliman, 'discerned through his bosom, which was as transparent as crystal, his heart enveloped in flames.' But when Arthur Coleridge suggested this influence to Tennyson, he replied: 'No, merely spectral visions' (*Tennyson and His Friends*, ed. H. Tennyson, 1911, p. 264).

242. *fretted:* 'worm-fretted' (Tennyson).

100 255. Tennyson commented: 'Some old writer calls the Heavens "the Circumstance" . . . Here it is more or less a play on the word.' Cp. Milton's astronomy: 'the hollow Universal Orb', *Paradise Lost*, VII, 257.

257. Probably referring to the scorpion's stinging itself to death when surrounded by fire. Tennyson calls a

NOTES

100 scorpion a 'serpent' of the mind in an early poem, *The Passions* (1827). Cp. Byron, *The Giaour* 422-3 (1813):
>The Mind, that broods o'er guilty woes,
>Is like the Scorpion girt by fire.

LADY CLARA VERE DE VERE

101 Published *1842*, but 'written early' (Hallam Tennyson). Probably about 1835 like *Lady Clare* (p. 256), slightly later than *The Lord of Burleigh* (p. 259). 'A dramatic poem drawn from no particular character' (Tennyson).

THE MAY QUEEN

104 Published *1832*, the *Conclusion* being added in *1842*. 'An early poem written in Lincolnshire' (Hallam Tennyson).

[New-Year's Eve]

106 12. *Charles's Wain:* the constellation, the Great Bear.

[Conclusion]

109 17. From *1842* to *1848*, 'taught' and 'show'd' had been transposed; Tennyson did not altogether remove an unhelpful ambiguity by this change in *1850*.

18. The foolish virgins, *Matthew* 25:1-13.

110 21. *death-watch:* 'a beetle ... whose ticking is supposed to forebode death' (Tennyson).

111 60. *Job* 3:17, 'There the wicked cease from troubling; and the weary be at rest.' Contrast the context of Job's bitter wish that he had died at birth.

THE LOTOS-EATERS

112 Published *1832*. The important revisions in *1842* were the addition of lines 114-32, and the re-writing of lines 150-73. The main source was *Odyssey*, IX, 82-104. Loeb translation:

>We set foot on the land of the Lotus-eaters, who eat a flowery food ... So they went straightway and mingled

NOTES

112 with the Lotus-eaters, and the Lotus-eaters did not plan death for my comrades, but gave them of the lotus to taste. And whosoever of them ate of the honey-sweet fruit of the lotus, had no longer any wish to bring back word or to return, but there they were fain to abide among the Lotus-eaters, feeding on the lotus, and forgetful of their homeward way. These men, therefore, I brought back perforce to the ships, weeping.

Tennyson was also influenced by Washington Irving's life of Columbus (1828), which described the idyllic life on Haiti. Spenser was the major influence on the style and tone; note the stanza-form, and in particular the cave of Morpheus (*Faerie Queene*, I, i, xli); the 'Idle lake' and its enervating island (II, vi, x); the blandishments of Despair (I, ix, xl); and the mermaids and the Bower of Bliss (II, xii, xxxii). There are a few touches from James Thomson's Spenserian imitation, *The Castle of Indolence*, I, v-vi.

3. Tennyson commented: ' "The strand" was, I think, my first reading, but the no rhyme of "land" and "land" was lazier.'

8. Tennyson said that this line, like line 11, was 'taken from the waterfall at Gavarnie, in the Pyrenees, when I was 20 or 21.'

23. *galingale:* a herb.

24. Lucretius, *De Rerum Natura*, III, 945: *eadem sunt omnia semper.* See line 155 note.

113 34. Cp. the ghosts in *Aeneid*, VI, 492: *pars tollere vocem exiguam.*

51. Tennyson commented: ' "tiërd" '; but he later said: 'making the word neither monosyllabic nor disyllabic, but a dreamy child of the two'.

53-6. The effect of the rhymes, and the subject-matter, suggest the end of Marvell's *Thyrsis and Dorinda* (1659), which—after 44 lines of couplets—concludes:

> Then let us give Carillo charge o' th Sheep,
> And thou and I'le pick poppies and them steep
> In wine, and drink on't even till we weep,
> So shall we smoothly pass away in sleep.

114 60-9. Cp. *Faerie Queene*, II, vi, xvii, on the relaxing island:

> Why then dost thou, O man, that of them all
>   Art Lord, and eke of nature Soveraine,
>   Wilfully make thy selfe a wretched thrall,
>   And wast thy joyous houres in needlesse paine,
>   Seeking for daunger and adventures vaine?

70-83. For Nature's effortlessness, cp. *Faerie Queene* (again the island, II, vi, xv):

> Behold, O man, that toilesome paines doest take,
>   The flowres, the fields, and all that pleasant growes...
>   They spring, they bud, they blossome fresh and faire...
>   Yet no man for them taketh paines or care,
> Yet no man to them can his carefull paines compare.

80. Cp. *Psalm* 21:4, 'He asked life of thee, and thou gavest it him, even length of days for ever and ever.'

84-5. Cp. *Aeneid*, IV, 451: *taedet caeli convexa tueri*.

86. A commonplace, but note the context of Spenser's 'Death is the end of woes': Despair's easeful seductions, I, ix, xlvii. Lines 96-8 below are tinged with Spenser's stanza xl:

> Sleepe after toyle, port after stormie seas,
> Ease after warre, death after life does greatly please

115 114-32. These lines were not in *1832*, but added in *1842*.

116-9. A life-long preoccupation of Tennyson's. It is the theme of *In Memoriam* XC (1850) and of *Enoch Arden* (1864).

116 120-1. Cp. *Odyssey*, XI, 115, the wooing of Penelope in Ithaca: 'proud men that devour thy livelihood' (Loeb).

133. *amaranth:* 'the immortal flower of legend' (Tennyson), as in Milton's Heaven, *Paradise Lost*, III, 352.

moly: 'the sacred herb of mystical power, used as a charm by Odysseus against Circe' (Tennyson), mentioned in *Comus* 636.

142. *acanthus:* a Greek plant.

117 150-73. In *1832*:

> We have had enough of motion,
>   Weariness and wild alarm,

NOTES

117
Tossing on the tossing ocean,
Where the tuskèd seahorse walloweth
In a stripe of grassgreen calm,
At noon tide beneath the lee;
And the monstrous narwhale swalloweth
His foamfountains in the sea.
Long enough the winedark wave our weary
 bark did carry.
This is lovelier and sweeter,
Men of Ithaca, this is meeter,
In the hollow rosy vale to tarry,
Like a dreamy Lotos-eater, a delirious
 Lotos-eater!
We will eat the Lotos, sweet
As the yellow honeycomb,
In the valley some, and some
On the ancient heights divine;
And no more roam,
On the loud hoar foam,
To the melancholy home
At the limit of the brine,
The little isle of Ithaca, beneath the day's
 decline.
We'll lift no more the shattered oar,
No more unfurl the straining sail;
With the blissful Lotos-eaters pale
We will abide in the golden vale
Of the Lotos-land, till the Lotos fail;
We will not wander more.
Hark! how sweet the horned ewes bleat
On the solitary steeps,
And the merry lizard leaps,
And the foamwhite waters pour;
And the dark pine weeps,
And the lithe vine creeps,
And the heavy melon sleeps
On the level of the shore:
Oh! islanders of Ithaca, we will not wander more.
Surely, surely slumber is more sweet than toil,
 the shore

NOTES

117 Than labour in the ocean, and rowing with the oar.

Oh! islanders of Ithaca, we will return no more.
155-70. The Gods are based on Lucretius's account of Epicureanism. Hallam Tennyson compared III, 18-22. In Loeb translation:

> Before me appear the gods in their majesty, and their peaceful abodes, which no winds ever shake nor clouds besprinkle with rain, which no snow congealed by the bitter frost mars with its white fall, but the air ever cloudless encompasses them and laughs with its light spread wide abroad.

Cp. Tennyson's poem *Lucretius* 109-10 (1868): 'Nor sound of human sorrow mounts to mar / Their sacred everlasting calm!'

A DREAM OF FAIR WOMEN

118 Published *1832*. In one manuscript, it has the title *The Legend of Fair Women*, which brings out the (slight) affinities with Chaucer's *Legend of Good Women* (see lines 2-3). As Tennyson commented, of Chaucer's women 'Cleopatra alone appears in my poem.'

1. In *1832* this opening was preceded by four stanzas:

As when a man, that sails in a balloon,
  Downlooking sees the solid shining ground
Stream from beneath him in the broad blue noon,—
  Tilth, hamlet, mead and mound:

And takes his flags and waves them to the mob,
  That shout below, all faces turned to where
Glows rubylike the far-up crimson globe,
  Filled with a finer air:

So, lifted high, the Poet at his will
  Lets the great world flit from him, seeing all,
Higher thro' secret splendours mounting still,
  Selfpoised, nor fears to fall,

Hearing apart the echoes of his fame.
  While I spoke thus, the seedsman, memory,
Sowed my deepfurrowed thought with many a name,
  Whose glory will not die.

NOTES

118 3. Arthur Hallam had called Chaucer 'our beautiful morning star,' echoing John Denham: 'Old Chaucer, like the morning Star' (*On Cowley* 1, 1645).

5. Hallam Tennyson compared *Faerie Queene*, IV, ii, xxxii: 'Dan Chaucer, well of English undefiled.'

16. Following this line, *1832* had two stanzas which anticipate the concerns with womanhood in Tennyson's *The Princess* (1847):

> In every land I thought that, more or less,
>   The stronger sterner nature overbore
> The softer, uncontrolled by gentleness
>   And selfish evermore:
>
> And whether there were any means whereby,
>   In some far aftertime, the gentler mind
> Might reassume its just and full degree
>   Of rule among mankind.

18. *the hollow dark*: the phrase occurs in Keats, *The Fall of Hyperion*, I, 455 (not published, though, till 1856), which suggests that it is romantic poetic diction.

27. *tortoise*: 'the "testudo" of ancient war. Warriors with shields upheld on their heads' (Tennyson).

119 52. Cp. Shelley, *Queen Mab*, IX, 175: 'the transient gulf-dream of a startling sleep'.

54. Tennyson said: 'The wood is the Past'; and he referred to lines 83-4, 'i.e. time backward'.

120 61-4. 'Refers to the early past' (Tennyson).

67. Cp. *Isaiah* 60:2, 'The darkness shall cover the earth, and gross darkness the people.'

77-80. Cp. *Song*, which immediately followed this poem in *1832* but which Tennyson did not reprint:

> Who can say
> Why Today
> Tomorrow will be yesterday?
> Who can tell
> Why to smell
> The violet, recalls the dewy prime
> Of youth and buried time?
> The cause is nowhere found in rhyme.

NOTES

121 87. Helen of Troy, 'daughter of Zeus and Leda' (Tennyson).

100. 'Iphigenia, who was sacrificed by Agamemnon to Artemis' (Tennyson). The sacrifice was to bring the winds that would carry Agamemnon's ships to Troy.

107. Hallam Tennyson commented: 'No doubt my father had in his mind the famous picture by Timanthes, *The Sacrifice of Iphigeneia*.'

113-6. The final version was adopted in *1853*. From *1832* to *1851*, it read:

> 'The tall masts quivered as they lay afloat,
>   The temples and the people and the shore.
> One drew a sharp knife thro' my tender throat
>   Slowly,—and nothing more.'

'I thought [it] too ghastly realistic,' said Tennyson. But it had been ridiculed by the reviewer J. W. Croker in 1833: 'what touching simplicity—what pathetic resignation—he cut my throat—"*nothing more!*" One might indeed ask, "What *more*" she would have?'

122 117-20. Adapting the words of Helen in *Iliad*, VI, 345 ff: 'I would that on the day when first my mother gave me birth an evil storm-wind had borne me away to some mountain or to the wave of the loud-resounding sea, where the wave might have swept me away or ever these things came to pass' (Loeb translation).

127. Tennyson commented: 'I was thinking of Shakespeare's Cleopatra:

>   Think of me
> That am with Phoebus' amorous pinches black.
>   (*Antony and Cleopatra*, I, v, 27-8).

Millais has made a mulatto of her in his illustration. I know perfectly well that she was a Greek. "Swarthy" merely means sunburnt.'

128. Cp. *Coriolanus*, II, ii, 96: 'Browbound with the oak.'

123 141-4. In *1832*:

> 'By him great Pompey dwarfs and suffers pain,
>   A mortal man before immortal Mars;
> The glories of great Julius lapse and wane,
>   And shrink from suns to stars.

NOTES

123 146. *Canopus:* 'in the constellation of Argo' (Tennyson). Known as 'the star of Egypt'. Canopus was also the name of a city of the Lower Egypt 'remarkable for lewdness' (Charles Rollin's *Ancient History*, 1789 translation, of which a copy was at Somersby).

149-52. Cp. *Antony and Cleopatra*, IV, viii, 14-16:
Chain mine armed neck; leap thou, attire and all,
Through proof of harness to my heart, and there
Ride on the pants triumphing!

161-4. Tennyson compared *non humilis mulier* (Horace's *Odes*, I, xxxvii, 32), on the death of Cleopatra.

181-4, 216-20. Adapted from lines originally written for *Margaret* (see p. 128). Jephtha's daughter was sacrificed by him because of his vow to God: 'If thou shalt without fail deliver the children of Ammon into mine hands, Then it shall be, that whatsoever cometh forth of the doors of my house to meet me, when I return in peace from the children of Ammon, shall surely be the Lord's, and I will offer it up for a burnt offering' (*Judges* 11: 30-1).

225. Hallam Tennyson compared Horace's *Odes*, I, xxxiv, 5-6: *Diespiter / igni corusco nubila dividens*.

126 242-4. Cp. *Job* 38:7, 'When the morning stars sang together, and all the sons of God shouted for joy.'

243. Tennyson compared *Comus* 313: 'every bosky bourn'.

251. Rosamond de Clifford, the mistress of Henry II, was said to have been poisoned by Queen Eleanor.

127 259. *Fulvia:* 'wife of Antony, named by Cleopatra as a parallel to Eleanor' (Tennyson).

263. *The captain:* 'Venus, the star of morning' (Tennyson).

266. Tennyson commented: 'Margaret Roper, daughter of Sir Thomas More, who is said to have transferred his headless corpse from the Tower to Chelsea Church. Sir Thomas More's head had remained for fourteen days on London Bridge after his execution, and was about to be thrown into the Thames to make room for others, when she claimed and bought it . . . [Her] vault was opened, and it is stated that she was found in her coffin, clasping

NOTES

127 the small leaden box which inclosed her father's head.'
269-72. Tennyson commented: 'Eleanor, wife of Edward I, went with him to the Holy Land (1269), where he was stabbed at Acre with a poisoned dagger. She sucked the poison from the wound.'

MARGARET

128 Published *1832*; from *1870*, among 'Juvenilia'. It is a companion-poem to *Adeline* (p. 40); see line 48.
21. Cp. Milton's *Il Penseroso* 72: 'stooping thro' a fleecy cloud'.

129 25-6. The notion that gunfire stills the waves.
34. Richard I, a troubadour and hero of troubadours, was imprisoned in Dürenstein on the Danube in 1192-3.
35. After this line, an early manuscript had:

> Or when the Gileadite returned,
> Whether Jephtha's daughter mourned
> Two moons beside the heavy flow
> Of torrent brooks in purple glens
> Of Judah, leaving far below,
> Leaving the fruitful olive plains,
> Leaving the hope of her bride bower
> In royal Mizpeh's battled tower.

Tennyson adapted these lines as *A Dream of Fair Women* 181 ff. (p. 124).
37. *Chatelet:* for Chastelard, executed in 1563 for importuning Mary Queen of Scots.

130 61. *leavy:* Tennyson compared *Much Ado*, II, iii, 72: 'since summer first was leavy'.

THE BLACKBIRD

130 Published *1842*. Written about 1833 (Hallam Tennyson). The stanza-form is that of *In Memoriam*.
5. *espaliers:* trees trained on lattices. *standards:* erect trees.
7. *black-hearts:* cultivated cherries.
12. *jenneting:* an early apple.

THE DEATH OF THE OLD YEAR

131 Published *1832*.

NOTES

TO J.S.

133 Published *1832*. Tennyson noted: 'Addressed to James Spedding, the biographer of Bacon. His brother was Edward Spedding, a friend of mine, who died in his youth.' Edward died 24 Aug. 1832. The belief that the dead 'sleep sweetly' is discussed in *In Memoriam* XLIII: 'If Sleep and Death be truly one.' For the opening of *To J.S.*, Tennyson adapted the opening (all he had written) of a poem which he had already sent to James Spedding ('Dear friend'); this had been quoted by Spedding in a letter to his brother Edward in 1831, so will have been particularly appropriate.

134 19-24. Tennyson commented: 'The death of my father', in March 1831.

45-8. Cp. *In Memoriam*, VI, 1-4:
> One writes, that 'Other friends remain,'
>   That 'Loss is common to the race'—
> And common is the commonplace,
> And vacant chaff well meant for grain.

135 49-52. Cp. Henry Vaughan's poem on the same theme, *They are all gone into the world of light:*
> Their very memory is fair and bright . . .
> Or those faint beams in which this hill is drest,
>   After the Sun's remove.

67. In *1832*: 'Altho' to calm you I would take'. This hyperbole aroused Edward FitzGerald's scepticism; he wrote in his copy of *1842* (Trinity College): 'I used to ask if this was not *un peu trop fort*. I think it's altered or omitted in future Editions. It is all rather affected.'

76. Cp. *Paradise Lost*, IV, 791: 'asleep secure of harme'.

'YOU ASK ME, WHY, THO' ILL AT EASE'

136 Published *1842*. Written about 1833 (Hallam Tennyson); it is one of Tennyson's many political poems of this date (the Reform Bill, 1832), including the two that immediately follow. Tennyson feared the results of the political agitation which had led to the Bill.

NOTES

'OF OLD SAT FREEDOM ON THE HEIGHTS'

137 Published *1842*. Written 1833 (Hallam Tennyson). See the preceding and succeeding political poems of this date. Tennyson draws on the traditional association of freedom and the mountains, as in Milton's 'mountain-nymph, sweet Liberty' (also in Wordsworth and Coleridge).

15. Tennyson commented: 'Like Zeus with his *trisulca fulmina*, the thunderbolts.'

'LOVE THOU THY LAND, WITH LOVE FAR-BROUGHT'

138 Published *1842*. Written about 1833. See the two preceding political poems of this date.

12. *lime:* to catch a bird with quicklime.

17-8. Tennyson later adapted these lines for *In Memoriam: Prologue* 25-6:

> Let knowledge grow from more to more,
> But more of reverence in us dwell.

139 27. *guerdon:* to reward.

33. *That:* i.e. the law.

37-40. G. R. Potter has warned against taking this as Darwinian evolution, since there is no suggestion that one develops from the other.

140 68. *the rising wind:* 'of revolutionary change' (Hallam Tennyson).

76. The path between battle-lines, *Iliad*, VIII, 553: so translated by Tennyson in 1863.

141 95. *Earn:* glean (Yorkshire dialect).

THE GOOSE

141 Published *1842*. Written 1833. It is probably an attack on radicalism and the Reform Bill agitation; see the three preceding political poems of this date. The political fable has an 18th-century air; cp. Thomas Yalden's *The Blind Woman and Her Doctors* (1702):

> Like a stuck pig the woman star'd
> And up and down she run:
> With naked house and walls quite scar'd,
> She found herself undone.

NOTES

THE EPIC

143 Published *1842*; from *1853*, among 'English Idyls'. It was probably written in 1837-8. Edward FitzGerald said that it was provided as an introduction to *Morte d'Arthur* 'to anticipate or excuse the "faint Homeric echoes" ', and 'to give a reason for telling an old-world tale.' He compared the frame of *The Day-Dream* (p. 228). This frame for *Morte d'Arthur* (both introduction here, and conclusion—see p. 153) did not accompany the poem in Tennyson's trial-edition of *1842*. For Leigh Hunt's strictures on Tennyson's evasive framing, see *Godiva* (p. 350). *The Epic* hints at Tennyson's ambitions for an epic on Arthur, though the *Morte* was to be the last, not the penultimate book (line 41). The poem opened the second volume of *1842*.

15. An inquiry was set up in 1835; the Ecclesiastical Commissioners Act was passed in 1836, and revised in 1840-1.

16. Geology was held to constitute a threat to the Bible long before Darwin published *The Origin of Species* in 1859.

144 50-1. Tennyson describes his own reading, as Fitz-Gerald observed.

MORTE D'ARTHUR

145 Published *1842*; from *1853*, among 'English Idyls'. It was written 1833-4 (*Memoir*, i, 129, 138), under the shock of Arthur Hallam's death, the news of which reached Tennyson on 1 October 1833. Cp. *Merlin and the Gleam* 77-80 (1889):

> Arthur had vanish'd
> I knew not whither,
> The king who loved me.
> And cannot die.

The poem is Tennyson's first major Arthurian work, later incorporated in full into the *Idylls of the King* as *The Passing of Arthur* (1869), where it was preceded by 169 lines and followed by 29 lines. Cp. *The Palace of Art* 105-8, *1832* text:

> Or that deepwounded child of Pendragon

NOTES

145
      Mid misty woods on sloping greens
      Dozed in the valley of Avilion,
        Tended by crownèd queens.

It is based closely on Malory's *Morte d'Arthur*, XXI, 4-5 (1484). Quotations are from the 3-vol. edition of 1816, of which a copy was at Somersby; Caxton's numbering is given below. For the Arthurian traditions, see R. S. Loomis, *The Development of Arthurian Romance* (1963). The poem is introduced in *The Epic* as including 'Homeric echoes'. Among these may be noted: set epithets, and set lines introducing and closing speeches; the words of one speaker being quoted by another; repetition of words and lines; and soliloquies. John Sterling's adverse comments on *Morte d'Arthur* in the *Quarterly Review* discouraged Tennyson from proceeding with his epic (E. F. Shannon, *Tennyson and the Reviewers*, 1952, p. 91). Sterling said that the poem's 'inferiority' was not compensated for by any 'stronger human interest'; 'the miraculous legend of "Excalibur" does not come very near to us, and as reproduced by any modern writer must be a mere ingenious exercise of fancy.' Shannon (p. 95) also quotes Leigh Hunt's criticisms: 'It treats the modes and feelings of one generation in the style of another, always a fatal thing, unless it be reconciled with something of self-banter in the course of the poem itself, or the mixture of light with grave.'

1. One of the 'Homeric echoes': *Iliad*, VI, 1; XVII, 384. Cp. Tennyson's translation: 'All day the men contend in grievous war,' *Achilles Over the Trench* 9 (1877).

4. *Lyonnesse*: 'the country of legend that lay between Cornwall and the Scilly Islands' (Tennyson).

5-12. Malory, XXI: 'And the noble King Arthur fell in a swoon to the earth. And there he swooned often times. And Sir Lucan and Sir Bedivere oftentimes heaved him up, and so weakly they led him between them both unto a little chapel not far from the sea side.'

14-7. Malory, XX, 9: 'For I have now lost the fairest fellowship of noble knights that ever held christian King together.'

NOTES

145 23. Malory, XXI, 7: 'Some men yet say in many parts of England that King Arthur is not dead, but by the will of our Lord in another place. And men say that he will come again.'

28-33. Malory, I, 25: 'So they rode till they came to a lake, which was a fair water, and a broad, and in the midst of the lake King Arthur was ware of an arm, clothed in white samite, that held a fair sword in the hand.'

146 36-44. Malory, XXI (subsequent quotations from Malory, unless noted otherwise, run on consecutively without omissions): ' "Therefore take you Excalibur, my good sword, and go with it unto yonder water side, and when thou comest there, I charge thee throw my sword into that water, and come again and tell me what thou shalt see there." "My lord," said Sir Bedivere, "your command shall be done, and lightly bring you word again." '

45-65. Malory: 'And so Sir Bedivere departed, and by the way he beheld that noble sword, where the pomel and the haft were all of precious stones, and then he said to himself: "If I throw this rich sword into the water, thereof shall never come good, but harm and loss." And then Sir Bedivere hid Excalibur under a tree, and as soon as he might he came again unto King Arthur, and said he had been at the water, and had thrown the sword into the water.'

60. Tennyson compared *Aeneid*, IV, 285: *atque animum nunc huc celerem, nunc dividit illuc*. From *Iliad*, I, 188.

61. G. G. Loane compared Pope's *Iliad*, IV, 570: 'In act to throw; but cautious, look'd around.'

147 66-81. Malory: ' "What sawest thou there?" said the King. "Sir," said he, "I saw nothing but waves and wind." "That is untruly said of thee," said King Arthur, "therefore go thou lightly and do my command, as thou art to me lief and dear, spare not but throw it in." '

82-112. Malory: 'Then Sir Bedivere returned again, and took the sword in his hand; and then he thought it

329

NOTES

147 sin and shame to throw away that noble sword. And so after he hid the sword, and returned again, and told to the King that he had been at the water, and done his command.'

148 104. The friendly sorceress of Malory, I, 25 (out of the sequence): ' "That is the *Lady of the Lake*," said Merlin, "and within that lake is a rock, and therein is as fair a place [palace] as any is on earth, and richly beseen." '

105-6. Cp. Pope's *Iliad*, XVIII, 468-72 (1720), where Vulcan is about to make the shield of Achilles:

Chains, bracelets, pendants, all their toys I wrought.
Nine years kept secret in the dark abode,
Secure I lay conceal'd from man and God.
Deep in a cavern'd rock my days were led;
The rushing ocean murmur'd o'er my head.

113-32. Malory: ' "What saw ye there," said the King. "Sir," said he, "I saw nothing but the water wap and the waves wan." "Ah traitor, untrue," said King Arthur, "now hast thou betrayed me two times, who would have wend [weened] that thou hast been unto me so self [lief] and dear, and thou art named a noble Knight, and wouldest betray me for the rich sword. But now, go again lightly, for thy long tarrying putteth me in great jeopardy of my life, for I have taken cold. And but if thou do as I command thee, and if ever I may see thee, I shall slay thee with mine own hands, for thou wouldest for my rich sword see me dead." '

149 133-66. Malory: 'Then Sir Bedivere departed, and went to the sword, and lightly took it up, and went to the water side, and there he bound the girdle about the hilt. And then he threw the sword into the water as far as he might, and there came an arm and an hand above the water, and met it and caught it, and so shook it thrice and brandished. And then the hand vanished away with the sword in the water. So Sir Bedivere came again to the King and told him what he had seen. "Alas," said the King, "help me from hence, for I dread me I have tarried over long." '

NOTES

149 139. Cp. this simile with Scott's *Lay of the Last Minstrel*, II, viii (1805), of which a copy was at Somersby:

> And red and bright the streamers light
>   Were dancing in the glowing north.
> So had he seen, in fair Castile,
>   The youth in glittering squadrons start,
> Sudden the flying jennet wheel,
>   And hurl the unexpected dart.
> He knew, by the streamers that shot so bright,
> That spirits were riding the northern light.

155. Tennyson compared *Odyssey*, III, 245.

150 167-203. Malory: 'Then Sir Bedivere took King Arthur upon his back, and so went with him to the water's side. And when they were at the water's side, even fast by the bank, hoved a little barge, with many fair ladies in it, and among them all was a Queen, and all they had black hoods, and they wept and shrieked when they saw King Arthur.'

183. *Larger than human: humano maior*, like the ghost of Romulus in Ovid, *Fasti*, II, 503. Cp. an unpublished poem which Tennyson wrote, also on the death of Arthur Hallam, *Hark! the dogs howl* 20-1:

> Larger than human passes by
> The shadow of the man I loved.

Also Tennyson's projected essay on Ghosts for the Cambridge 'Apostles': 'Forth issue from the inmost gloom the colossal Presences of the Past *majores humano*, some as they lived . . .'

192. Betty Miller compared Dryden, *Aeneis*, I, 10: 'And the long Glories of Majestick Rome.' Henry Boyd quoted Dryden's line prominently in his translation of Dante (1802), of which a copy was at Somersby.

151 204-25. Malory: ' "Now put me into the barge," said the King. And so he did softly, and there received him three Queens with great mourning, and so these three Queens set him down, and in one of their laps King Arthur laid his head. And then that Queen said: "Ah, dear brother, why have ye tarried so long from me. Alas, this wound on your head hath taken over much cold." '

NOTES

151 205-6. Malory, XXI, 6 (out of the sequence): 'Thus was he led away in a barge wherein were three Queens. That one was King Arthur's sister Morgan le Fay; the other was the Queen of Northgalis; and the third was the Queen of the Waste Lands.' Tennyson commented: 'Some may say that the three Queens are Faith, Hope, and Charity ... They are three of the noblest of women. They are also those three Graces, but they are much more.'

215. *greaves and cuisses:* armour for shin and thigh.

152 226-38. Malory: 'And so then they rowed from the land. And Sir Bedivere beheld all these ladies go from him, then Sir Bedivere cried: "Ah, my lord Arthur, what shall become of me now ye go from me, and leave me here alone among mine enemies."'

234-5. Malory, XIV, 2 (out of the sequence): 'Also Merlin made the *Round Table* in token of the roundness of the world. For by the *Round Table* is the world signified by right.'

239-64. Malory: ' "Comfort thyself," said King Arthur, "and do as well as thou mayest, for in me is no trust for to trust in, for I will into the vale of Avilion, for to heal me of my grievous wound. And if thou never hear more of me, pray for my soul." '

242. Tennyson commented: 'e.g. chivalry, by formalism of habit or by any other means.'

255. A commonplace found variously in Homer, Plato, Chaucer, Spenser, Milton—though none exactly parallels Tennyson's use.

259. 'From which he will some day return—the Isle of the Blest' (Tennyson).

153 265-72. Malory: 'But evermore the Queens and the ladies wept and shrieked, that it was pity for to hear them. And as soon as Sir Bedivere had lost sight of the barge, he wept and wailed, and so took the forest, and so he went all the night.'

270. *Revolving:* Miltonic; cp. 'much revolving', *Paradise Lost*, IV, 31; deriving from *Aeneid*, I, 305: *per noctem plurima volvens.*

NOTES

[The Epic]

282-3. Cp. *Hamlet*, I, i, 157-60:
> It faded on the crowing of the cock.
> Some say that ever 'gainst that season comes
> Wherein our Saviour's birth is celebrated
> This bird of dawning singeth all night long.

290-1. A traditional belief; cp. Shelley, *Hellas* 122: 'The truth of day lightens upon my dream.'

THE GARDENER'S DAUGHTER

Published *1842*; from *1853*, among 'English Idyls'. Written 1833-4 (*Memoir*, i, 103, and manuscript). Tennyson said that he had begun it at Cambridge. It brings together Tennyson's friendship for Arthur Hallam (the narrator's for Eustace), Hallam's love for Tennyson's sister Emily (Eustace's for Juliet), and Tennyson's love for Rosa Baring (the narrator's for Rose). Tennyson's love was still in its early stages, but Rosa's wealth and position were to be a bar, and Tennyson later expressed his disillusionment. He had thought of a series of 'Daughter' poems; see *The Miller's Daughter* (p. 71). Like Tennyson's other 'English Idyls', it is indebted to Theocritus, especially the 7th Idyll. Tennyson said: 'The centre of the poem, that passage describing the girl [lines 124-40], must be full and rich. The poem is so, to a fault, especially the descriptions of nature, for the lover is an artist, but, this being so, the central picture must hold its place'. Aubrey de Vere recorded of the poem (*Memoir*, i, 508-9):

> The poet had corrected it as carefully as he had originally composed it in his head, where he was in the habit of keeping more than one poem at a time before he wrote down any of them. I found him one day in James Spedding's rooms. He shewed me the MS and said, 'The corrections jostled each other, and the poem seemed out of gear. Spedding has just now remarked that it wants nothing but that this passage, forty lines, should be omitted. He is right.' It was omitted.

NOTES

154 As this suggests, the poem in its earlier drafts had been considerably longer.

6. Horace, *Epodes*, XI, 7-8: *per urbem ... fabula quanta fui*.

155 14. Shakespeare's Juliet has 'so light a foot', *Romeo and Juliet*, II, vi, 16.

47. Cp. Keats, *Ode to a Nightingale* 50: 'The murmurous haunt of flies on summer eves.'

156 67-9. Suggesting *Paradise Lost*, II, 400-2: balm, air, delicious. *fitful blast:* as twice in Shelley.

158 143. Cp. Eve in Paradise, where the flowers 'toucht by her fair tendance gladlier grew,' *Paradise Lost*, VIII, 47.

159 167. Titian's painting in Florence.

174-5. Cp. *The Talking Oak* 213: 'the swarming sound of life'.

160 181. Cp. *Love and Duty* 56: 'The slow sweet hours that bring us all things good.' Based on Theocritus XV, 104.

187. R. W. Rader has suggested that 'garden of Eden' hinted at Rosa Baring, since her home was that of her stepfather Arthur Eden.

162 263. Shelley has 'the baby Sleep', *Queen Mab*, I, 40.

DORA

163 Published *1842;* from *1853*, among 'English Idyls'. It was written by 1835 (*Memoir*, i, 151), and is unlikely to be earlier. Tennyson said that it was partly suggested by Mary Russell Mitford's story *Dora Creswell* (*Our Village*, iii, 1828), 'which is cheerful in tone, whereas this is sad'. From line 72 to the end, 'I have not followed Miss Mitford'; but this is misleading, since the scene with the wreath of flowers is in Mitford. After the dialogue, she cuts to the same place the next day when the farmer is playing with the child, watched by Dora and Mary, all now being well. Tennyson attempts a Wordsworthian simplicity, such as that of *Michael* (which he read to FitzGerald in 1835); he said that '*Dora*, being the tale of a nobly simple country girl, had to be told in the simplest possible poetical language, and therefore was one of the poems which gave most trouble' (*Memoir*, i, 151, 196). The best

NOTES

163 comparison of the poem with Wordsworth is by Matthew Arnold, in *On Translating Homer: Last Words* (1862), where he contrasts the genuine simplicity of Wordsworth with the 'semblance of simplicity,' the *simplesse* of *Dora*.
8-14. H. A. Mason has pointed out the Biblical phrasing: 'There came a day when'; 'called his son and said ... before I die ... now therefore', cp. *Genesis* 27:1-4. 'Well to look to', cp. 'goodly to look to', *1 Samuel* 16:12.
16-7. 'This quarrel is not in Miss Mitford' (Tennyson).
27-31. The final reading, adopted in *1843*. In *1842*:
> Consider: take a month to think, and give
> An answer to my wish; or by the Lord
> That made me, you shall pack, and nevermore
> Darken my doors again.' And William heard,
> And answer'd something madly ...

Tennyson's alteration of the line-endings here suggests an arbitrariness in the rhythms of *Dora*.

165 78. Cp. the setting and story in *Ruth*, e.g. 2:5, 'Then said Boaz unto his servant that was set over the reapers, Whose damsel is this?' Thomas Carlyle suggested the likeness in 1842 (*Memoir*, i, 213).

AUDLEY COURT

168 Published *1842*; from *1853*, among 'English Idyls'. It was written in autumn 1838 at Torquay (*Memoir*, i, 165), 'partially suggested by Abbey Park at Torquay in the old time' (Tennyson). In form and mood, it is based on Theocritus's 7th Idyll, where Simichidas's song (lines 96-127) resembles Francis's here. Cp. the setting of *The Princess* (1847), with its picnic and songs, especially the swallow-song (IV).
15. Cp. *Paradise Lost*, IX, 1106: 'pillar'd shade'.
18. *leafy vine:* traditional, as in Shelley.

169 34-5. There was Corn-Law agitation in 1837, the year in which William IV was gravely ill for a month and then died.

170 86. Tennyson added this line in *1869*. 'The little buoy appearing and disappearing in the dark sea' (Tennyson).
88. Cp. the image of moon and stars ending *Iliad*, VIII, as in Tennyson's *Specimen of a Translation*

NOTES

170 (1863): 'and the Shepherd gladdens in his heart.'

WALKING TO THE MAIL

171 Published *1842*; from *1853*, among 'English Idyls'. It was probably written 1837-8, as was *Audley Court;* see lines 63-8 note. It has affinities with Theocritus's 4th Idyll. The poltergeist story (lines 27-38) is widespread; Tennyson probably derived it from T. C. Croker's *Fairy Legends* (1825; the 1834 edition was at Somersby), the word 'flitting' being suggested by the words of the Scandinavian Nis, 'see, idag flytter vi' ('see, today we're moving').

15. Cp. Milton's Melancholy, 'commercing with the skies', *Il Penseroso* 39.

22-30. The final reading, adopted in *1853*. From *1842* to *1851*:

> ... You saw the man but yesterday:
> He pick'd the pebble from your horse's foot.
> His house was haunted by a jolly ghost
> That rummaged like a rat: no servant stay'd:

172 33. *tilt:* the waggon's awning or cover.

59. The Reform Bill of 1832.

173 63-8. Recalling the French Revolution; Carlyle has a section 'The Feast of Pikes' in *The French Revolution* (1837). Miss M. J. Donahue refers to the Chartist agitations in 1838.

75-92. 'This is an Eton story' (Hallam Tennyson).

91. All of Niobe's children were killed by the gods.

ST. SIMEON STYLITES

174 Published *1842*. Written 1833 (it is dated in manuscript), by November (*Memoir*, i, 130). Simeon was the first and most famous of the pillar-hermits (*Stylites* from the Greek for pillar). Hallam Tennyson gave as the sources William Hone's *Every-Day Book* (1825), which supplied almost all the details (under 'January 5'), and Gibbon's *Decline and Fall of the Roman Empire*, Chapter 37. FitzGerald said that 'this is one of the Poems A.T. would read with grotesque Grimness, especially at such passages as "Coughs, Aches, Stitches, etc." [lines 13-6],

NOTES

174 laughing aloud at times.' J. H. Buckley has suggested that it was influenced by contempt for Charles Simeon, a notoriously exclamatory and influential preacher at Cambridge in Tennyson's day. In his review of *1842*, Leigh Hunt called the poem

> a powerfully graphic, and in some respects appalling satire on the pseudo-aspirations of egotistical asceticism and superstition ... We do not recollect to have met with a more startling picture of the sordid and the aspiring—the selfish and the self-sacrificing—the wretched, weak body and mind and resolute soul—the abject, the dominant, the stupid, the imaginative—and, alas, the misgiving ... all mixed up in the poor phantom-like person of the almost incredible Saint of the Pillar.

2. Based on *Deuteronomy* 28:35, 'The Lord shall smite thee in the knees, and in the legs, with a sore botch that cannot be healed, from the sole of thy foot unto the top of thy head.' *Job* 2:7, 'and smote Job with sore boils from the sole of his foot unto his crown.' *Isaiah* 1:6, 'From the sole of the foot even unto the head there is no soundness in it; but wounds, and bruises, and putrifying sores.'

12-3. A reminiscence of Prospero to Caliban: 'to-night thou shalt have cramps, / Side-stitches ... I'll rack thee with old cramps, / Fill all thy bones with aches,' *The Tempest*, I, ii, 326-7, 370-1.

175 20. *Revelation* 7:9, 'clothed with white robes, and palms in their hands.'

40. 'One of his thighs rotted a whole year, during which time he stood on one leg only' (Hone).

46. *Matthew* 19:25, 'When his disciples heard it, they were exceedingly amazed, saying, Who then can be saved?'

176 56. Based on *Romans* 7:17-8, 'sin that dwelleth in me. For I know that in me (that is, in my flesh) dwelleth no good thing.'

61. Where according to Hone he was thought over-austere.

NOTES

176 81. *Acts* 8:7, 'Many taken with palsies, and that were lame, were healed.'

83. *Psalm* 85:2, 'Thou hast forgiven the iniquity of thy people, thou hast covered all their sin.'

177 86. *cubit:* about 18 inches.

93. Simeon thinks of the pillar as a sun-dial.

107. Simeon likens himself to Christ: 'The foxes have holes, and the birds of the air have nests; but the Son of man hath not where to lay his head,' *Matthew* 8:20.

109. According to Hone and Gibbon, one thousand two hundred and forty-four.

113. Cp. Gray's *The Descent of Odin* 31-3 (1768):
Long on these mould'ring bones have beat
The winter's snow, the summer's heat,
The drenching dews, and driving rain!

116. As shown in the illustration to Hone.

117. *Genesis* 32:24, 'And Jacob was left alone; and there wrestled a man with him until the breaking of the day.'

118. *Acts* 22:16, 'Arise, and be baptized, and wash away thy sins.'

178 120. *Psalm* 51:5, 'I was shapen in iniquity; and in sin did my mother conceive me.'

122. Contrast the martyrdom of Stephen: 'And he kneeled down, and cried with a loud voice, Lord, lay not this sin to their charge,' *Acts* 7:60.

146-7. Suggesting *Leviticus* 23:10-1, 'reap the harvest thereof . . . And he shall wave the sheaf before the Lord, to be accepted for you.'

179 168. Cp. Bunyan's *Grace Abounding* (1666): 'I have in my bed been greatly afflicted, while asleep, with the apprehensions of Devils, and wicked spirits.'

169. *Revelation* 9:11, 'The angel of the bottomless pit, whose name in the Hebrew tongue is Abaddon.' *Tobit* 3:8, 'Asmodeus the evil spirit.'

170-5. Cp. Caliban, on Prospero's 'spirits', *The Tempest*, II, ii, 8-10:
For every trifle are they set upon me—
Sometime like apes, that mow and chatter at me,
And after bite me.

See lines 12-3 note.

179 178. *Isaiah* 58:1, 'Cry aloud, spare not, lift up thy voice like a trumpet, and shew my people their transgression, and the house of Jacob their sins.'

179. As Simeon did, in Hone.

180 197-200. Cp. Keats, *Endymion*, II, 323-4:
  Before mine eyes thick films and shadows float—
  O let me 'noint them with the heaven's light!

200. The angel is mentioned in Hone.

205. Based on *Revelation* 2:7-10, 'To him that overcometh will I give to eat of the tree of life . . . And I will give thee a crown of life.'

208. 'When Simeon died, Anthony smelt a precious odour emanating from his body' (Hone).

217. The prophecy is not in Gibbon or Hone. See *Bede*, ed. A. Hamilton Thompson (1935), pp. 211-3: 'Sometimes the day was prophesied by the appearance of angels in a vision . . . This particular form of prophecy is of course a commonplace in the lives of the saints from the Life of St. Antony onwards . . . The idea underlying this widespread tradition was that the saint was thus granted time to prepare himself for the great change and to be fortified by receiving the Communion.'

218-9. *Psalm* 74:18, 'O Lord, and that the foolish people have blasphemed thy name.' *Jeremiah* 5:21, 'Hear now this, O foolish people.'

THE TALKING OAK

181 Published *1842*. Written by 1837 or early 1838 (*Materials*, i, 246); cp. the other jocular poems of this date, *Will Waterproof* (p. 247) and *Amphion* (p. 238). Tennyson called it 'an experiment meant to test the degree in which it was in [his] power as a poet to humanise external nature.' It was influenced by *As You Like It*, III, ii, 1-10:
  O Rosalind! these trees shall be my books,
  And in their barks my thoughts I'll character . . .
  Run, run, Orlando, carve on every tree
  The fair, the chaste and unexpressive she.

Tennyson's manuscript jotting 'P.V. 832' refers to Aeschylus, *Prometheus Vinctus* 832: 'that marvel,

NOTES

181 passing all belief, the talking oaks, by which thou clearly, and in no riddling terms, wast saluted as the renowned spouse of Zeus that was to be' (Loeb translation).

182 45. *Peter's-pence:* tax paid to the Pope, abolished just before Henry VIII's dissolution of the monasteries, the subject of lines 47-8.

47. *spence:* 'the monks' buttery' (Tennyson).

51. *offset:* a young shoot, here Queen Elizabeth.

54-6. 'That old Tory the oak calls him a brewer, as the old Cavaliers did' (Tennyson). Tennyson also pointed out that: 'The stork, a republican bird, is said to have gone out of England with the Commonwealth. And though the Commonwealth did not expire till some months after the death of Oliver, it practically went out with him. The night when he died was a night of storm.'

183 63. 'Queen Anne's times' (Tennyson).

186 175. Horace's *Odes*, III, xxvii, 21-2: *caecos sentiant motus.*

187 183. 'Vegetable Love', Marvell's *To His Coy Mistress* 11.

190 267. *culmination:* reaching the meridian.

292-4. The oaks at Dodona, where the dove 'pronounced that in this place should be set up an oracle of Zeus' (Tennyson).

LOVE AND DUTY

191 Published *1842*. Written about 1840. At this time Tennyson broke off his engagement to Emily Sellwood (whom he did not marry till 1850); the difficulties were partly financial, but not only so. The poem resembles Tennyson's letter to Emily, December 1839: 'How should this dependence on thy state coexist with my flying from thee? ask not. Believe that it does. 'Tis true, I fly thee for my good, perhaps for thine, at any rate for thine if mine is thine. If thou knewest why I fly thee there is nothing thou would'st more wish for than that I should fly thee. Sayest thou "are we to meet no more?" I answer I know not the word nor will know it. I neither

NOTES

191 know it nor believe it. The immortality of man disdains and rejects it—the immortality of man to which the cycles and the Aeons are as hours and as days' (Sir Charles Tennyson, p. 181). Tennyson's brother Charles added 'that the love between your father and mother continued unshaken, and that but for an overstrained, morbid scrupulousness as to what was conceived to be duty, they might have been contented to wait (an engaged couple) and so both might have been spared much suffering' (*Materials*, ii, 38).

5. *shout:* a noun.

15-8. The mentally ill whom Tennyson saw at this time in Dr Matthew Allen's asylum near High Beech.

192 28. *took . . . pastime:* this has erotic connotations for Tennyson, as in an early poem, *Almighty Love* (1827).

193 56-7. Tennyson compared Theocritus XV 104-5. Loeb translation,

The Seasons, the Seasons, full slow they go and come,
But some sweet thing for all they bring, and so they are welcome home.

71-4. Cp. Wordsworth, *Vaudracour and Julia* 97-101 (1820):

              meanwhile the galaxy display'd
Her fires, that like mysterious pulses beat
Aloft; momentous but uneasy bliss!
To their full hearts the universe seemed hung
On that brief meeting's slender filament.

73-4. G. G. Loane compared Chapman, *Bussy D'Ambois*, II, ii, 157-65 (1607):

Now all ye peaceful regents of the night . . .
    . . . this charm'd hour
Fix like the Centre; make the violent wheels
Of Time and Fortune stand.

Also Keats, *Hyperion*, I, 72-4:

As when, upon a tranced summer-night
. . . branch-charmed by the earnest stars.

82. *pathos:* suffering, 'used in opposition to *apathetic*' in line 18 (Tennyson).

84. Cp. *Paradise Lost*, VIII, 633: 'Live happy and love';

NOTES

193 where line 631 is 'Beyond the Earth's green Cape and verdant Isles'—cp. line 98 below.

194 97. *rack:* floating cloud, as in Shakespeare's Sonnet 33, which begins:

> Full many a glorious morning have I seen
> Flatter the mountain-tops with sovereign eye,
> Kissing with golden face the meadows green ...

Leigh Hunt speaks of 'rounded rack', and Shelley of 'crudded rack'.

ULYSSES

194 Published *1842*. It was written 20 October 1833 (it is dated in manuscript), soon after Tennyson heard the news of Arthur Hallam's death. Tennyson made two slightly different comments. First, 'The poem was written soon after Arthur Hallam's death, and it gives the feeling about the need of going forward and braving the struggle of life perhaps more simply than anything in *In Memoriam*' (Eversley edition). Second, comparing *In Memoriam*, 'There is more about myself in *Ulysses*, which was written under the sense of loss and that all had gone by, but that still life must be fought out to the end. It was more written with the feeling of his loss upon me than many poems in *In Memoriam*' (*Nineteenth Century*, 1893, xxxiii, 182). As sources, he specified *Odyssey*, XI, 100-37, and Dante's *Inferno*, XXVI, 90 ff. Tiresias speaks, *Odyssey*, XI, 112-37 (Loeb translation):

> Late shalt thou come home and in evil case, after losing all thy comrades, in a ship that is another's, and thou shalt find woes in thy house—proud men that devour thy livelihood, wooing thy godlike wife, and offering wooers' gifts. Yet verily on their violent deeds shalt thou take vengeance when thou comest. But when thou hast slain the wooers in thy halls, whether by guile or openly with the sharp sword, then do thou go forth, taking a shapely oar, until thou comest to men that know naught of ... ships ... And death shall come to thee thyself far from the sea [possibly 'from out of the sea'], a death so gentle, that shall lay thee low when

NOTES

194   thou art overcome with sleek old age, and thy people shall dwell in prosperity around thee.

On this 'mysterious voyage', Hallam Tennyson commented: 'This is elaborated by the author of the *Telegoneia*. My father, like Eugammon, takes up the story of further wanderings at the end of the *Odyssey*. Ulysses has lived in Ithaca for a long while before the craving for fresh travel seizes him. The comrades he addresses are of the same heroic mould as his old comrades.' The last sentence is meant to meet the objection that Ulysses' companions were dead. In a note Hallam Tennyson added: 'Perhaps the *Odyssey* has not been strictly adhered to, and some of the old comrades may be still left.' Dante is the more important source. Tennyson probably used H. F. Cary's translation (1805); there was a copy at Somersby. Ulysses speaks, XXVI, 90-124: nothing

> ... Could overcome in me the zeal I had
> T' explore the world, and search the ways of life,
> Man's evil and his virtue. Forth I sail'd
> Into the deep illimitable main,
> With but one bark, and the small faithful band
> That yet cleav'd to me. As Iberia far,
> Far as Marocco either shore I saw,
> And the Sardinian and each isle beside
> Which round that ocean bathes. Tardy with age
> Were I and my companions, when we came
> To the strait pass, where Hercules ordain'd
> The bound'ries not to be o'erstepp'd by man.
> The walls of Seville to my right I left,
> On th' other hand already Ceuta past.
> 'O brothers!' I began, 'who to the west
> Through perils without number now have reach'd,
> To this the short remaining watch, that yet
> Our senses have to wake, refuse not proof
> Of the unpeopled world, following the track
> Of Phoebus. Call to mind from whence ye sprang:
> Ye were not form'd to live the life of brutes,
> But virtue to pursue and knowledge high.'

194 With these few words I sharpen'd for the voyage
  The mind of my associates, that I then
  Could scarcely have withheld them. To the dawn
  Our poop we turn'd . . .

Ulysses then describes the last and fatal voyage. It has been much discussed whether or not we are to find Tennyson's Ulysses altogether noble; the most scrupulous account of the arguments is by J. Pettigrew, *Victorian Poetry* (1963), i, 27-45. For Robert Langbaum's important discussion of the poem, see p. 373 below.

4. *Unequal:* not 'unjust', but 'not affecting all in the same manner or degree,' a primitive state of law consequent upon the Ithacans' being 'a savage race'.

5. Cp. *Hamlet*, IV, iv, 33-9, which not only has 'sleep and feed', but is also apt to the theme of the poem:

> What is a man,
> If his chief good and market of his time
> Be but to sleep and feed? a beast, no more:
> Sure he that made us with such large discourse,
> Looking before and after, gave us not
> That capability and god-like reason
> To fust in us unused.

6-7. J. Pettigrew compared *Macbeth*, II, iii, 94-5: 'The wine of life is drawn, and the mere lees / Is left this vault to brag of.'

10. Tennyson quoted *Aeneid*, I, 744: *pluviasque Hyadas;* the rising of these stars was thought to mean storm.

10-1. Cp. Shelley, *Revolt of Islam*, III, xxxii, 3-4: 'the starry giant dips / His zone in the dim sea.'

11. *Vext:* cp. *The Tempest*, I, ii, 229: 'the still-vexed Bermoothes'. The application to the sea is very common, and is found in Milton, Pope and Shelley.

13-4. *Odyssey*, I, 3: 'Many were the men whose cities he saw and whose mind he learned, aye, and many the woes he suffered in his heart upon the sea' (Loeb translation).

195 18. Tennyson cited Aeneas's account of his experiences, *Aeneid*, II, 5-6: *quaeque ipse miserrima vidi / et quorum pars magna fui.* Cp. Byron, *Childe Harold*, III, lxxii, 1-2

NOTES

195 (1816): 'I live not in myself, but I become / Portion of that around me.' Byron's passage has lines relevant to *Ulysses* (lxx 6-9, lxxv 1-2):

>   on the sea
> The boldest steer but where their ports invite—
> But there are wanderers o'er Eternity,
> Whose bark drives on and on, and anchor'd
>   ne'er shall be . . .
> Are not the mountains, waves, and skies, a part
> Of me and of my Soul.

19-21. Matthew Arnold commented on these lines: 'It is no blame to their rhythm, which belongs to another order of movement than Homer's, but it is true that these three lines by themselves take up nearly as much time as a whole book of the *Iliad*. No; the blank verse used in rendering Homer must be a blank verse of which perhaps the best specimens are to be found in some of the most rapid passages of Shakespeare's plays—a blank verse which does not dovetail its lines into one another, and which habitually ends its lines with monosyllables' (*On Translating Homer*, III, 1861).

20. J. Pettigrew compared 'the unpeopled world' in Cary's Dante, above.

23. Ulysses' words, *Troilus and Cressida*, III, iii, 150-3:
>   Perseverance, dear my lord,
> Keeps honour bright: to have done, is to hang
> Quite out of fashion, like a rusty mail
> In monumental mockery.

Douglas Bush compared *Hamlet* (quoted at line 5 note).

30. F. J. Rowe and W. T. Webb, in their *Selections* (1888), described the syntax as 'absolute case'; Tennyson wrote: 'No, the accusative after *store* etc.' Hallam Tennyson confusingly notes: 'accusative absolute'.

31-2. See Cary's Dante above.

196 55. Douglas Bush remarked that 'Homeric voyages commonly begin in the evening; here the accent is on the evening of life.' Contrast Cary's Dante: 'To the dawn / Our poop we turn'd', where Ulysses' account of his fatal voyage goes on to mention the moon and the stars.

NOTES

196 58-9. Translating, as Tennyson acknowledged, a Homeric commonplace, *Odyssey*, IV, 580 etc.

60-1. Adapting *Odyssey*, V, 270: Odysseus 'watched the Pleiads, and late-setting Bootes, and the Bear, which men also call the Wain, which ever circles where it is and watches Orion, and alone has no part in the baths of Ocean' (Loeb translation).

63. The Isles of the Blest were thought to lie beyond the Pillars of Hercules (Gibraltar), and it is beyond the Pillars that Dante's Ulysses urges his companions to sail with him.

66-9. Recalling a poem by Arthur Hallam, *To J.M.G.* (written 1829):

> We are not as we were...
>
> We are not as we were: our silent tombs
> Shall have us not, till we have drunk our fill
> Of a new glorious joy, restoring heart and will!

LOCKSLEY HALL

196 Published *1842*. Written 1837-8. The main biographical impetus came from Tennyson's unhappy love-affair with Rosa Baring (see *The Gardener's Daughter*, p. 154), which precipitated many poems, including most notably *Maud* (1855). R. W. Rader has pointed out that Rosa's was an arranged marriage, and that the Hall was suggested by her Harrington Hall. Sir Charles Tennyson notes that the story of 'family estrangement owes much of its form and atmosphere to the feud between Somersby and Bayons' (p. 194), the latter being the home of Charles Tennyson-d'Eyncourt, in whose favour Tennyson's father had virtually been disinherited. Tennyson maintained that it was 'an imaginary place and imaginary hero': 'The whole poem represents young life, its good side, its deficiencies, and its yearnings.' Source: 'Sir William Jones's prose translation of the *Moâllakât*, the seven Arabic poems... hanging up in the temple of Mecca, gave the idea of the poem' (Hallam Tennyson). The 1799 edition of Jones's *Works* was at Somersby. Jones summarized the first poem, of Amriolkais: 'The poet...

196 supposes himself attended on a journey by a company of friends; and, as they pass near a place, where his mistress had lately dwelled . . . he desires them to stop awhile, that he might indulge the painful pleasure of weeping over the deserted remains of her tent. They comply with his request, but exhort him to show more strength of mind, and urge two topicks of consolation; namely, that he had before been equally unhappy, and that he had enjoyed his full share of pleasures: thus by the recollection of his passed delight his imagination is kindled, and his grief suspended.' Then follows an account of Amriolkais's amours (among them 'Fathima' —cp. *Fatima*, p. 79); the poem ends, like Tennyson's, with a violent storm. E. F. Shannon has suggested that 'Locksley' is from Scott's *Ivanhoe*, where it is Robin Hood's pseudonym (from his birthplace): 'Locksley is the pseudonym of a man alienated from society . . . indict[ing] the corruption and self-seeking of his day.' Reminiscences of *Hamlet*, too, were apt to an attack on a corrupt society, dealing with an unhappy love-affair; cp. Tennyson's description of *Maud* (a poem similar to *Locksley Hall*) as 'a little *Hamlet*'. As to the metre: 'Mr Hallam [Arthur's father] said to me that the English people liked verse in trochaics, so I wrote the poem in this metre.' The spur to its use may well have been the fact that, in the poem of Amriolkais, Jones's prose fell naturally into it: 'Thus I spoke, when my companions stopped their coursers by my side.' Tennyson's acute receptiveness to rhythms is famous (the origins of *The Charge of the Light Brigade* are an example), and Jones's prose probably ran in his head. In 1886 Tennyson published a sequel, *Locksley Hall Sixty Years After*.

3-4. Tennyson said that this means '*while* dreary gleams', not in apposition to 'curlews'.

197 8. Horace's *pronus Orion* (*Odes*, III, xxvii, 18).

9-10. From the *Moâllakât*: 'It was the hour, when the Pleiads appeared in the firmament, like the folds of a silken sash variously decked with gems.'

12. Cp. *The Day-Dream: L'Envoi* 10-2: 'science . . . / As wild as aught of fairy lore'.

NOTES

197 19-20. Recalling the effect of spring in James Thomson's *Spring* 786-8 (1728):

> the cooing dove
> Flies thick in amorous chase, and wanton rolls
> The glancing eye, and turns the changeful neck.

The imagery is traditional; Sir Cecil Clementi pointed out the likeness to the opening of the *Pervigilium Veneris*, a poem which may have influenced the metre of *Locksley Hall*.

198 31. *glowing hands:* traditional diction, used twice by Tennyson in poems of *1827*. Cp. Keats, *Eve of St. Agnes*, 271: 'These delicates he heap'd with glowing hand / On golden dishes.'

37. *the stately ships: Break, break, break* 9.

38. A traditional notion; cp. *Fatima* 19-21 and note (p. 301).

199 43-4. Cp. *Hamlet*, I, v, 50-2: 'To decline / Upon a wretch whose natural gifts were poor / To those of mine.'

50. A common indictment; E. F. Shannon compared *Ivanhoe*, Chapter 29: 'His war-horse—his hunting hound are dearer to him than the despised Jewess!'

200 68. Cp. the 'treble dated Crow' in Shakespeare's *The Phoenix and Turtle*; Horace's *annosa cornix* (*Odes*, III, xvii, 13).

69. Cp. *Hamlet*, I, v, 98-9: 'From the table of my memory / I'll wipe away all trivial fond records.'

201 75-6. *the poet:* Dante. Tennyson's note quoted *Inferno*, V, 121-3. These lines are in effect a retort to the *Moâllakát's* 'consolation'—see above.

79. The dreaming dog is from Lucretius, *De Rerum Natura*, IV, 991 ff.

202 89-90. The baby as 'rival' was suggested by the *Moâllakát's* very different tone: 'Many a lovely mother have I diverted from the care of her yearling infant . . . When the suckling behind her cried, she turned round to him with half her body; but half of it, pressed beneath my embrace, was not turned from me.'

203 103-4. Cp. the aspiration, contrasted with despair, in *The Two Voices* 149-56: 'To perish . . . like a warrior

NOTES

203 overthrown' (also 'foeman', 'smoke'). *laid:* the notion that gunfire stills the waves.

204 122. *Pilots . . . twilight:* in manuscript, 'Merchants in a rosy sunset.' Tennyson translates into prophetic fact the *Moâllakât's* beautiful simile for rain: 'The cloud unloads its freight on the desert of Ghabeit, like a merchant of Yemen alighting with his bales of rich apparel.' Cp. also *The Mermaid* 44: 'the purple twilights under the sea'.

123. Cp. the blood from the battle in an early poem, *The Vale of Bones* 77 (1827): 'the red dew o'er thee rain'd.' Byron, *Childe Harold*, IV, cxxvi: 'The skies which rain their plagues on men like dew.'

124. E. F. Shannon referred to the balloon stanzas for *A Dream of Fair Women* (p. 118), and argued that Tennyson was thinking mainly of balloons here.

205 133. *Hamlet*, I, v, 188-9:
> The time is out of joint, O cursed spite,
> That ever I was born to set it right.

206 155. *Mahratta:* soldiers of Bombay who were conquered in 1818.

207 180. *Joshua* 10:12.

208 182. Tennyson commented: 'When I went by the first train from Liverpool to Manchester (1830) I thought that the wheels ran in a groove. It was a black night, and there was such a vast crowd round the train at the station that we could not see the wheels. Then I made this line.'

190. *roof-tree:* the main beam; Tennyson's hero may include the meaning 'the whole family, the house.'

GODIVA

209 Published *1842*. It was written after a visit to Coventry in June 1840 (*Memoir*, i, 176). Detailed historical information was sent at Tennyson's request by one T. Lord. The poem is a short epyllion (minor epic) in the manner of Theocritus; cp. Tennyson's opening with that of the 13th Idyll (on Hylas), a poem which Tennyson much admired (*Memoir*, ii, 495):

From what God soever sprung, Nicias, Love was

NOTES

209 not, as we seem to think, born for us alone; nor first unto us of mortal flesh that cannot see the morrow, look things of beauty beautiful. (Loeb translation).

Tennyson's trial-edition of *1842* did not have the 4 introductory lines. In his review of *1842*, Leigh Hunt wrote acutely about the framing of *Godiva* and *Morte d'Arthur* (p. 145):

> a certain air of literary dandyism, or fine-gentlemanism, or fastidiousness, or whatever he may *not* be pleased to call it, which leads him to usher in his compositions with such exordiums as those to *Morte d'Arthur*, and *Godiva*; in the former of which he gives us to understand that he should have burnt his poem but for the 'request of friends' [Pope]; and, in the latter, that he 'shaped' it while he was waiting 'for the train at Coventry,' and hanging on the bridge 'with grooms and porters'. Really this is little better than the rhyming fine-ladyism of Miss Seward, who said that she used to translate an ode of Horace 'while her hair was curling' . . . This kind of mixed tone of contempt and nonchalance, or, at best, of fine-life phrases with better fellowship, looks a little instructive, and is, at all events, a little perilous . . . We suspect that these poems of *Morte d'Arthur* and *Godiva* are among those which Mr Tennyson thinks his best . . . and therefore it is that he would affect to make trifles of them. The reader's opinion is at once to be of great importance to him, and yet none at all.

28. *Genesis* 27:23.

210 45-9. Reminiscent of a poem by 'G.M.', *Godiva*, which was quoted from *The Etonian* in the *Quarterly Review* (1821), xxv, 107—this Review was a source for many of Tennyson's early poems.

> And let the traces of her raven hair
> Flow down in wavy lightness to the ground,
> Till half they veil'd her limbs and bosom fair,
> In dark and shadowy beauty floating round,
> As clouds, in the still firmament of June,
> Shade the pale splendours of the midnight moon.

NOTES

211 72. Cp. *The Two Voices* 42: 'Is cancell'd in the world of sense.'

THE TWO VOICES

211 Published *1842*, when it was dated '1833'. Hallam Tennyson described it as 'begun under the cloud of his overwhelming sorrow after the death of Arthur Hallam,' news of which reached Tennyson on 1 October 1833. This statement has not hitherto been disputed, but that Tennyson had begun it before Hallam's death is clear from a letter by J. M. Kemble (the manuscript belongs to Mrs C. B. Johnson). The letter is dated 22 June, and from internal evidence cannot but be June 1833:

> Next Sir are some superb meditations on Selfdestruction called *Thoughts of a Suicide* wherein he argues the point with his soul and is thoroughly floored. These are amazingly fine and deep, and show a mighty stride in intellect since the *Second-Rate Sensitive Mind* [1830].

Clearly a version of *The Two Voices* was already in existence. But Tennyson's writing of it may well have been affected by the death of Hallam. Two of the manuscripts stop after line 309 with three lines added; this would be a feasible ending, and conceivably a better one. The published ending was developed later, probably in 1837 or 1838 (*Materials*, i, 246). Hallam Tennyson said that the poem, 'describing the conflict in a soul between Faith and Scepticism, was begun under the cloud of his overwhelming sorrow after the death of Arthur Hallam, which, as my father told me, for a while blotted out all joy from his life, and made him long for death.' In his handling of the theme, Tennyson was indebted to Lucretius's discussion of death (III, 830-1094); to the solicitations of Despair in *Faerie Queene*, I, ix; and to Hamlet's 'To be or not to be . . .'. The tone of the poem was influenced by *Job* (as Carlyle suggested in 1842), *Psalms*, and *Ecclesiastes*. There are many similarities, in idea and phrasing, to *In Memoriam*, especially XLIII-XLVII. The triplet had been used by Tennyson's

NOTES

211 brother Charles in a poem of *1827*, *Ode on the Death of Lord Byron*. Lewis Carroll wrote a brilliant parody, *The Three Voices*.

1. Contrast *1 Kings* 19:12, where the 'still small voice' is the Lord's.

5-6. *Psalm* 139:11-4, 'If I say, Surely the darkness shall cover me; even the night shall be light about me ... I will praise thee; for I am fearfully and wonderfully made.'

8-15. Tennyson tacitly adapts a traditional emblem for 'the renewal of life, and the immortality of the soul.' Jacob Bryant, whose *New Analysis of Ancient Mythology* (1807 ed.) was at Somersby, says: 'at the return of spring it bursts its bonds, and comes out with new life, and in the most beautiful attire. The Egyptians thought this a very proper picture of the soul of man, and of the immortality, to which it aspired' (iii, 247-8).

212 16-8. Invoking science as well as religion, as M. Millhauser has said, 'the "creative eras" which Buffon and his English followers equated with the 6 creative days of Genesis.'

21. *Psalm* 8:6, 'Thou madest him to have dominion over the works of thy hands.'

39. *thy deficiency:* 'the want of thee' (Tennyson).

213 52-3. Cp. *Job* 14:20, 'Thou prevailest for ever against him, and he passeth: thou changest his countenance, and sendest him away.'

215 119-20. Note the Miltonic 'abyss', and 'waste wide anarchy', *Paradise Lost*, X, 282-3.

216 124-56. On the moral certainties of battle, cp. *Locksley Hall* 103-4 (p. 203).

138. Cp. *In Memoriam*, XXIV, 15: 'And orb into the perfect star'.

142. Cp. *Hamlet*, I, v, 32-3:
Duller shouldst thou be than the fat weed
That rots itself in ease on Lethe wharf.

217 152. Horace's *Odes*, II, i, 22: *non indecoro pulvere sordidos* (which Tennyson had quoted in a note to *The Vale of Bones* in *1827*).

NOTES

217 170. *The Palace of Art* 213: 'The riddle of the painful earth.'

218 192. *fold:* 'cloud' (Tennyson).

193. Tennyson commented: 'I pronounce "oblique" *oblīque*,' on the analogy of *oblige/obleege*. Wordsworth rhymed *strike/oblique* in the manuscript of *An Evening Walk* (1793).

195. 'Ixion embraced a cloud, hoping to embrace a goddess' (Tennyson).

196-9. Combining *Ecclesiastes* 3:19, 'For that which befalleth the sons of men befalleth beasts; even one thing befalleth them: as the one dieth, so dieth the other;' with *Psalm* 8:4-5, 'What is man, that thou art mindful of him? and the son of man, that thou visitest him? For thou hast made him a little lower than the angels.'

219 210. Horace's *Odes*, I, i, 30: *dis miscent superis*.

219. Stephen, the first Christian martyr.

222-5. *Acts* 7:55, 'But he, being full of the Holy Ghost, looked up steadfastly into heaven, and saw the glory of God.'

228. *Julius Caesar*, V, v, 73-5:
      The elements
    So mixed in him that Nature might stand up
    And say to all the world 'this was a man!'
Tennyson remarked: 'Some have happier dispositions.'

220 239. *Ecclesiastes* 5:15, 'naked shall he return to go as he came.'

243. Cp. Pope, *Epistle to Oxford* 24 (1722): 'Above all Pain, all Passion, and all Pride.'

247. *A Dirge* 2: 'Fold thy palms across thy breast'.

221 256-7. *Job* 14:21, on the dead man: 'His sons come to honour, and he knoweth it not; and they are brought low, but he perceiveth it not of them.'

264. *Psalm* 103:16, 'the place thereof shall know it no more'—man as a dead flower.

277-9. 'The simple senses made death a king' (Tennyson). Contrast *Revelation* 1:8, 'I am Alpha and Omega, the beginning and the ending, saith the Lord.'

280. Cp. the quotation from *Hamlet*, line 142 note above.

NOTES

222 284. Cp. *In Memoriam*, CXXIV, 13-4:
>A warmth within the breast would melt
>The freezing reason's colder part.

297. Cp. *In Memoriam*, CXXVIII, 24: 'toil cöoperant to an end'.

301-3. Combining *Romans* 7:18, 'For I know that in me (that is, in my flesh), dwelleth no good thing;' with *Galatians* 5:17, 'For the flesh lusteth against the Spirit, and the Spirit against the flesh: and these are contrary the one to the other: so that ye cannot do the things that ye would.'

305-6. Cp. *Paradise Lost*, II, 1035-9:
>from the walls of Heav'n
>Shoots far into the bosom of dim Night
>A glimmering dawn—

making Chaos a 'brok'n foe'. Cp. the end of *The Vision of Sin*:
>And on the glimmering limit far withdrawn
>God made Himself an awful rose of dawn.

224 349. Pythagoras's theory of the transmigration of souls; and Plato's myth of Er (*Republic* X).

351. Cp. *In Memoriam*, LXXXII, 6: 'From state to state the spirit walks.'

225 364. G. R. Potter has argued that Tennyson 'is writing about the transmigration of souls, and the lines refer not so much to material as to spiritual progress—a sort of semi-evolutionary idea that appears more than once in the writings of eighteenth-century thinkers.' The word *frame* 'injects the idea of physical change into these speculations concerning the soul. But from the lines themselves we cannot be at all sure whether Tennyson was thinking of changes in species, or of the same idea that he reflects in his Cambridge discussion, that the human body in its embryonic stages has resemblances to lower organisms.'

378. Arthur Hallam spoke of 'the material prime' in a poem of 1829.

226 395-6. *Job* 3:20-1, 'Wherefore is light given to him that is in misery, and life unto the bitter in soul; Which long for death but it cometh not.'

NOTES

226 397-9. Cp. *Ulysses* 24-5: 'Life piled on life / Were all too little.'

399. *John* 10:10, 'I am come that they might have life, and that they might have it more abundantly.'

227 424. Cp. the Ancient Mariner's release from guilt when he 'blessed them unaware. / The self-same moment I could pray' (lines 287-8).

228 462. *Philippians* 4:4, 'Rejoice in the Lord alway: and again I say, Rejoice;' *Ecclesiastes* 11:9, 'Rejoice, O young man, in thy youth.' Cp. Keats, *Sleep and Poetry* 37-9 (1817):

Sometimes it gives a glory to the voice,
And from the heart up-springs 'Rejoice! rejoice!'
Sounds which will reach the Framer of all things.

Edmund Blunden has observed that Coleridge's *Dejection* (1802) ends with the word 'rejoice'.

THE DAY-DREAM

228 One section, *The Sleeping Beauty*, was published in *1830*; the whole sequence was published *1842*. It was completed by about June 1834 (*Memoir*, i, 134), except for the *Prologue* and *Epilogue*, which were 'added after 1835 (when the poem was written), for the same reason that caused the Prologue of the *Morte d'Arthur*, giving an excuse for telling an old-world tale' (FitzGerald). This resemblance to *The Epic* might suggest 1837-8 for the *Prologue* and the *Epilogue*. On Tennyson's frames, see Leigh Hunt (*Godiva*, p. 350).

[THE SLEEPING PALACE]

229 9. Cp. Shelley, *Rosalind* 832: 'lustre bright and soft', a passage which might have come to Tennyson's mind because it describes how 'Sudden sleep would seize him oft / Like death, so calm.'

230 17. Cp. *Macbeth*, I, vi, 4: 'temple-haunting martlet'.

NOTES

[THE DEPARTURE]

234 4. 'The world of Love' (Tennyson).

235 13. *sliding*: traditional diction in such a context. Cp. Dryden, *Palamon and Arcite*, III, 129-33 (1700):

'Creator Venus, genial pow'r of love,
The bliss of men below and gods above!
Beneath the sliding sun thou runn'st thy race,
Dost fairest shine, and best become thy place;
For thee the winds their eastern blasts forbear . . .

[L'ENVOI]

236 10-2. Cp. *Locksley Hall* 12: 'With the fairy tales of science, and the long result of Time.'

16. Cp. *Locksley Hall* 128: 'the Parliament of man, the Federation of the world.'

237 19-20. A famous paradox. Cp. Bacon's *Advancement of Learning*, I, v, 1 (1605): 'These times are the ancient times, when the world is ancient, and not those which we account ancient *ordine retrogrado*, by a computation backward from ourselves.'

47. 'A recollection of the bust of Clyte' (Tennyson). Clyte watches Apollo leaving her; Tennyson had a bust of her (*Memoir*, i, 151).

[EPILOGUE]

238 7-8. In legend they do not alight.

AMPHION

238 Published *1842*. It was probably written about 1837-8, like the similar poems *The Talking Oak* and *Will Waterproof*. Amphion was the musician to whose lyre the stones moved to build Thebes; here a type of the poet, the moral being that 'Genius must not deem itself exempt from work' (Tennyson's wife Emily). Tennyson may have mingled Amphion and Orpheus, but in Skelton's *Garland of Laurel* (1523) Amphion too made the trees dance.

NOTES

239 37. *long order:* Tennyson mocks the usual solemnity of the term. Cp. Gray, *Ode for Music* 37-8:
> High Potentates and Dames of royal birth
> And mitred Fathers in long order go.

240 64. *scirrhous:* hard with cancer.

241 84. *Van Diemen:* Tasmania was discovered in 1642 by the Dutch navigator Tasman, who named it Van Diemen's Land after his patron.

93-4. Cp. Wordsworth, *Immortality Ode* 206: 'to me the meanest flower that blows'. Echoing Gray, *Ode on Vicissitude* 49 (1754): 'The meanest flowret of the vale.'

ST. AGNES' EVE

242 Published November 1836, in *The Keepsake* for 1837, as *St. Agnes*; then *1842*. The title was expanded in *1855*. It was written September 1833 (dated in manuscript). St. Agnes was a martyr at thirteen; her refusal to marry caused her to be violated before execution, but by a miracle she remained a virgin. A maiden who fasted on her Eve might see a vision of her destined lover. A draft-note by Tennyson said: 'Here the legend is told by a nun.' Tennyson's source was William Hone's *Every-Day Book* (1825), which quoted Keats's *Eve of St. Agnes*. Tennyson said the poem was a 'pendant to *Sir Galahad*' (p. 243).

19. *earthly house:* 2 Corinthians 5:1.

31. *Revelation* 21:9, 'I will shew thee the Bride, the Lamb's wife.'

243 33. *Hebrews* 4:9-11, 'There remaineth therefore a rest ['or, keeping of a Sabbath'] to the people of God ... Let us labour therefore to enter into that rest.'

35. *the shining sea:* Revelation 15:2.

SIR GALAHAD

243 Published *1842*. It was written by 1834 (*Memoir*, i, 139). Tennyson said it was 'intended for something of a male counterpart to *St. Agnes*' (*Memoir*, i, 142). Cp. the *Idylls of the King: The Holy Grail* (1869).

NOTES

EDWARD GRAY

246 Published *1842*. In 1840 Tennyson sent it to Emily Sellwood (who became his wife in 1850), as 'a virgin-ballad never yet written down . . . simple enough at any rate' (*Memoir*, i, 176). It is a ballad of the type of *Barbara Allen's Cruelty*, which is in Percy's *Reliques:*

> When he was dead, and laid in grave,
>   Her heart was struck with sorrow . . .
> And sore repented of the day,
>   That she did ere deny him.

WILL WATERPROOF'S LYRICAL MONOLOGUE

247 Published *1842*. It was written about 1837, ten years after the death of Canning (lines 101-4). The Cock Tavern, Fleet Street, had long been a favourite resort for men of letters.

8. *Lusitania:* the classical name for Portugal.

248 27. *master-chord:* cp. *Henry VIII*, III, ii, 105-6: 'the string, / The master-cord on's heart.'

42. *Unboding:* not anticipating (the only such sense in *Oxford English Dictionary*).

249 55-6. *Romans* 8:28, 'And we know that all things work together for good.'

63. The 'whirligig of Time' is from *Twelfth Night*, V, i, 376.

69. *Temple-bar:* historic site in London, at the junction of the Strand and Fleet Street.

250 78. *stiffer:* stronger, as in 'stiff port' (which survives in 'a stiff drink').

80. *peptics:* digestive organs.

100. 1815. Such dating was a classical commonplace, e.g. Horace's *Odes*, III, xiv, 18.

101. George Canning, famous for his oratory, died in 1827.

251 119. *Ganymede:* the youth snatched up by the eagle to be Jove's cupbearer.

127. Tennyson commented: 'As the bird drinks he holds up his neck. There is accordingly an old English saying about the cock "praising God" when he drinks.'

NOTES

251 132. 'The game of marbles' (Tennyson).
197. Invoking the full-blooded magnanimity and wit of Falstaff: 'The second property of your excellent sherris is the warming of the blood . . .' (*2 Henry IV*, IV, iii, 99-101).

253 199. *ana:* as in 'Shakespeariana' (Tennyson). *swarm'd:* bred a swarm of.
219-20. 'Latter days', 'increased', 'go down': all Biblical in mock-seriousness.

254 223. *boxes:* 'the pews where the diners sit' (Tennyson).
230. *pewit:* with the common pronunciation 'piū it'.

255 243. *unctuous:* here both spiritual and greasy.

LADY CLARE

256 Published *1842*. Tennyson said it was founded on Susan Ferrier's novel *The Inheritance* (1824), where the substituted baby becomes an heiress; Tennyson alters the fact that the lover spurns her on discovering the secret of her birth. It was probably written about 1835, like *Lady Clara Vere de Vere* (p. 101), following *The Lord of Burleigh* (p. 259).

THE LORD OF BURLEIGH

259 Published *1842*. It was written 1833-4 (from the evidence of the manuscripts). It is based, as Tennyson acknowledged, on the true story of Sarah Hoggins, who married in 1791 and died in 1797. Hazlitt told the story in *New Monthly Magazine* (April 1822), reprinted in *The Picture Galleries in England* (1824), of which Tennyson had a copy. FitzGerald said: 'When this poem was read from MS. in 1835 I remember the Author doubting if it were not too familiar with its "Let us see the handsome houses, etc.," for public Taste. But a Sister, he said, had liked it: *we* never got it out of our heads from the first hearing; and now, is there a greater favourite where English is spoken?'

260 63-4. Tennyson commented: 'The mood changes from happiness to unhappiness, and the present tense changes to the past.'

NOTES

SIR LAUNCELOT AND QUEEN GUINEVERE

262 Published *1842*. 'Partly if not wholly written in 1830' (Hallam Tennyson), but the manuscripts make it clear that Tennyson was still working on it in 1833. The manuscript at Trinity College (which may not be quoted) explains the subtitle 'A Fragment', since it describes the meeting of Launcelot and Guinevere with Merlin, and their journey. A letter by J. M. Kemble speaks of the poem as 'a companion to *The Lady of Shalott*' and describes the projected poem. The affinities with *The Lady of Shalott* (p. 57) are emphasised by the use of the same stanza, except that here the 5th and 9th lines are not refrains.

A FAREWELL

263 Published *1842*. It is written to the brook at Somersby (Hallam Tennyson), so it was presumably written in early 1837 when the family left. Cp. *In Memoriam*, CI, 9-10, on the same parting:
   Unloved, by many a sandy bar,
      The brook shall babble down the plain.

264 10. Leaving Somersby, Tennyson may have remembered a book which had been in the library there: Thomas Gisborne's *Walks in a Forest: Spring* (1794): 'And rustling aspens shiver by the brook.'

THE BEGGAR MAID

264 Published *1842*. Written September 1833 (dated in manuscript). Tennyson gave the reference to *Romeo and Juliet*, II, i, 14:
   Young Adam Cupid, he that shot so trim,
      When King Cophetua loved the beggar-maid.
Tennyson would have met the ballad in Percy's *Reliques*.

THE VISION OF SIN

265 Published *1842*. It was not completed until after 1839. Tennyson said: 'This describes the soul of a youth who has given himself up to pleasure and Epicureanism.

NOTES

265 He at length is worn out and wrapt in the mists of satiety. Afterwards he grows into a cynical old man afflicted with the "curse of nature", and joining in the Feast of Death. Then we see the landscape which symbolizes God, Law and the future life.' In a letter he mentioned that it 'has always been a favourite with myself'. FitzGerald remarked that 'Johnson's "Long-expected one-and-twenty" has the swing, and something of the spirit of the old sinner's lyric'. Cp. section IV with the drinking-song at the end of Burns's *The Jolly Beggars* (published in full in 1802):

> What is title? what is treasure?
> What is reputation's care?
> If we lead a life of pleasure,
> 'Tis no matter, how or where!

14. *mellow sound:* rhyming with 'ground', in Keats, *Endymion*, I, 146.

268 91. *Galatians* 2:16.

270 147-8. Cp. Shelley, *Alastor* 158-9:
> Knowledge and truth and virtue were her theme,
> And lofty hopes of divine liberty.

271 193. *heavy Ignorance:* Shakespeare, Sonnet 78.

272 210. A nightmarish reversal of evolution.

211. Cp. the landscape of Milton's Hell, *Paradise Lost*, I, 672, 704: 'shone with a glossy scurf', 'scumm'd the Bullion dross'.

213-4. 'The sensualist becomes worn out by his senses' (Tennyson).

220-4. Hallam Tennyson related this to *In Memoriam*, LV, 20: 'When he speaks of "faintly trusting the larger hope," he means by "the larger hope" that the whole human race would through, perhaps, ages of suffering be at length purified and saved, even those who "better not with time;" so at the end of this Vision we read: "God made Himself an awful rose of dawn".' G. G. Loane compared Keats, *Hyperion*, I, 203-12:
> Hyperion, leaving twilight in the rear,
> Came slope upon the threshold of the west;

272
>Then, as was wont, his palace-door flew ope ...
>And like a rose in vermeil tint and shape,
>In fragrance soft, and coolness to the eye,
>That inlet to severe magnificence
>Stood full blown, for the God to enter in.

Cp. also *The Two Voices* 304-6:
>Heaven opens inward, chasms yawn,
>Vast images in glimmering dawn,
>Half shown, are broken and withdrawn.

The 'voice' is a traditional folk-motif; cp. *The Voyage of Maildun* (translated in P. W. Joyce's *Old Celtic Romances*, 1879): 'After this they heard some one speaking on the top of the pillar, in a loud, clear, glad voice; but they knew neither what he said, nor in what language he spoke.'

THE SKIPPING-ROPE

272 Published *1842*. Tennyson reprinted it from *1843* to *1850*, but then dropped it and never subsequently reinstated it. He wrote it at the end of John Walker's *Rhyming Dictionary* (1800), of which his copy is at Lincoln; it includes in the index, under 'ope', all of Tennyson's rhymes. The poem was written about 1836.

'MOVE EASTWARD, HAPPY EARTH, AND LEAVE'

273 Published *1842*. Written 1836-8. It is an epithalamium. Probably it dates from the marriage of Tennyson's brother Charles in May 1836. Alternatively, Tennyson's engagement to Emily Sellwood was recognized early in 1838.

6. *sister-world:* 'the moon' (Tennyson). Perhaps Tennyson chose the word because he fell in love with Emily, who was the bride's sister, at the wedding of Charles (and wrote a poem, *The Bridesmaid*, at this time).

9. Cp. *Paradise Lost*, VIII, 166, where the earth, advancing from the west, 'bears thee soft with the smooth air along.'

NOTES

'BREAK, BREAK, BREAK'

273 Published *1842*. It was written in Lincolnshire one spring (*Memoir*, i, 190), so presumably before 1837, and after September 1833 since it is on the death of Arthur Hallam. Probably spring 1834. Cp. *In Memoriam*, especially for lines 11-2; and also the lines which Hallam Tennyson gave as the 'germ' of *In Memoriam* (*Memoir*, i, 107):

> Where is the voice I loved? ah, where
> Is that dear hand that I would press?
> Lo, the broad heavens cold and bare,
> The stars that know not my distress!

Richard Holt Hutton said in 1871: 'No poet ever made the dumb speak so effectually . . . Observe how the wash of the sea on the cold gray stones is used to prepare the mind for the feeling of helplessness with which the deeper emotions break against the hard and rigid element of human speech; how the picture is then widened out till you see the bay with children laughing on its shore, and the sailor-boy singing on its surface, and the stately ships passing on in the offing to their unseen haven, all with the view of helping us to feel the contrast between the satisfied and the unsatisfied yearnings of the human heart. Tennyson, like every true poet, has the strongest feeling of the spiritual and almost mystic character of the associations attaching to the distant sail which takes the ship on its lonely journey to an invisible port, and has more than once used it to lift the mind into the attitude of hope or trust. But then the song returns again to the helpless breaking of the sea at the foot of crags it cannot climb, not this time to express the inadequacy of human speech to express human yearnings, but the defeat of those very yearnings themselves.'

THE POET'S SONG

274 Published as the last poem of volume II in *1842*.

Critical Extracts

A. H. HALLAM

Mr. Tennyson belongs decidedly to the class we have already described as Poets of Sensation. He sees all the forms of nature with the 'eruditus oculus', and his ear has a fairy fineness. There is a strange earnestness in his worship of beauty which throws a charm over his impassioned song, more easily felt than described, and not to be escaped by those who have once felt it. We think he has more definiteness and roundness of general conception than the late Mr. Keats, and is much more free from blemishes of diction and hasty capriccios of fancy. He has also this advantage over that poet and his friend Shelley, that he comes before the public unconnected with any political party or peculiar system of opinions. Nevertheless, true to the theory we have stated, we believe his participation in their characteristic excellences is sufficient to secure him a share of their unpopularity.

The volume of 'Poems, chiefly Lyrical', does not contain above 154 pages; but it shews us much more of the character of its parent mind, than many books we have known of much larger compass and more boastful pretensions. The features of original genius are clearly and strongly marked. The author imitates nobody; we recognise the spirit of his age, but not the individual form of this or that writer. His thoughts bear no more resemblance to Byron or Scott, Shelley or Coleridge, than to Homer or Calderon, Firdúsí or Calidasa.

We have remarked five distinctive excellencies of his own manner. First, his luxuriance of imagination, and at the same time his control over it. Secondly his power of embodying himself in ideal characters, or rather moods of character, with such extreme accuracy of adjustment, that the circumstances of the narration seem to have a natural correspondence with the predominant feeling, and, as it were, to be evolved from it by assimilative force. Thirdly his vivid, picturesque delineation of objects, and the peculiar skill with which he holds all of them *fused*, to borrow a metaphor from science, in a medium of strong emotion. Fourthly, the variety of his lyrical measures, and exquisite modulation of harmonious words and cadences to the swell and fall of the feelings expressed. Fifthly, the elevated habits of thought, implied in these compositions, and imparting a mellow soberness of tone, more impressive, to our minds, than if the author had drawn up a set of opinions in verse, and sought to instruct the understanding rather than to communicate the love of beauty to the heart.

From: The Englishman's Magazine, August, 1831

GERARD MANLEY HOPKINS

I am meditating an essay, perhaps for the *Hexameron*, on some points of poetical criticism, and it is with reference to this a little that I have composed my thoughts on Tennyson. I think then the language of verse may be divided into three kinds. The first and highest is poetry proper, the language of inspiration. The word inspiration need cause no difficulty. I mean by it a mood of great, abnormal in fact, mental acuteness, either energetic or receptive, according as the thoughts which arise in it seem generated by a stress and action of the brain, or to strike into it unasked. This mood arises from various causes, physical generally, as good health or state of the air or, prosaic as it is, length of time after a meal. But I need not go into this; all that it is needful to mark is, that the poetry of inspiration can only be written in this mood of mind, even if it only last a minute, by poets themselves. Everybody of course has like moods, but not being poets what they then produce is not poetry. The second kind I call *Parnassian*. It can only be spoken by poets, but is not in the highest sense poetry. It does not require the mood of mind in which the poetry of inspiration is written. It is spoken *on and from the level* of a poet's mind, not, as in the other case, when the inspiration, which is the gift of genius, raises him above himself. For I think it is the case with genius that it is not when quiescent so very much above mediocrity as the difference between the two might lead us to think, but that it has the power and privilege of rising from that level to a height utterly far from mediocrity: in other words that its greatness is *that it can be* so great. You will understand. *Parnassian* then is that language which genius speaks as fitted to its exaltation, and place among other genius, but does not sing (I have been betrayed into the whole hog of a metaphor) in its flights. Great men, poets I mean, have each their own dialect as it were of Parnassian, formed generally as they go on writing, and at last—that is the point to be marked,—they can see things in this Parnassian way and describe them in this Parnassian tongue, without further effort of inspiration. In a poet's particular kind of Parnassian lies most of his style, of his manner, of his mannerism if you like. But I must not go farther without giving you instances of Parnassian. I shall take one from Tennyson, and from *Enoch Arden*, from a passage much quoted already and which will be no doubt often quoted, the description of Enoch's tropical island.

> The mountain wooded to the peak, the lawns
> And winding glades high up like ways to Heaven,
> The slender coco's drooping crown of plumes,
> The lightning flash of insect and of bird,
> The lustre of the long convolvuluses
> That coil'd around the stately stems, and ran
> Ev'n to the limit of the land, the glows
> And glories of the broad belt of the world,
> All these he saw.

Now it is a mark of Parnassian that one could conceive oneself writing it if one were the poet. Do not say that *if* you were Shakespear you can imagine yourself writing Hamlet, because that is just what I think you *cannot* conceive. In a fine piece of inspiration every beauty takes you as it were by surprise, not of course that you did not think the writer could be so great, for that is not it,—indeed I think it is a mistake to speak of people admiring Shakespear more and more as they live, for when the judgment is ripe and you have read a good deal of any writer including his best things, and carefully, then, I think, however high the place you give him, that you must have rated him equally with his merits however great they be; so that all after admiration cannot increase but keep alive this estimate, make his greatness stare into your eyes and din it into your ears, as it were, but not make it greater,—but to go on with the broken sentence, every fresh beauty could not in any way be predicted or accounted for by what one has already read. But in Parnassian pieces you feel that if you were the poet you could have gone on as he has done, you see yourself doing it, only with the difference that if you actually try you find you cannot write his Parnassian. Well now to turn to the piece above. The glades being 'like ways to Heaven' is, I think, a new thought, it is an inspiration. Not so the next line, that is pure Parnassian. If you examine it the words are choice and the description is beautiful and unexceptionable, but it does not *touch* you. The next is more Parnassian still. In the next lines I think the picture of the convolvuluses does touch; but only the picture: the words are Parnassian. It is a very good instance, for the lines are undoubtedly beautiful, but yet I could scarcely point anywhere to anything more idiomatically Parnassian, to anything which I more clearly see myself writing *qua* Tennyson, than the words

> The glows
> And glories of the broad belt of the world.

What Parnassian is you will now understand, but I must make some more remarks on it. I believe that when a poet palls on us it is because of his Parnassian. We seem to have found out his secret. Now in fact we have not found out more than this, that when he is not inspired and in his flights, his poetry does run in an intelligibly laid down path. Well, it is notorious that Shakespear does not pall, and this is because he uses, I believe, so little Parnassian. He does use some, but little. Now judging from my own experience I should say no author palls so much as Wordsworth; this is because he writes such an 'intolerable deal of' Parnassian.

If with a critical eye and in a critical appreciative mood you read a poem by an unknown author or an anonymous poem by a known, but not at once recognisable, author, and he is a real poet, then you will pronounce him so at once, and the poem will seem truly inspired, though afterwards, when you know the author, you will be able to distinguish his inspirations from his Parnassian, and will perhaps think the very piece which struck you so much at first mere Parnassian. You know well how deadened, as it were, the critical faculties become at times, when all good poetry alike loses its clear ring and its charm; while in other moods they are so enlivened that things that have long lost their freshness strike you with their original definiteness and piquant beauty.

I think one had got into the way of thinking, or had not got out of the way of thinking, that Tennyson was always new, *touching*, beyond other poets, not pressed with human ailments, never using Parnassian. So at least I used to think. Now one sees he uses Parnassian; he is, one must see it, what we used to call Tennysonian. But the discovery of this must not make too much difference. When puzzled by one's doubts it is well to turn to a passage like this. Surely your maturest judgment will never be fooled out of saying that this is divine, terribly beautiful—the stanza of *In Memoriam* beginning with the quatrain

> O Hesper o'er the buried sun,
>   And ready thou to die with him,
>   Thou watchest all things ever dim
> And dimmer, and a glory done.

I quote from memory. Inconsequent conclusion: Shakespear is and must be utterly the greatest of poets.

From a letter to A. W. M. BAILLIE, 10 September, 1864

WALT WHITMAN

Let me assume to pass verdict, or perhaps momentary judgment, for the United States on this poet—a remov'd and distant position giving some advantages over a nigh one. What is Tennyson's service to his race, times, and especially to America? First, I should say—or at least not forget—his personal character. He is not to be mention'd as a rugged, evolutionary, aboriginal force—but (and a great lesson is in it) he has been consistent throughout with the native, healthy, patriotic spinal element and promptings of himself. His moral line is local and conventional, but it is vital and genuine. He reflects the uppercrust of his time, its pale cast of thought—even its *ennui*. Then the simile of my friend John Burroughs is entirely true, 'His glove is a glove of silk, but the hand is a hand of iron.' He shows how one can be a royal laureate, quite elegant and 'aristocratic', and a little queer and affected, and at the same time perfectly manly and natural . . .

To me, Tennyson shows more than any poet I know (perhaps has been a warning to me) how much there is in finest verbalism. There is such a latent charm in mere words, cunning collocations, and in the voice ringing them, which he has caught and brought out, beyond all others—as in the line,

'And hollow, hollow, hollow, all delight,'

in *The Passing of Arthur*, and evidenced in *The Lady of Shalott*, *The Deserted House* and many other pieces . . . His mannerism is great, but it is a noble and welcome mannerism . . .

His very faults, doubts, swervings, doublings upon himself, have been typical of our age. We are like the voyagers of a ship, casting off for new seas, distant shores. We would still dwell in the old suffocating and dead haunts, remembering and magnifying their pleasant experiences only, and more than once impell'd to jump ashore before it is too late, and stay where our fathers stay'd, and live as they lived.

From: 'A Word About Tennyson', *The Critic*, 1 January, 1887

HAROLD NICOLSON

For although the great mass of Tennyson's poetry, however skilful it may be in form, appears in substance to be lacking in these important qualities of impulse, reality and emotion; although one must admit that his prosperous assurance, his laborious and careful revisions, his accuracy and caution, lead one at times to doubt the compelling force of his inspiration, and even, perhaps, to question his sincerity; although he was apt on all occasions to exploit sentiments and situations which were certainly superficial and perhaps unreal; although he flinched alike before the flame of passion and the cold nakedness of truth, yet there are sudden panting moments when the frightened soul of the man cries out to one like some wild animal caught in the fens at night-time—moments when he lies moaning in the half-light in an agony of fear. And at such moments the mystical genius of Tennyson comes upon one in a flash, and there can be no question of the reality of his emotion and his impulse.

I advance this theory not as a paradox but, for what it is worth, as an absolute personal conviction. For me, the essential Tennyson is a morbid and unhappy mystic. He is the hero of *The Sensitive Mind*, of *The Two Voices* and above all of *Maud*. He is a spirit for whom there was an 'ever-moaning battle in the mist'—a soul whose fancies mingled

> 'with the sallow-rifted glooms
> Of evening, and the moanings of the wind';

and thus at times there comes

> 'A cry that shiver'd to the tingling stars,
> And, as it were one voice, an agony
> Of lamentation, like a wind, that shrills
> All night in a waste land, where no one comes
> Or hath come, since the making of the world.'

For those who accept this theory no great difficulty will arise in reconciling the essential Tennyson with the Tennyson of the legend. One would prefer not to fall back upon the jargon of the psycho-analysts, but the application of the

Freudian system to the case of Tennyson is quite illuminating. For Tennyson was afraid of a great many things: predominantly he was afraid of death, and sex, and God. And in all these matters he endeavoured instinctively to sublimate his terrors by enunciating the beliefs which he desired to feel, by dwelling upon the solutions by which he would like to be convinced. The point does not require further elaboration: my contention is merely that once one accepts the realisation of Tennyson, and particularly the younger Tennyson, as a man who was morbidly afraid, one must admit that the processes by which he conquered his afflictions cannot by any possibility be described as consciously insincere. And once one is able to dispose of this fatal suspicion of insincerity, the real beauty of Tennyson's poetry will triumph of itself.

From: Tennyson (Constable, 1923: Grey Arrow edition, 1960), pp. 33-4

T. S. ELIOT

Tennyson is a great poet, for reasons that are perfectly clear. He has three qualities which are seldom found together except in the greatest poets: abundance, variety, and complete competence. We therefore cannot appreciate his work unless we read a good deal of it. We may not admire his aims: but whatever he sets out to do, he succeeds in doing, with a mastery which gives us the sense of confidence that is one of the major pleasures of poetry. His variety of metrical accomplishment is astonishing. Without making the mistake of trying to write Latin verse in English, he knew everything about Latin versification that an English poet could use; and he said of himself that he thought he knew the quantity of the sounds of every English word except perhaps *scissors*. He had the finest ear of any English poet since Milton. He was the master of Swinburne; and the versification of Swinburne, himself a classical scholar, is often crude and sometimes cheap, in comparison with Tennyson's. Tennyson extended very widely the range of active metrical forms in English: in *Maud* alone the variety is prodigious. But innovation in metric is not to be measured solely by the width of the deviation from accepted practice. It is a matter of the historical situation: at some moments a more violent change may be necessary than at others. The problem differs at every period. At some times, a violent revolution may be neither possible nor desirable; at such times, a change which may appear very slight, is the change which the important poet will make. The innovation of Pope, after Dryden, may not seem very great; but it is the mark of the master to be able to make small changes which will be highly significant, as at another time to make the radical changes, through which poetry will curve back again to its norm.

From: 'In Memoriam', in *Essays Ancient & Modern* (Faber, 1936); reprinted in Killham's collection (see Bibliography, p. 379)

ROBERT LANGBAUM

Most characteristic of Tennyson is a certain life-weariness, a longing for rest through oblivion. This emotional bias is all the more powerful because it appears to be subconscious. Not only does it conflict with the poet's often stated desire for personal immortality, but it even conflicts in a poem like *Ulysses* with what seems to be his intent. Yet Tennyson exploits this emotional bias beyond any English poet before him; it informs not only his best lyrics—*Break Break Break, Tears Idle Tears*, and the best of *In Memoriam*—but also his best dramatic monologues. The longing for oblivion is certainly an element in Keats' *Nightingale* but it is kept in balance by a countervailing sense of the hard reality which must in the end be returned to, and is in every instance sublimated into the imaginative construction of a realm where death is defied—the regressive urge leads after all to the vision of the 'magic casements'. In Tennyson, however, the longing for oblivion is not a first step toward a vision of transformed being but an end in itself, overwhelming us and dispelling all other considerations[. . .]

The same weariness and longing for rest is the emotional bias of Tennyson's finest dramatic monologue, *Ulysses;* though here the emotion is couched in the contrasting language of adventure, giving an added complexity of meaning to the poem. To read *Ulysses* as a poem of strenuousness in the manner of Browning, as some critics have done, is to read with the head only and not the sensibility. For its music bears the enervated cadence of *Tithonus* and *The Lotos-Eaters*. The speaker is the old Ulysses whose glories are behind him; and though he has still the appetite for life that makes him dissatisfied with the domestic hearth, it is an old man's appetite exceeding potency. We miss the emotional meaning of his final journey unless we see that it is undertaken with a sense of diminished strength, as the last thing possible:

Tho' much is taken, much abides; and tho'
We are not now that strength which in old days
Moved earth and heaven; that which we are, we are.

It is a mystical journey undertaken by night with an old crew. They are to sail beyond the limits of the world until they die, it is a journey to death. But death here is not the culminating experience that it is in Browning's *Prospice;* it is as much experience as is possible to old men. Nor is death a fight as in *Prospice*, 'the best and the last,' but a decline, a sinking below the horizon. The poet is inevitably moved toward death in *Prospice*, but in *Ulysses* death is deliberately sought for.

The story of Ulysses' final journey comes from Dante, whose account of it in the *Inferno* Tennyson follows so closely that his poem is in places a paraphrase. Yet the difference in emotional meaning is especially apparent just because the facts and even the thoughts are analogous.

CRITICAL EXTRACTS

Ulysses' famous exhortation of his crew as they are about to cross the limit of the habitable world: 'Consider your origin: you were not made to live like brutes, but to follow virtue and knowledge' (xxvi, 118), is admirably represented by Tennyson's lines:

> and vile it were
> For some three suns to store and hoard myself,
> And this gray spirit yearning in desire
> To follow knowledge like a sinking star,
> Beyond the utmost bound of human thought.

But the informing image and emotion of the passage are not in Dante—the *gray* spirit indicating an old man's tired yearning, and the *sinking* star directing the yearning toward disappearance, extinction.

What is incidental in Dante, that Ulysses is old, caught Tennyson's imagination to become the central fact from which his meaning emerges. There is no sign of diminished vigour in Dante's Ulysses. He is destroyed, as a matter of fact, as punishment for his too vigorous presumption in daring to sail beyond the limit assigned to man. The tempest that destroys him is the disaster he has risked in going adventuring. But even before embarking, Tennyson's Ulysses holds out death in one form or another as the inevitable goal of the journey. They may be washed down by the gulfs, or they may touch upon the Happy Isles of the dead; in any case his purpose holds

> To sail beyond the sunset, and the baths
> Of all the western stars, until I die.

Tennyson's Ulysses picks himself up from his Ithacan somnolence to make the choice for life; he will carry on, he will make the last effort, but with the same cry of pain that stirs Eliot's vegetable world in April, and with the same endurance of life only because it leads to death.

From: *The Poetry of Experience* (Chatto & Windus, 1957), pp. 89-91

Bibliography

For Tennyson's main publications, see the list of dates (p. 13). There are also two volumes edited by Sir Charles Tennyson: *The Devil and the Lady* (Macmillan, 1930), a pseudo-Elizabethan play written by Tennyson in his teens; and *Unpublished Early Poems* (Macmillan, 1931), an important selection from poems then in manuscript. The two volumes have been reissued, as one, by Indiana University Press (1964).

Editions, Works of Reference, etc.

The Works of Tennyson (Macmillan, 1894). Includes his final revisions and his posthumous volume.

The Eversley Edition of the Works of Tennyson, edited by Tennyson's son, Hallam Lord Tennyson (Macmillan, 1907-8), 9 vols. The standard edition, differing in text only very slightly from *1894*. Very occasionally a reading in *1894* is to be preferred, and *Eversley* sometimes lacks punctuation. It has lengthy notes by Tennyson and Hallam Tennyson, and from Edward FitzGerald's remarks.

The Works of Tennyson, with notes by the author, edited by Hallam Lord Tennyson (Macmillan, 1913). A one-volume version of *Eversley*, with a few changes in the notes.

Poetical Works, Including the Plays (Oxford University Press, 1953). Oxford Standard Authors. No notes or variant readings, but it reprints some of the poems which Tennyson suppressed.

The Poems of Tennyson, edited by Christopher Ricks. Forthcoming in 1968, in the series 'Longmans' Annotated English Poets' (General Editor, F. W. Bateson). It includes all the poems Tennyson published, plus those printed by his son Hallam and his grandson (Sir Charles Tennyson), together with unpublished poems, manuscript and published variants, and full notes on dates of composition, publication, sources, biographical context, etc. It makes use of the two important Tennyson collections, at Harvard and at the Tennyson Research Centre, Lincoln.

BIBLIOGRAPHY

T. J. WISE, *A Bibliography of the Writings of Alfred, Lord Tennyson* (London: Printed for Private Circulation, 1908), 2 vols. Still not superseded, though it is marred by Wise's errors and omissions and by his including many of his own forgeries.

PAULL F. BAUM, in *The Victorian Poets: A Guide to Research* (ed. F. E. Faverty, Harvard University Press, 1956). An excellent account of Tennyson studies till that date. In the forthcoming revision of this *Guide*, the chapter on Tennyson is by E. D. H. Johnson.

ARTHUR E. BAKER, *Concordance to the Poetical and Dramatic Works of Alfred, Lord Tennyson* (Kegan Paul, 1914; reissued by Routledge & Kegan Paul, 1966). Useful, but it has 5 separate alphabetical sequences, and is very careless (many words are simply left out).

HALLAM TENNYSON, *Alfred Lord Tennyson: A Memoir* (Macmillan, 1897), 2 vols. A mine of information, using diaries and letters. Decorous but indispensable. Hallam Tennyson created the *Memoir* from an earlier version which he printed privately about 1895: *Materials for a Life of A.T.* *Materials* includes facts and poems dropped in the *Memoir*. A later assemblage by Hallam Tennyson of similar material is *Tennyson and His Friends* (Macmillan, 1911).

CHARLES TENNYSON, *Alfred Tennyson* (Macmillan, 1949). The standard biography, including much new material about Tennyson's early years and his family. Other essential studies by Sir Charles are: a series of articles in the *Nineteenth Century* (1931), and another in the *Cornhill Magazine* (1936); *Six Tennyson Essays* (Cassell, 1954); and 'The Somersby Tennysons', *Victorian Studies*, Supplement (Christmas 1963).

Criticism

(i) *Recommended for use in both schools and universities*

HAROLD NICOLSON, *Tennyson: Aspects of his Life, Character and Poetry* (Constable, 1923). A witty brief biography combined with a most influential view of Tennyson's true greatness as that of 'a morbid and unhappy mystic'.

W. P. KER, *Collected Essays* (1925). Contains Ker's lecture on Tennyson (1909), of particular interest on versification.

BASIL WILLEY, *More Nineteenth Century Studies* (Chatto & Windus, 1956). Tennyson in the context of Victorian religious thought.

(ii) *Recommended more particularly for university students*

The most acute criticism of Tennyson was by his contemporaries. Among the reviews, those by Arthur Hallam (*Englishman's Magazine*, 1831); 'Christopher North', John Wilson (*Blackwood's Magazine*, 1832); J. W. Croker (*Quarterly Review*, 1833); Leigh Hunt (*Church of England Quarterly Review*, 1842); and W. E. Gladstone (*Quarterly Review*, 1859). There are perceptive essays by R. H. Horne (*A New Spirit of the Age*, 1844); by Walter Bagehot (*Literary Studies*, 1879); and by Richard Holt Hutton (*Literary Essays*, 1888). Scattered comments in lectures and letters by Matthew Arnold and by Gerard Manley Hopkins have real value. For Walt Whitman, see p. 370. A forthcoming volume edited by Professor J. D. Jump assembles the important criticism of Tennyson from 1830 to 1892.

J. F. A. PYRE, *The Formation of Tennyson's Style* (University of Wisconsin, 1921). Valuable particularly on Tennyson's metrical development.

DOUGLAS BUSH, *Mythology and the Romantic Tradition* (Harvard University Press, 1937). A very informative chapter on Tennyson.

PAULL F. BAUM, *Tennyson Sixty Years After* (University of North Carolina Press, 1948). Undeferential and stimulating critical study.

HUMPHRY HOUSE, *All in Due Time* (Hart-Davis, 1955). Includes two notable essays on Tennyson.

ROBERT LANGBAUM, *The Poetry of Experience: The Dramatic Monologue in Modern Literary Tradition* (Chatto & Windus, 1957). A first-rate study (the best criticism yet of Browning), most illuminating on Tennyson's dramatic monologues.

BIBLIOGRAPHY

JOHN KILLHAM, *Critical Essays on the Poetry of Tennyson* (Routledge & Kegan Paul, 1960). Assembles some of the best modern criticism of Tennyson. Essays by G. M. Young, Arthur J. Carr, H. M. McLuhan, G. Robert Stange, Elizabeth Waterston, Lionel Stevenson, W. W. Robson, E. J. Chiasson, Cleanth Brooks, Graham Hough, Leo Spitzer, T. S. Eliot, John Killham, and F. E. L. Priestley.

JEROME HAMILTON BUCKLEY, *Tennyson: The Growth of a Poet* (Harvard University Press, 1960). The first study of Tennyson's development to make use of the Harvard manuscripts. Important for its facts about composition and revision.

A volume in the series 'Twentieth Century Views' (Prentice-Hall; General Editor, Maynard Mack) is forthcoming, edited by Mrs. M. M. Sussman.

(iii) *Recommended for advanced university students*

JOHN CHURTON COLLINS, *Illustrations of Tennyson* (Chatto & Windus, 1891). On Tennyson's verbal borrowings and allusions.

W. P. MUSTARD, *Classical Echoes in Tennyson* (Macmillan, 1904).

W. D. PADEN, *Tennyson in Egypt: A Study of the Imagery in his Earlier Work* (University of Kansas, 1942). Combines a shrewd psychoanalytical approach with a mass of important information about Tennyson's reading and sources.

E. D. H. JOHNSON, *The Alien Vision of Victorian Poetry* (Princeton University Press, 1952). An original discussion of the part played by, for example, dreams in Tennyson's poetry.

EDGAR F. SHANNON, *Tennyson and the Reviewers: A Study of His Literary Reputation and of the Influence of the Critics upon His Poetry 1827-51* (Harvard University Press, 1952).

JOHN KILLHAM, *Tennyson and 'The Princess': Reflections of an Age* (Athlone Press, 1958). Important not only for *The Princess*, but for Tennyson's place in Victorian social thought and for the sources of many poems.

BIBLIOGRAPHY

RALPH WILSON RADER, *Tennyson's 'Maud': The Biographical Genesis* (University of California Press, 1963). Discovers new facts about Tennyson's early life and his love for Rosa Baring, the importance of which extends beyond *Maud* itself into many of Tennyson's most interesting poems.

Index of Titles

Adeline, 40
Amphion, 238
Audley Court, 168

Ballad of Oriana, The, 50
Beggar Maid, The, 264
Blackbird, The, 130
'Break, break, break', 273

Character, A, 42
Circumstance, 53
Claribel, 19
Conclusion, 109

Day-Dream, The, 228
Death of the Old Year, The, 131
Dirge, A, 47
Dora, 163
Dream of Fair Women, A, 118
Dying Swan, The, 46

Edward Gray, 246
Eleänore, 66
Epic, The, 143

Farewell, A, 263
Fatima, 79

Gardener's Daughter, The, 154
Godiva, 209
Goose, The, 141

Isabel, 21

Lady Clara Vere de Vere, 101
Lady Clare, 256
Lady of Shalott, The, 57
Lilian, 20
Locksley Hall, 196
Lord of Burleigh, The, 259

Lotos-Eaters, The, 112
Love and Death, 49
Love and Duty, 191
'Love thou thy land, with love far-brought', 138

Madeline, 27
Margaret, 128
Mariana, 23
Mariana in the South, 63
May Queen, The, 104
Mermaid, The, 55
Merman, The, 53
Miller's Daughter, The, 71
Morte d'Arthur, 145
'Move eastward, happy earth, and leave', 273

New-Year's Eve, 106

Ode to Memory, 35
Œnone, 80
'Of old sat Freedom on the heights,' 137
Oriana, The Ballad of, 50
Owl, The, 28

Palace of Art, The, 91
Poet, The, 43
Poet's Mind, The, 45
Poet's Song, The, 274

Recollections of the Arabian Nights, 30

St. Agnes' Eve, 242
St. Simeon Stylites, 174
Sir Galahad, 243
Sir Launcelot and Queen Guinevere, 262
Sisters, The, 88

INDEX

Skipping-Rope, The, 272
Songs:
  A spirit haunts the year's last hours, 39
  It is the miller's daughter, 76
  Love that hath us in the net, 77
  The Owl, 28
  The Owl (Second Song), 29

Talking Oak, The, 181
To J.M.K., 57
To J.S., 133
To —— ('Clear-headed friend'), 26
To —— ('I send you here a sort of allegory'), 90
Two Voices, The, 211

Ulysses, 194

Vision of Sin, The, 265

Walking to the Mail, 171
Will Waterproof's Lyrical Monologue, 247

'You ask me, why, tho' ill at ease', 136

Index of First Lines

A spirit haunts the year's last hours, 39
A still small voice spake unto me, 211
Airy, fairy Lilian, 20
Altho' I be the basest of mankind, 174
At Francis Allen's on the Christmas-eve, 143

Break, break, break, 273

Clear-headed friend, whose joyful scorn, 26
Comrades, leave me here a little, while as yet 'tis early morn, 196
'Courage!' he said, and pointed toward the land, 112

Deep on the convent-roof the snows, 242

Eyes not down-dropt nor over-bright, but fed, 21

Flow down, cold rivulet, to the sea, 263
Full knee-deep lies the winter snow, 131

Her arms across her breast she laid, 264

I built my soul a lordly pleasure-house, 91
I had a vision when the night was late, 265
I knew an old wife lean and poor, 141
I read, before my eyelids dropt their shade, 118
I see the wealthy miller yet, 71
I send you here a sort of allegory, 90
I thought to pass away before, and yet alive I am, 109
I waited for the train at Coventry, 209
If you're waking call me early, call me early, mother dear, 106
I'm glad I walk'd. How fresh the meadows look, 171
In her ear he whispers gaily, 259
It is the miller's daughter, 76
It little profits that an idle king, 194
It was the time when lilies blow, 256

Lady Clara Vere de Vere, 101
Like souls that balance joy and pain, 262
Love that hath us in the net, 77
Love thou thy land, with love far-brought, 138

Move eastward, happy earth, and leave, 273
My father left a park to me, 238
My good blade carves the casques of men, 243
My heart is wasted with my woe, 50

INDEX

My hope and heart is with thee—thou wilt be, 57
Mystery of mysteries, 40

Now is done thy long day's work, 47

O blackbird! sing me something well, 130
O Lady Flora, let me speak, 228
O Love, Love, Love! O withering might, 79
O plump head-waiter at The Cock, 247
O sweet pale Margaret, 128
Of love that never found his earthly close, 191
Of old sat Freedom on the heights, 137
On either side the river lie, 57
Once more the gate behind me falls, 181

So all day long the noise of battle roll'd, 145
Sure never yet was Antelope, 272
Sweet Emma Moreland of yonder town, 246

The Bull, the Fleece are cramm'd, and not a room, 168
The plain was grassy, wild and bare, 46
The poet in a golden clime was born, 43
The rain had fallen, the Poet arose, 274
The wind, that beats the mountain, blows, 133
There is sweet music here that softer falls, 113
There lies a vale in Ida, lovelier, 80
This morning is the morning of the day, 154
Thou art not steep'd in golden languors, 27
Thou who stealest fire, 35
Thy dark eyes open'd not, 66
Thy tuwhits are lull'd, I wot, 29
Two children in two neighbour villages, 53

Vex not thou the poet's mind, 45

We were two daughters of one race, 88
What time the mighty moon was gathering light, 49
When cats run home and light is come, 28
When the breeze of a joyful dawn blew free, 30
Where Claribel low-lieth, 19
Who would be a mermaid fair, 55
Who would be a merman bold, 53
With a half-glance upon the sky, 42
With blackest moss the flower-plots, 23
With farmer Allan at the farm abode, 163
With one black shadow at its feet, 63

You ask me, why, tho' ill at ease, 136
You must wake and call me early, call me early, mother dear, 104